LIONEL
MESSI
AND THE ART OF LIVING

LIONEL
MESSI
AND THE ART OF LIVING

A N D Y   W E S T

First published by Pitch Publishing, 2018

Pitch Publishing
A2 Yeoman Gate
Yeoman Way
Worthing
Sussex
BN13 3QZ
www.pitchpublishing.co.uk
info@pitchpublishing.co.uk

A CIP catalogue record is available for this book
from the British Library.

ISBN 978-1-78531-450-6

Typesetting and origination by Pitch Publishing

Printed and bound in the UK by TJ International Ltd

Contents

Acknowledgements

Firstly, I would like to thank Paul and everyone at Pitch Publishing for giving me the opportunity to write this book.

I am sincerely grateful to the seven interviewees whose thoughtful insights have added an extra dimension to the pages that follow: John Carlin, Nando De Colo, Danny Kerry, Daniel Memmert, Adrian Moorhouse, Brendan Rodgers and Pablo Zabaleta. Thanks also to Simon Heggie, Iain Jamieson, Craig Mortimer-Zhika and Lisa Young for their assistance in arranging some of those interviews.

I have been fortunate to receive significant help and advice, in different ways, from friends and family, especially Jonathan Crook, Andrew Findlay, Barry Gale, Gavin Jamieson, Roland Nash and Andrew Smallbone.

There has been an endless supply of support and encouragement from my parents Gordon and Barbara, my wife Hannah and my daughters Lucy and Isabella. Thank you for everything.

And finally, of course, thank you – for the inspiration – to Lionel Messi.

Andy West
Barcelona, August 2018

Introduction

How can you even begin to describe Lionel Messi?

So many column inches and broadcast hours have been devoted to dissecting the Argentine's glittering career, prodding and probing at every possible aspect of his private and public life, it means that now attempting to conjure up new ways of capturing his genius is a thankless task.

Words are not even really necessary to evoke Messi's greatness because his achievements speak loud and clear for themselves. You are probably already aware that he is Barcelona's runaway all-time leading goalscorer, surpassing previous record holder Cesar Rodriguez Alvarez when he was only 24 years old and now more than doubling Cesar's tally.

You also know that Messi has won a dazzling array of trophies, including nine La Liga titles and four Champions League crowns. And there have, of course, been personal accolades galore, too, such as a record four consecutive Ballon d'Or awards between 2009 and 2012.

All of this and much more is well known and fully documented, and there isn't really anything new to be revealed about the incredible facts and figures of Messi's career.

But that doesn't have to be the end of the story.

We have seen his unstoppable shots, his mazy dribbles and his astonishing assists, but maybe we can also stop to consider how the achievements of this remarkable footballer resonate with our own lives. How we can study exactly what has allowed him to become the player that he is and draw lessons which can be meaningfully applied on an everyday basis.

At first glance, this suggestion might appear rather far-fetched. Messi is an elite professional sportsman of unparalleled genius whose talents have made him one of the most famous and worshipped people on the planet, earning him an estimated fortune of $280 million. How on earth can our own ordinary and unremarkable lives be realistically compared to someone seemingly so untouchable and unique?

But we should not forget that behind the glamour and the glory, underneath the thin layer of fame and fortune, there lies a human being. Just a normal human being.

Someone who has endured many hardships and challenges, and continues to do so every day. Someone who has encountered often unwarranted and occasionally spiteful scorn. Someone who has suffered infuriating frustrations and intense disappointments, as well as celebrating joyful successes and proud achievements. Someone who needs the love and support of those around him. Someone with frailties and insecurities, mingled together with hopes and dreams.

Someone just like you and me.

* * * * *

Over the course of this book we will examine some of the specific qualities which have allowed Lionel Messi to become arguably the greatest football player in history.

From his willingness to accept onerous personal responsibilities, to his ability to sacrifice selfish ambitions by working in a team, there are many inspirational lessons to be learned from the story of how a (very) small boy from a nondescript city in Argentina raised himself to the summit of human achievement in one of the most competitive arenas known to modern mankind.

For everything that he has done and continues to do, Messi truly is an inspiration. The idea that an athlete can be a role model is nothing new, but we often tend to apply that description to their conduct *off* the field of play, related to non-sporting activities such as charity work or lifestyle choices. In this book, we will focus instead on the great things Messi has done *on* the football pitch, and see how his feats with his feet can be related to normal life.

In addition to the glorious successes, though, we must also look at the other side of the coin and consider what we can learn from Messi's surprisingly numerous failures – especially in a book written in 2018, which saw him suffer serious heartache in his profession's two most prestigious competitions, the Champions League and the World Cup.

Never, indeed, has the frailty of Messi's exalted status among gods on earth been more evident than during the World Cup finals in Russia.

He headed into the tournament loaded with great expectations, fresh from a starring role in winning yet another league and cup double with Barcelona (although the successes of the season were somewhat overshadowed by a calamitous Champions League collapse in the quarter-finals against Roma) and assigned the task of single-handedly leading Argentina to their first title since 1986 – and his first at senior international level.

In their demands that he must emulate his legendary predecessor in the Argentina number ten shirt, Diego Maradona, most people were happy to blithely overlook the fact that Messi's national squad was relatively weak compared with many others, and that the team had no settled style of play after a frenetic qualifying campaign featuring three different managers. Despite those serious and significant imperfections, Messi was still saddled with an enormous amount of hype and hope, nonchalantly expected to carry the team on his shoulders all the way to the title. Anything less, the watching world agreed in advance, would be a failure.

And failure it was. Argentina never looked like potential world champions for even five minutes of the six hours their challenge lasted, which saw them draw against Iceland, suffer a hammering at the hands of Croatia, scrape past Nigeria with a late goal and then eliminated by France in a manner far more convincing than the 4-3 scoreline suggested.

Argentina had been chaotic, disorganised and largely terrible and, on an individual level, Messi had offered relatively little. Hampered by the individual and collective weaknesses of his team, he was a marginal presence for the majority of the action and only provided two highlight moments – and one of them, a missed penalty against Iceland, was a highlight for all the wrong reasons.

So, the team failed and Messi failed. Argentina did not look capable of vaguely challenging for the World Cup, never mind actually winning it, and Messi did little to inspire them, allowing those who are keen to doubt his abilities or believe that he is a spent force to shout their criticisms from the rooftops to an eagerly receptive audience.

Messi's ongoing failure to win a senior title with Argentina is one of the first things we can all relate to, because our lives are shaped in a similar way.

Minor events, fine details, trivial and unavoidable circumstances, happy or tragic coincidences ... together they conspire to make us successes or failures, wealthy or underprivileged, famous or anonymous.

In 2014, it wouldn't have taken many changes in circumstances for Messi to have won the World Cup. Just a few bounces of the ball here and there would have made all the difference, but that didn't happen. In both 2015 and 2016, he only needed Argentina to score more penalties than Chile to become a Copa America champion. But that didn't happen either, so his international career will therefore forever be regarded by most people as a failure, and there's nothing he can do about it.

Like Messi, all we can do is give our best efforts to exert an impact upon our own defining moments and control as many aspects of our lives as possible, but ultimately we cannot escape the harsh truth that many of those key turning points in life are decided by factors outside our influence – or simply by random chance.

From the moment we are born into one family or another, in one part of town or another, possessing certain genetic abilities or others, with some opportunities left wide open but others firmly closed, we have no choice but to accept our fate in the same way that Messi, to a significant degree, has no choice but to accept his fate with Argentina. He did his very best, of course, but in the end many of the decisive factors were, in large part, beyond his control.

Messi's endless quest to win trophies and accolades – sometimes wonderfully successful, at other times deeply disappointing – has many similarities, despite the wildly different contexts, with the chance events which give our own lives their specific direction: the dream job we didn't get because another candidate went to the same school as the interviewer; the future life partner we meet through a friend of a friend; the sudden and unpreventable illness afflicting a loved one to reduce us to sleepless nights and worried days.

These ups and downs just happen in life, and very often there is nothing we can do about them. They mostly cannot be anticipated or foreseen, cajoled or warded off, and our only option is to respond to the hand we have been dealt to the best of our abilities. Sometimes, the best of our abilities will be sufficient and allow us to achieve our ambitions, as they did with Messi's nine Spanish league title triumphs. But on many more occasions, like Messi in his four World Cups, we will fail, however much we try.

That does not mean we should just give up. Life without continual striving for self-betterment would not be worth living, and our instinctive compulsion to set goals and just *get things done* – a belief in our ability to shape the direction of our lives by exercising free will – is probably the most striking feature that separates sentient human beings from unconscious robots.

In the same way that we should not – we cannot – simply give up on our career aspirations despite knowing that we will probably never become a millionaire chief executive, Messi did not give up on his World Cup dream ahead of Russia 2018 despite knowing that the Argentina team he captained was badly flawed. Because there's always that tantalising chance that maybe, just maybe, if we work hard enough and keep on striving, we might end up with everything we have ever wanted.

* * * * *

One point should be emphasised before we go any further: this book is an examination of Messi's career, not his personality. It is not a chronologically ordered biography and makes no attempt to uncover his secrets or analyse his life off the pitch except where it directly relates to his sporting endeavours.

As the title suggests, this book is about the 'Art of Living' as much as it is about Lionel Messi, using his exploits on the field of play as a starting point to examine various aspects of the human condition.

For that reason, Messi only appears in the third person. We are talking *about* him, not to him. The book is not an effort to decipher his innermost thoughts and beliefs; rather, it is an attempt to better understand the potential we all possess by examining his immense list of achievements – and his frustrating failures – which are visible to us all.

When Messi is playing football, he is operating at the outer limits of human capability, and that is what interests us here. When he is conducting one of his few media interviews (generally at the behest of his sponsors) or choosing his latest tattoo, he returns to the realm of the ordinary. In this book, we are solely interested in the *extra*ordinary: Messi's sporting prowess, the arena in which he excels and which sets an example for us all to aspire towards.

We will not, therefore, be analysing what Messi says (which wouldn't take long, in any case) or attempting to understand what he thinks about the world and life in general. Instead, we will be looking at what he *does* – an appropriate exercise for a player who has always led by example, by action, rather than by words.

This explains the identity of the interviewees, one of whom features prominently in each chapter. Although there are a couple from the football world (Messi's long-time former team-mate Pablo Zabaleta and Celtic manager Brendan Rodgers), we will also hear from a diverse group (a writer, a sports scientist, a hockey coach, a swimmer-turned-businessman and a basketball player) who can shed light on how his successes and failures are relevant in other fields of endeavour.

In doing so, we will occasionally stray far away from football and dip into areas such as psychology and philosophy. In Chapter Four, for example, we consider the nature of human freedom – an endlessly complex topic which has occupied some of the greatest minds in history for thousands of years. It would be impossible to cover the entirety of that subject in one chapter of a book about a footballer, so please forgive any omissions or over-simplifications, which are entirely the responsibility of the author. It should become clear that the content covered is only intended as an introduction to these areas, and by no means a final word.

* * * * *

Messi's fruitless but relentless pursuit of the ever-elusive World Cup trophy is only one aspect of his career which is worthy of deeper contemplation.

On the brighter side, there is plenty of food for thought in the way that a genetic condition and burning ambition compelled him to break up his family and move to another continent, thousands of miles from home, at the age of 13.

We can learn a great deal from contemplating how he has given expression to his unique individual talents within the framework of a team sport, whilst continually accepting enormous amounts of personal responsibility. There is another fascinating case study in seeing how he has been forced to consistently change and adapt to new playing positions and different environments over the course of his career.

We can also study the way in which Messi makes decisions and solves problems, and think about how those processes can inform the humdrum details of our own lives. And we can draw inspiration from seeing how, when all the money and fame are stripped away, Messi has always been primarily motivated and captivated by one simple thing: his pure love of football.

In the pages that follow, we will closely examine all those topics and more, and reflect upon how they can be related to ordinary everyday life. We will be helped along by insights from our interviewees, some of whom know Messi personally and others who are experts in their specific fields and can therefore broaden our perspectives, illuminating the shared bond of humanity we all have in common.

We might never be able to use our left foot to artfully arrow a match-winning 20-yard shot into the bottom corner, and we might never become world-famous millionaires. But if we study his greatness and consider how it resonates with our own lives, we might all be able to, in our own modest way, unleash our inner Messi.

Chapter One
The Price of Success

Argentina 2-1 Brazil
FIFA World Youth Championship semi-final
Tuesday 28 June 2005, Galgenwaard Stadion, Utrecht
It is the summer of 2005, and the most talented young footballers on the planet have spent the last few weeks gathered in the Netherlands with dreams of winning the sport's most prestigious junior tournament: the FIFA World Youth Championship.

After 36 games of intense competition, they have been whittled down to just four remaining teams – and one of the semi-finals is being contested between South American neighbours Argentina and Brazil, the protagonists of perhaps international football's most famous and heated rivalry, whose brightest emerging stars are now going head to head for a place in the final.

With just six minutes played, the ball is passed to Argentina's diminutive number 18, who receives possession slightly right of centre, around 30 yards from goal. His name, the whole world will soon know, is Lionel Messi.

An attacking player for Spanish club FC Barcelona with a handful of first-team appearances already under his belt, Messi controls adroitly and looks up. Seeing space to run into, he cuts inside and dribbles towards the penalty area, always keeping the ball on his favoured left foot.

Two, three, four little touches, using his body to shield the ball away from the Brazilian defender who is trying to close him down. Then, with the opposition players tracking back towards their own goal to cover the danger, Messi decides to shoot. From 25 yards, he lets fly. The connection is sugar sweet and the ball rockets, without a trace of swerve or dip, straight into the top right corner, leaving Brazilian goalkeeper and captain Renan groping hopelessly at thin air.

'Look at where he's put that ball!' gushes the Argentine television commentator in admiring tones. 'Unstoppable for all the goalkeepers in Brazil's history!'

It is certainly a sensational strike, even drawing applause from some of the Brazilian fans inside the stadium in Utrecht. But it is not enough to seal victory and progression to the final, because Brazil bounce back to level the game with 15 minutes remaining through a set-piece header from midfielder Renato. 1-1.

With the clock winding down, extra time is looking inevitable. Deep inside stoppage time, however, Argentina have one more chance to attack as the ball goes out of play for a throw-in, midway inside Brazil's half. Swiftly, midfielder Neri Cardozo gathers the ball on the left touchline and hurls it down the line into the path of Messi, who has already started his run into space.

Messi gathers the ball on the left flank, level with the edge of the box. He drives towards goal, drops his shoulder to beat a challenge, reaches the byline and cuts back a low cross to the near post. Argentina's substitute striker Sergio Aguero can't connect cleanly, but the loose ball drops obligingly to the team's captain, Pablo Zabaleta, who twists to shoot and sees a deflection wrong-foot Renan, sending the ball bouncing into the back of the net.

Victory for Argentina, and a place in the final! And Messi, with a brilliant goal and an assist, is again the hero, just as he had been three days earlier – the day after his 18th birthday – in the quarter-final against a Spain team featuring his former Barcelona youth team-mate Cesc Fabregas and future full internationals David Silva, Juanfran and Fernando Llorente.

In that last-eight encounter, with the game tied at one apiece midway through the second half, Messi had delivered a delicately weighted pass to break open the Spanish defence and release Gustavo Oberman, who finished well to make it 2-1. Two minutes later, Messi completed the job himself with a superb solo strike, receiving the ball on the edge of the penalty area and taking two deft touches to create space for a low shot which he dispatched clinically into the far corner.

Even now, though, with Spain and Brazil both defeated and a place in the final assured, there is still work to be done before Argentina can be crowned world youth champions. Next, they have to play Nigeria in the final.

Messi, as Argentina's star turn and most in-form player, will inevitably be at the heart of the Albiceleste's efforts in the title decider against a Nigeria team which overcame Morocco and hosts the Netherlands to reach the final – and as soon as the game starts he's in the thick of the action, snapping into a challenge to win the ball and spark his team's first attack after just 15 seconds.

Predictably, Messi is the central character when the scoring is opened towards the end of the first half. Argentina launch a counter-attack and Messi receives possession on the halfway line, turning sharply to dribble past one defender, then another, and then advancing into the box before being felled by a reckless challenge from Nigeria centre-back Dele Adeleye. It's a clear penalty, and Messi picks himself up to convert from the spot, coolly sending goalkeeper Ambruse Vanzekin the wrong way.

But Nigeria fight back, levelling the game early in the second half, and tension rises as the game ticks into its final quarter. Then, with 20 minutes to play, comes the next big moment: Aguero breaks into the area from the right and is clumsily fouled by opposing full-back Monday James, giving referee Terje Hauge an easy decision: another penalty.

After a long delay during Nigerian protestations, Messi again steps up to take his second spot-kick of the game. And again his aim is true, as he slides the ball into the bottom right corner while Vanzekin dives to the left. 2-1 to Argentina.

This time there's no way back for the African team, and 20 minutes later the final whistle is blown: Argentina are the world champions, and 18-year-old Lionel Messi is the hero. Two goals in the final, a goal and an assist apiece in the semi- and quarter-finals, and individual awards for the best player and leading scorer of the tournament.

Superstardom beckons!

Chasing the dream

Lionel Messi's soaring success as a teenager with his national under-20 team that summer in the Netherlands, which he described at the time as the best moment of his life, can be seen as a reward for all the effort he had exerted to get that far. A pat on the back from the gods of football for a job well done, and a tantalising promise that even more exciting and rewarding glories would be forthcoming if he could stay on his current path.

That path, though, had not been an easy one for Messi to tread.

The story of his childhood is already well known. But it is worth recapping again here, to provide some context for the journey this precocious talent had to travel before he could hold aloft the world's most prestigious trophy in youth football that sunny summer day in 2005.

As a young boy growing up in a middle-class family in Rosario, a medium-sized city in central Argentina, Lionel Messi (born on 24 June 1987) was like many others of his age: obsessed with football, always with a ball at his feet, and spending every spare second out on the street or in the city's parks playing games with his cousins and older brothers – Rodrigo and Matias – or with the local club side, Grandoli, who he started to represent at the age of five before then joining the youth ranks of one of the city's top-flight clubs, Newell's Old Boys.

His parents, Jorge and Celia, were happy to support their sons' shared infatuation with the round ball, and when they were unable to make the journeys to drop off and collect little Leo, Rodrigo and Matias, their much-cherished maternal grandmother – also named Celia – would always step in to ensure the boys could train and play, giving them endless supplies of moral and emotional encouragement every step of the way.

All of this is perfectly commonplace. Nothing unusual so far. Boys who love football, show some talent for the game and enjoy the support of a doting grandparent – we've heard this one before.

But the story for Lionel, who had always been very small, took a sharp deviation away from the norm at the age of ten, when he was diagnosed with a growth deficiency which could only be treated by the daily injection of hormones. And that treatment was going to be very expensive – around £1,000 a month, more than half of his father Jorge's salary.

Without the treatment, he would continue to grow at an abnormally slow rate, which would also inevitably slow his progress on the football field, allowing opposition players to easily brush him off the ball as they grew into tall and strong teenagers while he remained underdeveloped. If Leo's dreams of becoming a top-level professional footballer were to be maintained, there was no option: he needed those injections, plain and simple.

Initially, Jorge's social security benefits were able to cover the cost. And for two years, Lionel personally undertook the task himself, uncomplainingly injecting himself every single day without fail, alternating on a daily basis from left leg to right before he went to bed at night.

When he was 12, though, problems ensued because the state welfare system would no longer pay for the treatment. Jorge approached Leo's club, Newell's, who made encouraging initial noises but then failed to be forthcoming with the cash. So Lionel travelled 200 miles from his home town of Rosario to the country's capital, Buenos Aires, for a trial with Argentina's most successful club, River Plate. They were impressed, but not enough to invest so much money in a player so young.

The Messi family was running out of options. If Lionel's treatment was discontinued, his chances of playing football at a decent level would almost certainly be over – he would just be too small and frail to compete with his peers, and it was highly unlikely that he would ever be able to catch up.

Eventually, Jorge, Celia and Lionel decided together that only one course of action was open to them: they would move, all of them, to Europe, where they would find a club with a well-managed youth system and the necessary resources to pay for the hormone injections. It was their only choice, especially in the aftermath of a deep economic crisis which had wiped away the disposable incomes of millions of Argentines.

So they jumped on 1a plane to Barcelona, where Lionel won 32 trophies, scored 600 goals and became the greatest player in history.

That simple? No. Far from it.

Moving to Barcelona, which sounds so easy when it is reduced to those mere three words, was an extremely painful and complex process on many levels for the whole Messi family. It took months to plan, and meant uprooting four children (the boys had a younger sister, Maria Sol). It meant Jorge leaving his good job as a manager at an engineering firm. It meant Celia leaving her beloved extended family.

The whole thing was an enormous risk for such a young boy, even more so because there was no guarantee of a contract, treatment or actually anything at all beyond a short trial waiting at the other end.

Through the influential agent Josep Maria Minguella (who had also facilitated Diego Maradona's move to the Camp Nou many years earlier), the Messi family had been in touch with Barcelona, who were willing to offer a two-week trial after liking what they saw on the video tapes of Leo in action. But a trial is only a trial, and that is a very long way from a commitment to a contract. Lionel was only just 13 years old, still very small, and in those days signing any players from overseas was extremely unusual even for the biggest of clubs – never mind a tiny youngster who needed expensive medical treatment and a relocation package for his entire family.

Once the trial started in the summer of 2000, Lionel was painfully quiet off the pitch – one of his new team-mates, Cesc Fabregas, has since jokingly claimed he initially thought Messi was mute – but he was sensational on it, routinely dribbling past desperate challenge after desperate challenge to score sensational solo goal after sensational solo goal. Very quickly, his new team-mates and coaches were won over by his talent.

The decision of actually signing him, though, with all the expensive complications that entailed, was not one that anybody at the Camp Nou was prepared to take. Finally, the club's technical director Charly Rexach – who missed the first part of Messi's trial because he was attending the Olympic Games in Sydney – was convinced.

After witnessing the little young Argentine score a dazzling goal in a practice game on the artificial pitch in the shadow of the Camp Nou, Rexach made the commitment the family had been waiting for: Barça would sign Leo, they would pay for his treatment, they would provide accommodation for the family to live, and they would find a job with a decent salary for Jorge.

The Messi family, hugely relieved but still very nervous, returned to Argentina to prepare for the permanent move, with the promise from Rexach that everything would be sorted and Lionel would soon be presented with an official contract to formally sign for FC Barcelona.

Even then, though, it was far from plain sailing. Rexach was confronted by serious internal disagreement from board members who were staunchly against making such a big financial commitment, breaking all the club's budgets, to sign an under-sized 13-year-old from thousands of miles away on the basis of a brief trial. It was weeks rather than days before Rexach was finally able to push the deal through, giving more sleepless nights to Jorge, who was understandably worried that the Spanish club would eventually refuse to honour the agreement and the family would be left stranded.

Things became even harder for Leo when he finally returned to Barcelona in February 2001, five months after his initial trial, to sign officially and begin his new life in Europe. Firstly, as a foreigner, he was only allowed to compete in regional league games and mediocre-quality friendlies, severely limiting his initial playing time. And then, in just the second of those low-key matches he was allowed to play, he suffered a broken leg – his first serious injury – to force him out of action for the rest of the season.

In the meantime, Jorge was still failing to receive the agreed financial support from the club, and Leo's younger sister Maria Sol was missing Argentina so badly that in the summer she moved back to Rosario with her mother and brothers, leaving Lionel and his father alone in Barcelona, splitting the family in half across the deep wide ocean.

Leo, very much a vulnerable young teenager, was very close to his mother and missed her terribly, with their regular phone calls and web chats proving an inadequate replacement for seeing her every day. He cried himself to sleep on many occasions, and when he woke up his daytime routines were complicated by his lack of familiarity with the local Catalan language, further slowing his integration process and making him miss the familiar comforts of home even more.

All things considered, the shy and small Lionel Messi's transition from the innocent happiness of childhood at home with his friends and family to a supposedly glamorous new life at one of the biggest and best football clubs in the world was anything but easy.

Dream move? At times during those early days, it must have felt more like a nightmare.

Talent is not enough

Brendan Rodgers has spent the last two decades helping talented young footballers develop into successful senior professionals.

After his own playing days were cut short by a chronic knee injury at the age of 20, Rodgers set himself upon a new career path by taking a low-level coaching position within the junior ranks at Reading. Over the next ten years he gradually climbed up the club's academy coaching ladder before, in 2004, he was hand-picked by Jose Mourinho's assistant Steve Clarke to coach the youth team at Chelsea.

He subsequently moved into senior management with Watford, before continuing his career with stints at Reading, Swansea, Liverpool and now Celtic.

Even though it's ten years since he last coached an underage team, Rodgers has never forgotten his roots and has always placed his trust in youth: at Reading, he launched the careers of Gylfi Sigurdsson and Ryan Bertrand; his hat-trick hero in Swansea's Championship play-off final victory (against, ironically, Reading) was a young player he had previously worked with at Chelsea, Scott Sinclair; Liverpool came agonisingly close to winning the Premier League in 2014 with a pair of players in their early twenties, John Flanagan and Philippe Coutinho, and teenager Raheem Sterling, and Rodgers' consecutive treble-winning teams at Celtic have prominently featured young stars such as Moussa Dembele, Kieran Tierney, Patrick Roberts and Odsonne Edouard.

And after overseeing the progress of several hundred young players during the course of his long coaching career, Rodgers strongly believes in a simple mantra: talent is not enough.

'The first thing you look for in a young player is talent, and as a boy Messi clearly had natural talent which could be nurtured,' Rodgers explains in an interview for this book.

'But there are thousands upon thousands of talents throughout the world of football, and if you can't dedicate your life to becoming a player, talent alone eventually won't be enough to make it. To become a successful professional, lots of different qualities are also needed. One of the first and most important is mental resilience.'

Messi, we have seen from the story of his childhood, certainly had that resilience. From the age of ten, he had to spend three years administering himself with hormone injections every single day. When the money for that treatment ran out, Newell's Old Boys would not pay. River Plate also rejected him. Barcelona offered him a trial but took months to follow it up with a formal contract. When that eventually came, his entire family had to uproot their lives and move 6,000 miles away from home. He struggled with the local language and was slow to integrate with his new team-mates. His sister hated Spain so much she moved back home, leaving Lionel in a new and strange city with no friends, no mother, no siblings and only his father for company.

How easy it would have been, at any stage during that long and arduous process, for Messi to have simply given up. To have decided that his childish fantasy of becoming a professional footballer, which had every chance of coming to nothing anyway, wasn't worth the aggravation to himself or his family. To have taken the easy option, refused the injections, stayed in Rosario, carried on playing for Newell's at whatever level he happened to reach and settled for that.

But he did not give up. He took each obstacle and setback in his stride and carried on. When he was too small, when he had to inject himself every day, when he was effectively rejected by two clubs in Argentina, when he was kept waiting for months by Barcelona, when he was desperately homesick, when he was unable to play for his new club, when he was badly injured, when he didn't understand the language in his new city, when he was forced to live apart from his mother and his brothers ... when all those things happened, he just carried on.

Messi's mental fortitude during his childhood was really quite unconnected from his ability to play football. Yes, he could dribble the ball past a row of defenders. Yes, he could shoot with deadly accuracy into the bottom corner. But if he hadn't also been able to handle the severe mental demands of suffering from a hormone deficiency, moving to a new continent and leaving behind his family and friends, those sporting skills would not have taken him very far.

In fact, Rodgers believes a wealth of pure talent can even prove to be a drawback for young players when they suddenly become confronted by how competitive the professional game is, and by how much work they will have to undertake if they want to enjoy a prolonged career at the top.

'Lots of players have natural ability,' he says. 'But that natural ability can sometimes even be a difficulty, especially in the modern world of sports science and psychology where everything is analysed and natural advantages can be challenged.

'If you've got natural ability and that's always been your greatest strength, it can become a problem because everything has always been easy, but then you reach professional level and it's not easy at all. To overcome that, you need to have a capacity to learn and grow. How quickly can you learn? If you get a player who is naturally gifted but also has a capacity to learn, develop and grow, then you've got real potential.

'But if you want to be successful, there's always a price to pay. You have to continually test yourself. You have to make sacrifices. With Messi, at a very young age he was moved into a new culture, away from his family and friends, and he had to devote his life to football in completely new surroundings. Lots of young players can't cope with that, and having that ability to persevere when things get difficult is so important.'

Messi was mentally equipped to cope with the various challenges he faced, and that – as much as his brilliance with the ball at his feet – was an absolutely fundamental aspect of his continued development after he made the move to Barcelona.

He soon flourished in the youth team at La Masia, the club's famed football academy, scoring goals at a rapid rate and helping his team, which also included Fabregas and

Gerard Pique, win every trophy available. Then he accelerated through five different youth teams in the course of just one season before, in November 2003, less than three years after permanently arriving in Spain, he was given his first-team debut by manager Frank Rijkaard as a substitute in a friendly against Porto. A competitive debut came the following year, then his first goal at senior level (against Albacete in May 2005) and then, a few weeks later, the World Youth Championship title with Argentina.

The bewildering speed of Messi's progress during his teenage years could fool us into thinking that his advancement from youth team football in Argentina to superstardom in Barcelona had been a merry and gentle waltz. In reality, as we have seen, it had been anything but easy.

And when we see Messi now, scoring goals and winning titles, driving luxury cars and living in an ultra-modern beachside mansion, earning countless millions and receiving daily adulation, it's easy to fool ourselves into thinking that he has an easy life. That he is a lucky man. That he has landed on his feet. But before you can land, it's necessary to jump, and one of the main reasons that Messi is now blessed with more of the best things that life has to offer is that he has also been prepared to endure more of the hardest things that life has to offer without complaint and without backing down.

In the modern world, where social mobility is supposedly more fluid than ever before, we are often told to follow our dreams and have big ambitions. Impossible is nothing. Just do it.

Often these emotive rallying cries are little more than catchy slogans dreamed up by marketing executives with a new product range to sell, but Messi provides evidence that just occasionally, if you have the right mentality as well as talent, even the grandest of dreams really can come true.

'Because he was resilient and prepared to persevere, the natural talent of Lionel Messi became a working talent,' says Rodgers. 'And that working talent being applied every day over many years made him the genius he is. Don't get me wrong, there's also lots of natural ability as well. But it's by being a working talent that he's become the greatest player in the history of the game.'

The passion for success

For Messi, being crowned world champion at youth level in 2005 was the end of one era, and the beginning of another.

After that summer, he never again returned to junior football. Within a couple of months he was a full international. By the end of the season he was a household name, a regular in Barcelona's starting eleven, a European champion and preparing to play in another world championship – this time the real deal, the World Cup.

So the triumphant tournament in the Netherlands was the end of the journey for Messi as a boy. It was now time for him to become a man and continue his ascent towards greatness.

At this point it might appear inevitable that Messi, having overcome his growing pains and triumphed at the World Youth Championship, would then automatically become a hugely successful global superstar, as though the rest of his story was predestined and nothing could possibly go wrong.

But that's not the case at all. Plenty of players are great at 18, among the best in the world at that age, but then – for a variety of reasons – they fail to progress any further.

Just look at the line-ups from Argentina's games that summer in 2005, starting with his Albiceleste team-mates. Some of them, like Sergio Aguero, Pablo Zabaleta, Ezequiel Garay and Lucas Biglia, went on to enjoy excellent careers at the highest level, continuing to play alongside Messi on a regular basis with the senior national team for many years and cramming their mantelpieces full of silverware won with an array of the biggest clubs in the world.

Not everybody was quite so fortunate. For example, the striker who converted Messi's pass against Spain in the quarter-final and then kept Aguero out of the starting eleven for the final, Gustavo Oberman, never really established himself as a top-level professional, playing for several clubs in Argentina without any great success and suffering a failed attempt to break into Europe with brief spells at Cluj in Romania and Cordoba in Spain.

Oscar Ustari, the team's goalkeeper, ended up spending most of his playing days as an understudy at unremarkable clubs like Getafe, Almeria and Sunderland, before returning to Argentina to join Newell's Old Boys and then moving to Mexico with Atlas. That's not a terrible career, by any means, but it is well below the heights he might have hoped to hit when he accompanied Messi, Aguero and Zabaleta to world championship glory back in 2005.

The same pattern is repeated with the other competing teams in that tournament. Spain, for example, in addition to containing well-known names such as Cesc Fabregas and David Silva, were captained by central defender Miquel Robuste, who only managed a handful of senior top-flight appearances for Levante before seeing his career disappointingly dwindle away – he now plays for Badalona, just up the coast from Barcelona, in the Spanish third tier.

Brazil's scorer in the semi-final meeting with Argentina, Renato, spent the next few years occasionally representing various lower-ranked clubs and was last seen with Sao Caetano in the Brazilian second tier before finishing his professional career, aged just 28, in 2013. And the Nigeria goalkeeper beaten twice by Messi from the penalty spot in the final, Ambruse Vanzekin, has passed his career in his home country, mostly with Warri Wolves, and never advanced into the senior national team.

This might be hard to contemplate, but the same underwhelming fate could also have befallen Messi. There was nothing inevitable or preordained about the way in which he advanced from that summer's triumph to become the all-time leading scorer in Barcelona's history.

It could have all gone wrong for him, just as it did for Robuste and Renato.

In fact, it is quite striking, looking back now at the footage from that tournament, just how much room for improvement there was for the teenage Messi.

He had some spectacular moments, of course, including the crucial goals and assists against Brazil and Spain described at the beginning of this chapter. He was obviously very talented and had huge potential. But he also made a lot of mistakes, regularly and needlessly conceding possession by running with the ball for too long, heading straight into traffic or taking the wrong passing option.

Back then, in the summer of 2005, he was clearly a very good player, and easily recognisable as the elite performer he duly matured to become, but there was not always the final delivery to go with his dazzling dribbling ability. He was nowhere near the finished product, and had some jagged rough edges which needed to be smoothed off before he could be considered a top-class professional. He might never have made that progression at all.

What separates Aguero, Zabaleta, Fabregas and Silva from Ustari, Robuste, Renato and Vanzekin? Why were the former quartet able to maintain their youthful status among the very best players in the world while the latter became relative also-rans? At the age of 18, all these players were competing at more or less the same level. What explains the stark divergence in fortunes once they moved into adulthood?

There is no simple or single answer. Many, many things can go wrong as a talented teenager treads the precarious path towards lasting success: injuries; loss of focus; poor management or coaching; bad advice; weak character; lack of discipline or temperament and plain bad luck ... they can all conspire to derail even the most talented of young performers.

Celtic boss Brendan Rodgers – whose own playing career was ended early by injury – has already identified mental resilience and perseverance as key ingredients in the quest to convert youthful promise into a successful career, and the next quality he pinpoints is that most basic of human qualities: passion.

'Lots of the most successful players I've worked with have that passion,' Rodgers says. 'Two of them are now Messi's team-mates, Luis Suarez and Philippe Coutinho. When I worked with them at Liverpool, you could clearly see they just loved football. They wanted to train every day and play every day and they would always be among the last to leave because of their love and passion for football.

'That passion is so important, especially now in the modern game where in many ways it's become a business. If you can retain that passion and pure enthusiasm for the game, even in the environment of a business where there's so much money flying around, that should allow you to do the right things as a professional.'

For young players, Rodgers believes that displaying passion and commitment both on the pitch and on the training ground also carries the additional benefit of earning the respect of the squad's established senior professionals, who do not take kindly to the sight of hot prospects from the youth team arriving at first-team level with a nonchalant sense of entitlement.

'When you're a young player, your aim should be to get in with the senior players and show them they can trust you,' says Rodgers. 'And that trust is not based only upon your talent but also upon how hard you're prepared to work. Messi has always been the type of player whose football did his talking and that would have made the process easier, just another part of his journey.'

Messi's passion for football, his unadulterated love of the game, has always been evident from the almost naïve enthusiasm he displays on the pitch, and at professional level one of the earliest signs of this quality – proving unequivocally to his team-mates and everyone else that he was worthy of respect – came in March 2007, when he took a starring role in a thrilling Clasico meeting with Real Madrid.

The two teams had been faltering in recent weeks with Madrid winning just one of their last six games and manager Fabio Capello consequently rumoured to be on the verge of losing his job, while hosts Barça were also under pressure after losing two of their previous three games. It was consequently expected to be a tight, nervy affair – but instead, Messi, despite only being 19 years old, turned it into a Clasico classic.

Ruud van Nistelrooy opened the scoring early on for Madrid, but Messi soon levelled by receiving a pass from Samuel Eto'o and sliding a precise low shot past Iker Casillas. Almost immediately, still with just 12 minutes played, van Nistelrooy restored the visitors' advantage from the penalty spot, only for Messi to pounce on a loose ball and fire home, making it 2-2 before half-time.

After Barça were reduced to ten men with the dismissal of Oleguer Presas, Madrid went ahead for the third time through Sergio Ramos's flicked header from a set piece, but irrepressible teenager Messi would not be denied: in the 91st minute he took Ronaldinho's pass in his stride, surged away from two defenders and thrashed a powerful strike past Casillas, before racing away in a frantic shirt-tugging, badge-kissing, shouting and screaming celebration which made it clear just how much the goal had meant to him.

That hat-trick in March 2007 showed that Messi, at the age of 19, was very much on the right track. He had the talent. He had the resilience and the perseverance. He had the passion and the willingness to work hard.

All the ingredients were coming together, but there were still more challenges to overcome.

From always injured to always available

An important side note to that Clasico hat-trick was that, even though the game came two and a half years after Messi's competitive first-team debut, it was the first time he had ever played against Real Madrid at the Camp Nou.

This was because the early years of his career were blighted by a series of injuries, mainly muscle strains with Messi struggling to grow into his body as he developed from a boy into a man – not helped by his poor diet, which featured an excess of junk food and not enough fruit and vegetables.

The regular recurrence of these relatively minor but frustrating injury absences was a warning sign for Messi: if he had allowed them to continue, he risked seriously testing the patience of Barcelona's fans, directors and coaches, who would have been very reluctant to hand out lucrative new contracts or give a more prominent playing role to a youngster who was nearly always injured, no matter how much talent he had.

Fortunately, Messi and his advisors were sharp enough to recognise the dangers and he took the necessary action, putting himself on a strict new diet and devising a tailored training programmes to look after his injury-prone muscles, and the apparent fragility of his youth has now been long forgotten: since 2008 he has never played less than 30 league games in a season, and he has made at least 50 appearances in all competitions in eight of the last ten campaigns.

Brendan Rodgers believes this durability, which has arisen from self-imposed discipline, is another key to Messi's success, saying: 'His availability has been remarkable.

'To achieve everything that he's achieved, and score the number of goals he's scored, he's had to be available to play 50 or 60 games a season every year for ten years. To do that you need to be at the top level of your fitness, and look after yourself in every aspect of your lifestyle.

'I've worked with some players who I believed were going to be top players but they could never find that availability, and with Messi it's very clear that he looks after himself in order to be available to play every week.'

Although he is too discreet and polite to name names or point fingers, one of the gifted players who worked with Rodgers but failed to always be available – and perhaps the starkest example of sadly squandered talent among Messi's contemporaries – is Mario Balotelli.

During his teenage years with Inter Milan, Balotelli was a genuine sensation. In 2008, at the age of 17, he scored twice to knock Juventus out of the Coppa Italia, prompting the website *sportslens.com* to gush: 'His touch and technique [are] already reminiscent of the greats of football history.' Later that year he became Inter's youngest ever scorer in the Champions League, and the club's president Massimo Moratti raved: 'The quality he has you cannot ignore and we must support him to the fullest.'

Inter's next manager Jose Mourinho – never noted for his ability to develop young players – did not fully agree with that sentiment, and after a series of disciplinary issues Balotelli was allowed to join Manchester City for £22.5m (a substantial sum in those days) in the summer of 2010, reuniting with his first professional manager Roberto Mancini. Balotelli was still only 20 years old, and this was his second chance to blossom into an elite performer – a possibility underlined when he was given the 2010 Golden Boy award for the best young player in the world, previously presented to Messi in 2005.

At first, there were hopeful signs that Balotelli would eagerly seize his latest opportunity as he quickly became a fixture in ambitious City's starting eleven and finished his first season in England by being named man of the match in the 1-0 FA

Cup Final victory over Stoke, playing a key role as his club won their first trophy in 35 years.

The following season also contained some memorable highlights, including two goals and a fabulous performance in an era-defining 6-1 victory over Manchester United at Old Trafford, and an assist to Aguero for the dramatic title-winning goal in the final minute of the final day of the Premier League campaign against Queens Park Rangers.

But his disciplinary problems persisted, and midway through the following season City's patience – just as Inter's had a couple of years previously – finally ran out. Balotelli returned to Italy with AC Milan, where the same cycle repeated itself: occasional flashes of brilliance overshadowed by a lack of discipline and inconsistent performances. A poor season under Rodgers in Liverpool was followed by a poor season back with Milan, and Balotelli, now 28 at the time of writing, has spent the last couple of years attempting to revive his career in France with Nice.

Balotelli's talent has never been in doubt. When he was 18, it could be argued that he was better than Messi had been at the same age. Even now, at his best he is unplayable. But his best has only been evident on rare occasions, and one of his greatest weaknesses has been his lack of availability: seven of his 12 professional seasons have seen him make less than 30 appearances in all competitions.

Balotelli is enjoying a good career as a top-flight player. He will earn many millions, win a few trophies and could yet resurrect his international career after recently being recalled by Italy for the first time in four years. But with his boundless talent he could have been a world-beater, one of the very best of his generation – perhaps even as good as Messi. The reason he so far has failed to do so has nothing to do with his ability, and everything to do with his application.

And his story is a stern reminder that world class at the age of 18 does not necessarily mean world class at the age of 28. The road to success is tough; staying on it is even tougher.

Ronaldinho's example to follow ... and avoid

Early in his professional career, Messi was given a close-up lesson about exactly what can happen if the necessary commitment to continued excellence is not sustained, with a high-profile team-mate swerving off the path in spectacular and tragic fashion.

When Messi progressed into the senior team, the undisputed king of the Camp Nou was Ronaldinho. The flamboyant Brazilian was a World Cup winner with Brazil in 2002, joined Barça from Paris St Germain a year later and proceeded to thrill and astound fans on a weekly basis with his joyfully audacious and endlessly inventive play.

Ronaldinho was at the peak of his powers, widely regarded as the best attacking player in the world – certainly the most thrilling – and he won the Ballon d'Or award by a landslide in 2005. He even earned the rarity of a standing ovation from Real Madrid fans after delivering a particularly astonishing two-goal display in Barcelona's 3-0 victory at the Bernabeu in November 2005 (a game which also marked Messi's Clasico debut).

Happily for Messi, Ronaldinho was also a commendably generous and open-hearted individual, who welcomed the young Argentine into the fold with open arms. Rather than jealously regarding him as a potential rival and usurper, the Brazilian superstar saw Messi as a little brother and did everything he could to make him feel comfortable, best illustrated when he brilliantly set up the teenager for his first goal at senior level against Albacete in May 2005 and then paraded him to the impressed crowd by lifting him high upon his shoulders – a touching gesture which also, with hindsight, became heavily symbolic.

Ronaldinho's arrival in Barcelona in 2003 had sparked a serious upturn in fortunes for the Catalan club, injecting a much-needed sense of optimism after a fallow few years, and he is still very much regarded as a hero figure by fans (many of whom, with a hint of embarrassed guilt, will quietly confide – when they're sure that nobody else is listening – that Messi might be the better player of the two, but that Ronaldinho was more exciting).

With Samuel Eto'o and Deco playing key supporting roles in the attacking positions, Frank Rijkaard steadying the ship from the sidelines and Messi's rich potential starting to unfold, Ronaldinho inspired Barcelona to consecutive La

Liga title triumphs in 2005 and 2006, as well as the second Champions League crown in the club's history in 2006. He looked untouchable.

But then, just as he reached the summit, came the fall. The problem was that Ronaldinho lived his life in the same way that he played his football: with a smile on his face, full of energy, full of exuberance, and above all else just wanting to enjoy himself. Reports started to circulate that he was spending more and more time in the nightclubs of Barcelona with a wide selection of the region's finest-looking ladies, sometimes arriving for training in such a bad state that he fell asleep in the changing room and couldn't take part in the session.

Inevitably, Ronaldinho started to lose his physical shape, and his performances dipped. He was still conjuring moments of magic, but they became less frequent, and his lack of professionalism also prompted rumours of divisions within the squad as some players became increasingly frustrated that their star man was not pulling his (rapidly growing) weight.

Ronaldinho could not regain his peak form, and in the summer of 2008 the club decided enough was enough: he was promptly sold to AC Milan. At the time it was a controversial decision but it was proven to be the correct one, with Ronaldinho never again returning to his best and only becoming a partial success during his three years in Italy, before returning to Brazil to while away the remainder of his career with a series of clubs in his homeland, occasionally winning trophies and scoring spectacular goals but never recapturing the form which had made him such a glorious sight between 2002 and 2006.

Watching Ronaldinho's descent very carefully was a young and impressionable Lionel Messi, who hugely admired the charismatic Brazilian during his early days in the senior squad and soon became a friend as well as a team-mate, joining Ronaldinho, Deco and Sylvinho at the 'Brazilian table' in the club's dining room and gratefully allowing himself to be taken under the superstar's wing.

This was a key time in both Messi's career and his life. He was 17 when Ronaldinho created his first goal and hoisted him high upon his shoulders in that game against Albacete; he had just turned 21 when, a little more than three years later, the Brazilian was sold. During that crucial period, Messi was leaving behind his childhood and entering adulthood. He was becoming a man, and also becoming a highly paid, hugely admired megastar footballer – with all the tempting off-the-pitch opportunities that entails. He also knew exactly how those opportunities could have been exploited, because he saw Ronaldinho do it nearly every night.

The high life, the good times, the glitz and glamour, the extra-curricular entertainment ... they were all opening up in front of Messi, who could have very easily taken advantage of a first-rate guide into this new and beguiling lifestyle in the form of his team-mate and friend.

If Messi had allowed Ronaldinho to become his mentor off the pitch as well as on the field of play, his story could have taken a very different path. He could, perhaps, have taken his eye off the ball to the extent that he became another version of Mario Balotelli, failing to fulfil his endless potential and instead spending more time enjoying his wealth and fame and everything they can offer to a young man who allows himself to be dazzled by the bright city lights on the sunny Mediterranean coast. He could have chosen fun over football, hijinks over high achievement, bedpost trophies over football trophies, the easy life over hard work.

Many people, in the same situation, would have done exactly that. How easy it would have been for such a young, naïve and inexperienced young man to start flashing his newly-earned cash, joining Ronaldinho in carousing until sunrise and neglecting to continue to do the things that had taken him to the top in the first place.

That would have been even easier for Messi due to the regular injuries, as mentioned earlier, he suffered during this period, restricting his availability for first-team action but increasing his availability for nightclub action.

Instead, though, he took the opposite course to Ronaldinho. Rather than yielding to temptation, he made even more sacrifices. He worked harder than ever to regain his fitness and didn't allow his head to be turned – he remained, and still is, a quiet, stay-at-home kind of guy, reserving his energies for training and playing rather than dancing vertically and horizontally in the nightclubs of Barcelona. He did everything that Ronaldinho didn't, setting himself up for a career of incredible durability rather than becoming a flame that shone brilliantly but quickly burned out.

In addition to Messi's mental fortitude, Brendan Rodgers believes the young Argentine was able to avoid following the example of Ronaldinho, whose decline was played out in vivid detail right in front of his eyes, in significant part thanks to the values he had been immersed in during his time with the club's youth team programme.

'Sometimes the greatest inspiration you can be given is when you have an example of what *not* to do,' emphasises the Celtic boss.

'When he came into the first team, Messi will have looked at Ronaldinho as an incredible talent and been inspired by him because, in those few years when he was at his absolute peak, Ronaldinho was the best player in the world, no doubt about it.

'But Messi was given an education by Barça, and by the time he reached the first team those values and principles were in place. That culture was all about humility and respect, not just for others but for themselves as well. And if you look at the generation of players who came through that culture at La Masia – people like Xavi, Iniesta, Busquets – they all have those qualities.'

Ronaldinho, with his increasing fondness for the excesses of life, was threatening to undermine that culture just as Messi was ready to explode towards greatness. So he had to go. And the differing directions their careers followed after they were separated in 2008 makes it clear that if you want to be the best and continue to be the best, it's necessary to make sacrifices. If you want to bask in the bright glow of the candle at both ends, sooner or later you'll end up getting burned.

Messi vs Ronaldo: the greatest rivalry?

Here is a rather obvious statement: if you want to be the best, you have to be better than everyone else. And if one of your competitors is very, very good indeed, you have no choice but to be even better.

By the summer of 2009, just a year after Ronaldinho's departure, Lionel Messi was already being widely lauded as the best player in the world having played a starring role in Barcelona's historic treble at the end of Pep Guardiola's spectacular first season in charge, including a brilliant headed goal in the Champions League Final victory over Manchester United in Rome.

That same summer, Real Madrid smashed the world transfer record by signing a player who was intended to provide some serious rivalry to Messi both on the pitch in terms of goals scored and trophies won, and off the pitch in terms of individual accolades and global marketing power.

And so was born one of the greatest rivalries in the history of sport: Lionel Messi and Cristiano Ronaldo.

Ronaldo was already a bona fide superstar when he was recruited by Madrid for £80m from Manchester United. Fittingly, his last game for the Red Devils had been that Champions League Final against Barça, where he dazzled in the early stages and repeatedly came close to netting the opener before a goal from Samuel Eto'o changed the complexion of the contest and allowed Messi and co to take over.

The Portuguese star had already won one Champions League crown, overcoming Chelsea in rain-sodden Moscow the previous year, and had just helped United to their third consecutive Premier League title, during which time he blasted home 91 goals in all competitions – 20 more than Messi in the same time frame.

What they have both achieved since then is truly mind-boggling.

By the end of the 2017/18 season, when he left Madrid to join Juventus, Ronaldo had scored 450 goals in Spain to surpass the Bernabeu club's previous record holder, Raul, who mustered a mere 323.

Messi, meanwhile, had plundered no less than 552 competitive goals for Barcelona, more than doubling the amount registered by the club's second-highest scorer, Cesar Rodriguez Alvarez (232).

And that's just the start of it. The outlandish figures recorded by these two intergalactic superhuman superheroes just keep on dripping off the page (stats accurate to the end of the World Cup). Between them, they have scored 694 league goals alone since Ronaldo's move to Spain in 2009. They have both scored at least 40 goals in every single season since 2010, a feat which earned gushing praise and awards galore for Mohamed Salah when he did it just once.

Messi has scored 30 hat-tricks in La Liga; only Ronaldo has more with 34. They have won five Ballon d'Or awards each, exercising an absolute duopoly over the honour for a decade. They are both the leading scorers for their respective countries: Messi with 65 goals for Argentina, Ronaldo with 84 for Portugal. They are the top two scorers in Champions League history, Ronaldo on 120 and Messi with 100, streets ahead of third-placed Raul (71).

The problem we have, sitting in the middle of all these outrageous accomplishments, is that statistics like those have become so well known and comfortably familiar we have started to take them for granted. Messi scored 45 goals last season? Well, that's below his usual standard. Ronaldo netted 15 in the Champions League? Of course he did.

Their goalscoring feats have become normalised, when really they are not normal at all. In the history of football, they are completely abnormal.

So let's step back for a moment, and get some perspective on what these two players have done over the last decade.

Barcelona and Real Madrid are two of the wealthiest, most prestigious and most demanding clubs in sport. They have won honours galore and their list of famous former forwards reads like a roll call of all-time greats: Alfredo Di Stefano, Ferenc Puskas, Johan Cruyff, Diego Maradona, Raul, Romario, Ronaldo Nazario, Ronaldinho ... these two mega-giants of the global sporting landscape have *always* been heavyweight contenders, and they have *always* boasted a plethora of world-class talent.

But over the last few years they have simultaneously possessed players who set new goalscoring records at such a dizzying pace it's not even a contest: Messi has recorded 320 *more* goals (and counting) than anyone else who has ever played for Barcelona; the iconic Hugo Sanchez didn't even manage *half* the total that Ronaldo plundered for Madrid. These are astronomical achievements amid some serious competition, and the fact that neither of them have suffered a single bad season, and neither of them have slowed down since they turned 30, makes it even more incredible.

Being granted the opportunity to watch just one of Messi or Ronaldo would be special enough, yet for nine years before Ronaldo's move to Juventus we had the pleasure of watching both of them in the same league at the same time. Real Madrid and Barcelona both boasting players who obliterate all their club's scoring records by averaging a goal per game for nearly a decade has never happened before, and it will never happen again.

Messi very much had the better of their early exchanges, claiming that Champions League victory over United in 2009, playing a starring role in the famous 'Manita' victory in 2010 (see Chapter Four), netting twice at the Bernabeu in a Champions League semi-final in 2011 (see Chapter Three) and winning La Liga three years in a row. During that period, Ronaldo's only significant scalp was a cup-clinching headed goal in the Copa Del Rey Final in 2010, and Messi's haul of four straight Ballon d'Or awards between 2009 and 2012 emphasised the gap between them.

Slowly, though, Ronaldo then started to claw back some of the lost ground, and their personal battle soon reached a dazzling crescendo which has somehow been maintained ever since.

The rivalry was perhaps best encapsulated in a Camp Nou Clasico in October 2012. Ronaldo struck first when he received a pass from Karim Benzema and beat Victor Valdes with a low shot inside the near post; Messi responded by latching on to a loose ball in the box to fire home; then Messi conjured more magic with a spectacular 25-yard free kick into the top right corner, only for Ronaldo to answer back with a crisp finish from Mesut Ozil's through ball. The game finished Barcelona 2-2 Real Madrid, Messi 2-2 Ronaldo, summing up both their incredible individual achievements and their unstoppable thirst for goals.

In the last five years, it has been more or less honours even in terms of trophies. Messi has been on top domestically, winning four more league titles to Ronaldo's one, but the Portuguese has dominated in Europe with four Champions League crowns to Messi's one, also registering the three highest-scoring seasons in the competition's history. Ronaldo has also tasted triumph on the international stage, winning Euro 2016 with Portugal (even though he was off the pitch, injured, when it happened) to eclipse Messi's three losing finals with Argentina.

Without wishing to enter the debate about which of the two players is better, it's clear that both of them have produced almost unheard-of levels of consistency for a very long period and, although this can only ever be a hypothetical discussion, it's interesting to consider whether Messi or Ronaldo would have been able to sustain such outrageous rates of productivity without one key factor: each other.

Their personal relationship is, by all accounts, distant but respectful. There's none of the malice or bitterness that tabloid sections of the media would sometimes like us to believe, and Messi has repeatedly stated that he does not regard himself and Ronaldo as rivals – he is only focussed on winning team trophies, he claims, and has no interest whatsoever in the media-hyped individual battle between himself and the Portuguese star.

But is that completely true? Although (as we will discuss in detail in a later chapter) Messi is very much a team player who is prepared to sacrifice individual ambitions for the good of the group, in the ultra-competitive world of elite sport it's difficult to imagine that Ronaldo's presence in Madrid for nine years had absolutely zero motivational impact.

Of course, Messi and Ronaldo would have both reached extremely high levels of performance if the other one didn't exist (there was no Ronaldo to inspire Messi on the playing fields of Rosario, or during the 2005 World Youth Championship, or during his Clasico hat-trick in 2007), but from Michelangelo and Leonardo Da Vinci to Taylor Swift and Katy Perry, history is full of examples of high achievers who have used personal rivalries as fuel for their own competitive juices. Simply stated, it's self-evident that if Messi wants to be the best player in the world, for the last decade that has necessarily entailed being better than Ronaldo.

The extent to which Messi and Ronaldo have inspired each other is an interesting if ultimately unprovable debate, but Brendan Rodgers believes internal aspirations rather than external rivalries have been more important in their astronomical achievements.

'I think we're fortunate that we've had two of the greatest players in the history of the game playing beside each other for so long, but I'm not sure how much they've influenced each other,' he says.

'Maybe subconsciously in some ways they've driven each other on, but I think both those players inherently have that hunger to be the very best players they can be. With the very elite performers, that drive comes from within.

'If you look at Messi, of course he's always been playing in a top quality team in a system that he knows so well, but he has still had this inner desire and hunger to keep on improving. And there's also a lot of humility – it clearly doesn't matter to him what he's already achieved, he still has the same desire and humility to know that he has to keep on working hard and practising.'

As we can't inhabit their brains, we will never know for sure – and perhaps neither will the players themselves – whether Messi and Ronaldo would have been quite so good without the other one. But perhaps rather than competing with each other as it has often been assumed, they have really been engaged in an even more intense battle: competing with themselves.

Dead-ball king ... eventually

One of the main reasons that Messi and Ronaldo have enjoyed such incredible longevity has been their ability to find ways of getting better with every passing year. Even as their bodies have inevitably slowed down, they have adapted to the passage of time and remained just as effective as ever, if not more so.

For a specific example of Messi's relentless quest for self-improvement, we can consider the remarkable transformation he has effected in his ability to score from set pieces.

It's surprising to learn that during his early days at Barcelona, he was not particularly good at free kicks and, in any case, he very rarely had the chance to take any because ownership of those duties belonged well and truly to the masterful Ronaldinho.

As England fans will ruefully remember from the 2002 World Cup quarter-final, the Brazilian was a sublime dead-ball expert, capable of curling, caressing or thrashing the ball into the net from practically any angle or distance. Over the course of his career he netted 66 free-kick goals, and it's striking just how varied they were – the top-right corner was Ronaldinho's favoured destination, but he could and did put them anywhere.

So Messi didn't really have much chance to start taking free kicks until after Ronaldinho left the Camp Nou in the summer of 2008, and he didn't need long to net his first: a cheeky, quickly taken effort before the wall had been set in a home win over Atletico Madrid two months into the new season.

At this stage, however, Messi's goals from set pieces initially only came in a slow trickle, and he was by no means a dead-ball specialist. It was only in 2009 – five years after his senior career got underway – that he started to improve his output, and that was partly thanks to advice he received from Diego Maradona during the former World Cup-winning captain's spell as Argentina manager.

According to Fernando Signorini, the national team's fitness coach at the time who was later interviewed by Spanish television channel La Sexta, during one training session Messi took three consecutive poor free kicks and started to walk away in frustration when Maradona accosted him. The old master put his arm around Messi and told him to try a few more, and to allow his foot to linger on the ball for a fraction of a second longer when he made contact, otherwise 'the ball won't know what you want it to do'.

Implementing that advice by committing himself to a lot of practice – which he continues on an almost daily basis – Messi transformed his free-kick-taking abilities beyond all recognition, and he is now one of the most prolific dead-ball experts in history: in the 2017/18 season he scored six goals from set pieces to equal a Spanish league record set 11 years earlier by ... guess who? ... Ronaldinho.

Like Ronaldinho, Messi has developed a wide repertoire of set pieces and can score anywhere the opposing defensive wall and goalkeeper happen to leave him with an opening. In the spring of 2018, for example, he netted free kicks in three consecutive games: the first, against Girona, was craftily drilled under the wall into the bottom left corner; the next at Las Palmas was a rocket into the top left corner; and then he defeated second-placed Atletico Madrid – effectively sealing the league title – with a wickedly dipping missile into the top right corner.

Interestingly, the inventive 'under-the-wall' free kick that Messi pulled out of the bag against Girona was a trick he had previously executed in a World Cup qualifying victory over Uruguay nearly six years earlier. But even then the idea wasn't original. In fact, he had stolen it from a former team-mate: in 2006, Messi was present in person to witness a free kick being rifled low under the wall during Barcelona's Champions League meeting with Werder Bremen. The taker? Ronaldinho, of course. The apprentice had learned from the master, in order to eventually overtake him.

This determination to learn and keep on improving is one of the keys to Messi's greatness, and perhaps the single most important key to his astonishing consistency and durability – and one of the greatest lessons he can teach us: you are never too good or too old to improve.

By the time he received Maradona's set-piece-taking advice in 2009, he was already the best player in the world, and we have already seen how much hard work had been necessary to propel him to that lofty status.

Even then, though, despite all the plaudits and tributes he was being showered with on a daily basis, Messi still didn't think he had reached the summit of his potential. He was still humble enough to remain receptive to new ideas, and the improvement in his free-kick technique effected by Maradona, along with the adoption of specific tricks of the trade such as Ronaldinho's under-the-wall creation, meant he was able to do something which didn't really seem possible but always is, whoever you are and however good you are: he became even better.

But we are now ready to discover that no matter how much determination, passion and commitment Messi has devoted to the challenge of making himself the best footballer he could possibly become, he will never be perfect.

Even the best dead-ball experts can't score from every free-kick, and sometimes the most important moments of them all result in heart-wrenching failure.

Chapter Two
Learning to Lose

Germany 1-0 Argentina (after extra time)
FIFA World Cup Final
Sunday 13 July 2014, Estadio Maracana, Rio de Janeiro

It is injury time of extra time in the World Cup Final. The final few seconds of the most important game in football.

Argentina, losing by one goal to nil against Germany, have possession inside their own half. Javier Mascherano drives forward, calling upon his final reserves of energy to break into opposition territory, and threads a short pass to Lionel Messi, who immediately turns and darts towards the German goal, desperately seeking one last chance to release a killer pass or to shoot.

Bastian Schweinsteiger, exhausted, tracks the opposition captain's run with everything he has left to give and lunges at him in desperation, knowing that allowing Messi to continue his dribble would give the world's best player the opportunity to advance menacingly towards the penalty area. Schweinsteiger succeeds in making contact, sends Messi sprawling, and Italian referee Nicola Rizzoli inevitably whistles for a free kick.

A free kick. Thirty yards from goal, right of centre – almost the perfect angle for a left-footed player like Messi, although a few yards further out than he would prefer, especially against an excellent goalkeeper like Germany's Manuel Neuer.

With 49 seconds of the additional two minutes already elapsed, the whole world knows this will be Argentina's last chance of equalising to force a penalty shoot-out. The whole world also knows that Messi will take the free kick, and that he will shoot. No cross. No clever routine carefully honed on the training ground. No attempted deceit. Just one man, a ball, a defensive wall, a goalkeeper and the goal.

As soon as the set piece is awarded, Messi is up, back on his feet. Alert and ready, looking for the ball so he can place it and prepare for the shot. Referee Rizzoli takes a few seconds to stand over Messi and make sure he doesn't stealthily nudge the ball a few inches forward – something he regularly does when the officials aren't looking – while Germany build their wall and the physically spent Schweinsteiger receives treatment.

A nervous hush has fallen over the vast stadium. German fans have pressed the pause button on the songs of celebration they were jubilantly roaring a few seconds earlier, now fearing their victory is not yet secure ... because Messi has a chance to shoot. Argentine supporters, silent and some already in tears, are clinging on to the dream that all might not yet be lost ... because Messi has a chance to shoot.

Due to Schweinsteiger's treatment, nearly two minutes elapse between the award of the free kick and Rizzoli blowing his whistle again to signal that it can be taken, giving Messi plenty of time to fully confront the enormity of the situation.

This is the moment Messi has spent his whole life preparing for. There could be no bigger stage and no bigger moment than right here, right now. This free kick and joyous glory, or this free kick and crushing disappointment.

What can possibly be going through his mind? Is he thinking back to everything he has gone through to reach this moment? Daydreaming about the personal and collective glory that lies within reach if he can arrow the ball beyond Neuer's grasp and into the top corner? Calculatingly his options for the placement of the shot and exactly how he should strike it? Or is he simply staying inside his bubble, trying very hard to think about nothing at all?

We will never know how many thousands of disconnected thoughts and images flashed through his mind in those two minutes but now, with the whistle blown, Messi is ready. The world is ready.

Messi brushes through his hair with his left hand, briefly rubs his face with his right, glances over his right shoulder as though he was expecting to see someone there, and begins his run-up. This is it.

Short, stuttering steps in his usual manner. Three paces and he's ready to strike. Right foot planted. Body leaning forward, head over the ball. He pulls back his famous left foot and shoots ... and the ball flies horribly high and wide, nowhere near the goal. Nowhere near the goal at all.

Messi trudges away, looks down to the ground in disbelief and then throws back his head in despair, closing his eyes to blot out the horror of the moment. Relieved German fans resume their raucous celebrations. Neuer slowly retrieves the ball, thumps it downfield, and a few seconds later Rizzoli whistles again, this time for the last time. The game is over. The World Cup is over, and Germany are champions.

Messi's shot was the last meaningful kick of the game. It could have been his Ultimate Hero Moment, the goal to cement his legacy as the greatest player in the history of football. Instead, it was one of the worst free kicks he's ever taken.

A few minutes later, he is standing alone. In fact, despite being engulfed by the gaze of 74,738 spectators, dozens of frantic flash bulb photographers and busy crews of invasive television cameras relaying live close-up images to the watching world, he has never been more alone than right now.

Everyone on the Argentine side of the pitch is hurting, of course. But the defeat they have just suffered is particularly painful for Messi because he is their captain, their leader and their all-pervasive, all-powerful emblem. This has partly been their World Cup, but it has really been *his* World Cup – his chance to reach his date with destiny.

For the last few weeks, Messi has given everything within his considerable powers to answer the challenge of leading his team – his country – to glory. The knowledge that everybody, including himself, has been expecting him to meet that challenge was an enormous burden to bear but he has shouldered it without complaint and he came close to succeeding. So, so close. But in the end, when a lifetime of dedication came down to a few minutes of competition, Messi and Gonzalo Higuain couldn't take their chances, sending the ball a few inches the wrong side of the post. Then Germany substitute Mario Gotze put his much more difficult opportunity exactly where he wanted to, and now the dream has been extinguished.

And so Messi is a broken man, standing a few paces in front of his silenced, motionless team-mates, who know that even attempting to console their talisman would be pointless. He is entirely beyond consolation; there is no possible consolation.

Sport can be unspeakably spiteful, and now Messi is subjected to the merciless, mocking, taunting cruelty of being forced to walk past the trophy – the object of his life's desires – so that he can be presented with the award for the competition's best player, a meaningless trinket that he has no interest in collecting.

There is Messi; there is the World Cup trophy ... *the* trophy. They are so close together he could stretch out his hands and grab it, but subject and object have been destined to remain apart. Within reach but cruelly out of reach – perhaps forever. As he glances vacantly towards the trophy he has coveted and chased for his entire life, the shock to Messi's system has shut down his senses, and his haunted, ghoulish, bloodless expression as he trudges blindly past the glittering gold is so striking, so vivid and so intense that an image capturing the moment is subsequently named the best photograph of the year.

That photograph captures a moment, but it is so powerful because it also does much more than that: it captures a lifetime. A lifetime of ruthlessly striving, relentlessly and without compromise, to be the best possible footballer. To score goals, to win games, to claim titles. To lift the World Cup.

And there, right in front of his eyes, there *is* the World Cup. But Messi won't be lifting it. Argentina have lost, and he has failed.

Professional losers

For any professional athlete, even the very best, losing is a way of life. Failure is normal and routine. And make no mistake, Lionel Messi has experienced more than his fair share of failure and losing.

Over the course of his career, Messi has failed in four World Cups and lost three Copa America finals, on one occasion missing a penalty in the decisive shoot-out. He has failed to win nine Champions League titles. He has lost the Spanish league five times, including once – in 2014 – when he scored a potentially title-winning goal in the latter stages of the last game of the season against direct rivals Atletico Madrid but saw it wrongly ruled out for offside.

Messi's failures far outweigh his successes, vividly demonstrating that even the very greatest of sporting heroes are forced to accept losses more regularly than they can celebrate glory.

Even those who are able to temporarily repel the demons of defeat for improbably long periods generally end up being overcome by its dark powers in the end: Muhammad Ali lost his last two fights; Usain Bolt didn't win his last individual race and couldn't finish his last relay due to injury; Martina Navratilova lost her last two Grand Slam finals and five of her last six; Donald Bradman, needing just four runs from his final innings before retirement to finish with a Test cricket batting average of 100, was out for 0 off the second ball.

Messi, Ali, Bolt, Navratilova, Bradman ... the greatest ever? A sorry bunch of losers, more like.

For even the greatest exponents of their crafts, losing is an integral part of sport and something they just have to get used to. Storybook endings, like Messi whipping his last-gasp World Cup Final free kick into the top corner and then scoring the winning penalty in the subsequent shoot-out, are usually confined to the realms of fairy tale fantasy rather than hard-nosed reality.

In the real world, it's far more common to see Messi sail his shot miles over the bar. To see Roberto Baggio, the world's best player at the time, do the same in the 1994 World Cup Final penalty shoot-out against Brazil. To see Diego Maradona sent home from his last World Cup in disgrace after failing a drugs test. To see Zinedine Zidane end his career by getting himself sent off for a violent headbutt in the 2006 World Cup Final, which his France team then lost on penalties to Italy. To see Cristiano Ronaldo nearly hit the corner flag with his last shot as Portugal limped out of the 2018 finals against Uruguay. In the real world, even the very best are forced to confront painful defeat more often than they are able to bask in the aftermath of heroic glory.

And if you stop to think about it, isn't that quite comforting?

In an increasingly competitive and unforgiving world where we all face relentless pressures to be persistently successful in every aspect of our lives – more beautiful, more wealthy, more healthy, more powerful, more admired and respected and popular – the realisation that Lionel Messi is a loser more often than he is a winner can provide a healthy sense of perspective.

When we suffer a personal or professional setback, or life just isn't working out the way we want, we can take solace from the knowledge that the most successful, highly paid, envied and iconic sporting superstars of our times and of all time know exactly how we are feeling – in fact, they've probably felt worse.

The realisation that even a genius like Messi can screw up by sending probably the most important single kick of his career high above the crossbar when he had the chance to become the comic book hero in the World Cup Final can be, surely, a significant consolation for those of us with lesser talents.

A consolation, and also an inspiration. When we allow ourselves to understand that everyone fails sometimes, it becomes apparent that the most important thing is not whether we succeed or fail, but how we react when it's our turn to confront the inevitability of defeat. Do we give up? Decide it's not worth the effort in the first place? Allow ourselves to become psychologically broken by the pain of losing?

For a professional athlete, that's not an option. The only option is to come to terms with the unavoidable occurrence of heart-breaking failure and get straight back to work, striving to do everything possible to ensure the next opportunity for disappointment is instead turned into a rare cause for celebration.

That attitude was best expressed by Michael Jordan, who is widely regarded as the greatest player in the history of basketball after winning six NBA titles and being named the league's Most Valuable Player on five occasions (note: that also means, over the course of his 15-year career, Jordan *didn't* win nine NBA titles and *wasn't* named the Most Valuable Player on ten occasions).

Rather than totting up his triumphs, Jordan preferred to bask in his failures. 'I've missed more than 9,000 shots in my career,' he famously commented. 'I've lost almost 300 games; 26 times, I have been trusted to take the game-winning shot and I missed. I've failed over and over and over again in my life.

'And that is why I succeed.'

Michael Jordan succeeded because he embraced failure. And if all-time greats like MJ and Messi can embrace failure, so can the rest of us.

Sent off, sidelined, snubbed

It did not take very long for Lionel Messi to become rudely acquainted with the fact that losing is an integral part of an elite sportsperson's life.

Immediately after the glorious 2005 World Youth Championship triumph we encountered in the opening chapter, Messi was confronted by a bittersweet season which unforgivingly hurled him between the extreme ends of the emotional spectrum and forced to him to experience a colourful variety of setbacks to make him fully aware – just in case he wasn't already – that his newly launched voyage as an elite footballer would be anything but plain sailing.

Messi's success with Argentina's youth team in the summer of 2005 naturally attracted a lot of attention, and it didn't take long for national team coach Jose Pekerman to decide that the young sensation's path into senior international football should be accelerated.

Pekerman wasted no time in calling Messi into his squad in August 2005, just two months after his triumph on the junior stage, for a friendly away to Hungary in Budapest. The rising star was ready to take his next step towards superstardom, but his senior international debut was not ready to follow that script.

In the 64th minute, with Argentina leading 2-1, Messi's big moment came. Pekerman summoned him from the bench, introducing him to replace another talented young player of whom great things were expected, Porto forward Lisandro Lopez (and this reminds us again, as already discussed, of the fragility of youth talent: Lopez ended up playing just seven games for Argentina, and by the age of 30 his club career had descended into a brief and unsuccessful spell with Al-Gharafa in Qatar).

Within seconds of entering the action, Messi received the ball midway inside Hungary's half and, as came naturally, dribbled towards goal, only for his shirt to be rudely tugged back by Hungary defender Vilmos Vanczak. Attempting to free himself of the opponent's unlawful attentions, Messi threw out his right arm in frustration just after German referee Markus Merk whistled for a foul. Messi's swinging forearm caught Vanczak in the face and the Hungarian did what most players do, exploiting the situation by rolling around on the turf in apparent agony.

As both sets of players surrounded Merk to vociferously air their complaints, the impatient official revealed his decision with a dramatic flourish: a yellow card was flashed towards Vanczak for the original foul, and a straight red to Messi for his retaliation.

Messi had been sent off, 40 seconds into his international debut.

Pulling on the Albiceleste shirt at senior level for the very first time, a dream he had cherished for as long as he could remember, was not supposed to work out like this, and Messi was distraught as he wandered in a trance-like daze to the sidelines – bearing the same disbelieving expression which would be seen by the whole world nine years later in Rio de Janeiro – to be met with a consoling hug from his coach Pekerman.

The red card was a harsh decision. There was frustration and a touch of petulance in Messi's swinging arm but no malice, and most referees in those circumstances – penalising an 18-year-old debutant seconds after he had been introduced in a low-key early-season friendly – would have settled for a yellow card at the most. But Merk was in no mood for leniency, and Messi was left in tears in the dressing room as he was struck by the injustice of his dream debut turning into a nightmare.

More bad dreams became reality for Messi in the next few months, starting with a Champions League last 16 meeting with Chelsea – his first knockout appearance in the competition – which was initially a high-profile triumph but soon descended into personal disaster.

The first leg, played at Stamford Bridge in February 2006, saw Messi make his first of many rude acquaintances with then-Chelsea coach Jose Mourinho, who accused the visiting starlet of cheating after the London club's full-back Asier Del Horno was sent off for a wild lunge on his young tormentor after just 37 minutes.

'Can we suspend Messi for play-acting?' blasted Mourinho in a typically provocative post-game rant. 'Barcelona is a very cultured city. It's a place where they understand all about the theatre.'

It was hard to sympathise with Mourinho because Messi had spent the first half constantly embarrassing Del Horno, repeatedly cutting inside from the right wing, lanky hair flapping behind him and oversized shirt appearing to engulf his entire body.

Eventually Messi's frequently beaten adversary lost patience and decided the only way of stopping the teenager was to brutally launch into him, nowhere near the ball, with an X-rated challenge by the corner flag. Del Horno probably should have already been sent off for a vicious knee-high, studs-up lunge on Messi a few minutes earlier, but he couldn't avoid punishment the second time and – whatever Mourinho might have claimed – the red card was the only possible decision for referee Terje Hauge.

The red card controversy aside, the breathtaking quality of Messi's precocious performance at Stamford Bridge, at the tender age of 18, served to further alert the wider footballing world to the awesome ability of this rapidly unfurling talent and, after Barcelona won the game 2-1 through an own goal by John Terry and a header from Samuel Eto'o, the return leg at the Camp Nou was set up to become the latest step in the young maestro's ascent towards greatness.

Instead, however, it became another personal calamity as he limped off with a thigh injury midway through the first half, bringing his first full senior campaign to a cruelly premature end.

The remainder of the season was a frantic race against the clock as Messi desperately attempted to recover his fitness in time for the Champions League Final in Paris, where his team were set to face Arsenal after overcoming Benfica and AC Milan without him.

He didn't make it. Having suffered a setback in training, Messi was ruled out of the first final of his senior career as Barça coach Frank Rijkaard regretfully but understandably decided it was simply too risky to select a player who had not set foot on the pitch for more than two months.

To say that Messi was devastated would be an understatement. This was his first big chance to secure major silverware at senior level, yet injury was keeping him on the sidelines, with Rijkaard's decision to omit him from the 18-man squad denying him even the hope of being introduced as a substitute. And although his team took the trophy with a come-from-behind 2-1 victory – in large part thanks to outstanding performances from the bench by veteran Swedish forward Henrik Larsson and promising youngster Andres Iniesta – Messi was in no mood to celebrate with his team-mates as they frolicked around the Stade de France turf.

In fact, Messi couldn't even bring himself to take part in the presentation ceremony, remaining resolutely and glumly inside the changing room, alone with his bitter thoughts, until team-mates Ronaldinho, Deco and Thiago Motta came to share the trophy with him, reminding him that it was a team game, that he had played a part in the season's wider success if not the final itself, and that he was being disrespectful towards his team-mates by refusing to celebrate their triumph.

Messi then belatedly joined the celebrations and later confessed that he felt embarrassed for the youthful petulance of his initial reaction, wishing he could turn back time to properly mark the victory when the final whistle blew in Paris. But his frustration was obvious: he believed that he was fit and ready to play, and could not accept Rijkaard's refusal to give him the chance to compete in the most prestigious club fixture in world football.

At least, though, he had the consolation of knowing that an even more prestigious event lay just around the corner: the World Cup.

By the summer of 2006, Messi was well established in the senior Argentina squad and the silver lining of his recovery from injury was that, although it had come too late for him to appear in the Champions League Final, he was fully fit and fresh for the World Cup finals, to be held in Germany.

Coach Pekerman's squad contained a plethora of well-established attacking talent, and it would be difficult for Messi to force his way into the starting line-up ahead of more experienced players like Juan Roman Riquelme, Javier Saviola, Carlos Tevez, Hernan Crespo and his idol Pablo Aimar. But he could certainly expect to be called upon as an impact sub from the bench, and that's exactly what happened in the second group game against Serbia, when Messi was introduced for the final 15 minutes and responded by creating a goal for Crespo before netting a well-taken effort to complete a comprehensive 6-0 victory, becoming Argentina's youngest-ever World Cup finals goalscorer at the age of 18 years and 357 days.

He was then selected to start the final group game, a dead rubber against the Netherlands which predictably ended as a goalless draw between two teams who had already qualified for the knockout stage. The last 16 meeting with Mexico – played on Messi's 19th birthday – was a tense affair, but Pekerman showed his faith in Messi by introducing him for Saviola towards the end of normal time with the game tied at one apiece. He was so nearly the hero, having a stoppage time goal wrongly ruled out for offside, but Argentina still prevailed thanks to a stunning long-range volleyed winner from Maxi Rodriguez in the first half of extra time.

And so Messi moved on to the World Cup quarter-final against hosts Germany at the Olympic Stadium in Berlin, with the speed of his progress such that just a year after taking the starring role in the World Youth Championship, he was now hoping to replicate that success at senior level.

But he never had the chance. Pekerman left Messi on the bench throughout the last-eight encounter, which finished 1-1 after 120 minutes as Roberto Ayala's header was cancelled out by a late leveller from Miroslav Klose. Inevitably, Germany won on penalties, converting all four of their attempts while Ayala and Esteban Cambiasso missed for Argentina, leaving Messi – not for the first time that year – in tears in the dressing room. They were partly tears of disappointment that the team's journey was over. But Messi's frustration was compounded because, for the second time in six weeks, he had been powerless to play any part in a massive occasion, condemned to watch from the sidelines.

Pekerman received a mountain of criticism for his failure to introduce Messi from the bench, but in fairness the coach's hands were partially tied by an injury to goalkeeper Roberto Abbondanzieri, forcing him to take the unusual step of using a substitution to bring on a keeper, Leo Franco. Pekerman still could have introduced Messi for Crespo a few minutes later, but instead opted for a more like-for-like replacement by introducing veteran centre-forward Julio Cruz, leaving the most highly rated young player in the world to sit and watch, wondering what might have been.

What might have been, indeed: if Abbondanzieri had not injured his chest in a collision with Klose, maybe Messi would have been the final throw of the dice from Pekerman; maybe he would have then been in position to score the golden chance that Rodriguez blasted into the side netting when Argentina still led 1-0; maybe Messi would have taken and converted the penalty that Ayala missed in the shoot-out; maybe an uninjured Abbondanzieri would have stopped one of the German penalties that his understudy Franco could not reach. Maybe, maybe, maybe ...

Whatever the rights and wrongs of Pekerman's use of his substitutions, Messi's failure to appear in the World Cup quarter-final was just another case of crucial circumstances lying beyond his control. As they had done in the Champions League Final a few weeks earlier, events had conspired against the teenager, preventing him from playing any part in what could have been the most important game of his career to date.

And so, in the space of 12 months by the end of the 2005/06 campaign, Messi had been sent off on his international debut, sidelined by a two-month injury absence at the key stage of the season, left out of the Barcelona squad for the Champions League Final and snubbed by Argentina for the World Cup quarter-final.

Those setbacks were desperate disappointments for the teenager, but they were also valuable learning experiences: after being shown a straight red card in his international debut, he learned to never again react to being fouled by swinging his arms in the direction of an opponent's face; after being gently admonished by his team-mates for failing to celebrate their triumph in the Champions League Final, he learned that collective successes should be celebrated even if he had played no part; and after sitting out the World Cup quarter-final due to a strange quirk of circumstances, he learned that sometimes, for unpredictable reasons, things just don't work out.

Sometimes, even when your name is Lionel Messi and the whole world appears to be at your feet, life comes at you hard. And, as we will now see, high achievers from all sorts of walks of life have been forced to learn that same lesson.

Mandela and Messi: the great pragmatists

There are, of course, far more serious ways of losing in life than on a football field. Nelson Mandela, for instance, lost more than a third of his adult life through imprisonment, before – to use footballing parlance – 'bouncing back' to gain his freedom, end apartheid, instigate free and racially open elections and become the first president of a democratic South Africa.

You may be thinking it's rather strange to introduce an iconic, era-defining politician in the middle of a story about a footballer, but on further examination there are plenty of similarities between Mandela and Messi – especially in the way they both learned to respond to adversity.

To understand why, and see how their shared characteristics also relate to our own lives, we will turn to one of the finest chroniclers of Mandela's remarkable life, and somebody who has also studied Messi's progress very closely: the writer and journalist John Carlin.

Carlin was born to an English father and a Spanish mother, spent most of his childhood in Argentina, took his first steps as a journalist in war-torn Central America, and in 1989 moved to South Africa as the on-the-ground correspondent for the recently launched UK newspaper *The Independent*.

As a young journalist, Carlin was fortunate to find himself in South Africa during a momentous period in world history. Within months of his arrival, Mandela was released from prison amid a blaze of international publicity to resume his position as leader of the African National Congress, subsequently negotiating with the ruling apartheid powers to initiate the country's first open elections, and then winning those elections to become a hugely popular president, globally hailed as the leader of a new world order based on peace, understanding and mutual tolerance.

Carlin was right there at the coalface, reporting on Mandela's every move and meeting him personally on several occasions, throughout that dramatic process. He eventually earned the respect of the leader to the extent that, when his time working in South Africa came to an end, Carlin was invited to an official function by Mandela so the leader could deliver a personal farewell.

Later, Carlin wrote a book – *Playing the Enemy* – which explored Mandela's appropriation of the 1994 Rugby World Cup, hosted by South Africa, as a powerful symbol of national unity. The book was later turned into a blockbuster movie, *Invictus*, directed by Clint Eastwood and starring Morgan Freeman and Matt Damon. More recently, Carlin published another book in the wake of the former president's death, *Knowing Mandela*, in which he captured the spirit of one of history's greatest statesmen.

After leaving South Africa, Carlin settled in Barcelona, where his many ventures included a long-running sports column, *The English Corner*, in Spain's top-selling newspaper, *El País*. He also became a friend of Rafael Nadal, later co-writing the tennis star's autobiography.

His work as a sportswriter in Barcelona and his Argentine roots also ensured that Carlin was perfectly placed to pursue the progress of Lionel Messi, in the same way that he had earlier tracked the remarkable career of Mandela. So when it comes to Messi and Mandela, this is a man who knows what he's talking about.

And although they obviously operated in markedly different fields of endeavour, Carlin believes that distinct parallels can be drawn between the way in which Messi and Mandela – a pair of globally heralded, richly talented and inordinately ambitious geniuses who operated at the outer limits of human achievement – interacted with the world and attempted to mould it into the shape of their desires, battling against many morale-sapping setbacks along the way.

'Messi and Mandela are two extreme examples of human beings taken to the ultimate test,' reflects Carlin when we meet at his north London home.

'Mandela endured so much suffering yet he still had that self-control, he still kept his eye on the goal. He played the cards he was dealt, which is all that any of us can do. Rather than pretending you've got four aces and a king ... no, you've got two sevens, a six, a nine and a three. See what you can make of that. He had a clear sense of what was possible and what wasn't possible. He was all about the results.'

Football, of course, is also all about the results. If you lose, you lose, and everyone loses sooner rather than later. But that doesn't mean you will lose forever, and for professional athletes who are sincerely committed to reaching the top, the only possible response to the inevitable disappointments which come along the way – rather than allowing themselves to wallow in bitterness and regret – is to take it on the chin, dust themselves down, pick themselves up and come back for more. Just like Mandela did when he was released from captivity.

When you *really* want to achieve something – like Mandela ending apartheid or Messi winning major titles – that's the only choice you can make. And if you are sufficiently focussed on your goals, you will not allow anything to blow you off course: for Messi, being left out of the team for a World Cup quarter-final and a Champions League Final was a source of immense frustration, but it was only a temporary obstacle which was eventually overcome; for Mandela, being imprisoned for three decades was a deeply challenging setback to put it rather mildly, but he didn't allow it to signify the final whistle in his life's quest.

'When Mandela was released from prison,' continues Carlin, 'there was naturally a part of him that was full of resentment and loathing for the apartheid leaders who had imprisoned him, especially for the way they had treated his family. Part of him wanted revenge. Mandela wasn't a saint, but above all else he had a vision which he achieved by submitting to reality. Everything was subordinate to Mandela's aim of multiracial elections and democracy. He very rarely let rip with his emotions because he knew that would undermine his objectives.'

Mandela was a passionate believer in his cause and he devoted his whole life, despite being forced to endure circumstances which few people could tolerate, to achieving his aims. But rather than lashing out with indiscriminate fury and anger, he learned to channel his considerable emotions and energies in a positive fashion, taking care not to do anything which would be detrimental to his greater goal.

'A classic case was when Chris Hani was killed,' explains Carlin. 'After Mandela, Hani was the most popular leader in South Africa, a brilliant guy who was destined to become Mandela's successor. But he was assassinated by white supremacists. And for Mandela that was an absolutely devastating blow because Hani was like a son to him.

'Yet he had to display the most extraordinary self-restraint, because he knew that if he gave vent to his feelings, all that rage and loathing he had inside, he would have unleashed a wave of revenge killings across the whole country. It could have sparked a racial war. Mandela understood that whatever short-term satisfaction he might get from that, it would come at the price of the ultimate goal of achieving elections and democracy.

'It was amazing to see how he battled to control his emotions. He put on this Sphinx-like face many times when I interviewed him. When he heard about Hani's death, his face became a statue and he was just processing everything – his personal feelings of pain, loss and anger, all battling internally against the pragmatist, the leader, the guy who is responsible and who wants a result. Mandela wanted a result and he was utterly focussed on that.

'And Messi is very much like that too. Messi also has an awareness of the limits of what's possible and he doesn't waste his energy on histrionics because he knows they don't have any practical value. Messi is a very practical, pragmatic player. Have you ever seen him do a stepover? No, because everything he does has a purpose. There's no excess energy whatsoever. And if he fails, he knuckles down and works out what he can do in the next game, the next competition.'

Like Mandela, albeit in a very different sphere of activity, Messi has committed his whole life to achieving his ambitions: winning football trophies. Like Mandela, he has been forced to endure serious setbacks along the way. Like Mandela, he has never allowed himself to be knocked out of his stride by those setbacks, instead preferring to pick himself up and try again. Like Mandela, he learned the importance of controlling his emotions (such as his childish tantrum after the 2006 Champions League Final) and channelling his energies in a constructive fashion, at all times keeping his eye on the goal.

Like Mandela, he came to understand that victory doesn't always come easily, but that it will never come at all if you just give up.

Why should the rest of us be any different?

Two forms of defeat

Lionel Messi was certainly not prepared to give up on his dreams after the tough few months he encountered in 2006.

Even as a teenager, he had already developed (or been born with) a thick skin and a determination to overcome adversity, and those qualities quickly came to the fore: within a month of his omission from the World Cup quarter-final he was back at work in Barcelona, devoting himself to the task of pursuing the silverware which had eluded him in the previous months.

As we all know, Messi eventually succeeded in that aim to achieve a long list of glittering triumphs on a personal and collective level: nine league titles, four Champions League crowns and five Ballon d'Or awards among many more.

But success didn't come quickly – after the 2006 Champions League Final that he missed, he didn't win another trophy with Barcelona until 2009 (although he did claim an Olympic gold medal with Argentina in 2008) and, seen from another perspective, his career is a long list of failures. Even when he became universally lauded as the greatest player in the world, the devastating defeats continued to pile up, one on top of the other, year after year.

To appreciate the scale of his losses, it's worth seeing some of his most shattering lowlights, presented chronologically:

2005: Sent off 40 seconds into his international debut.

2006: Left out of the team for the Champions League Final and World Cup quarter-final.

2007: Lost the Copa America Final 3-0 against Brazil. Won nothing with Barcelona.

2008: Again won nothing with Barcelona, resulting in the firing of coach Frank Rijkaard.

2009: The glorious exception: won all six possible trophies with Barcelona and his first Ballon d'Or in a faultless season.

2010: Lost 4-0 against Germany in the World Cup quarter-final. Lost the Champions League semi-final against Inter Milan.

2011: Lost against Uruguay in the Copa America quarter-final, staged at home in Argentina, resulting in brutal and widespread personal criticism from his fellow countrymen. Lost the Copa Del Rey Final against Real Madrid.

2012: Lost the Champions League semi-final against Chelsea, missing a decisive penalty in the second leg. Lost La Liga to Real Madrid.

2013: Lost the Champions League semi-final 7-0 on aggregate against Bayern Munich. Lost the Ballon d'Or to Cristiano Ronaldo for the first time since 2008.

2014: Failed to win any trophies with Barcelona, having a potentially title-winning goal wrongly disallowed for offside against Atletico Madrid in La Liga's final game. Lost the Copa Del Rey Final against Real Madrid. Lost the Champions League quarter-final against Atletico. Lost the World Cup Final against Germany.

2015: Lost the Copa America Final against Chile after a penalty shoot-out.

2016: Lost the Copa America Final against Chile after a penalty shoot-out ... again. This time he missed his spot kick in the shoot-out. Lost the Champions League quarter-final against Atletico ... again.

2017: Lost La Liga to Real Madrid. Lost the Champions League quarter-final against Juventus.

2018: Lost the Champions League quarter-final against Roma despite winning the first leg 4-1, leaving Messi with just one Champions League crown in the last seven seasons. Lost in the World Cup last 16 against France, missing a penalty in the opening 1-1 draw against Iceland and scoring just once in four games.

When viewed like that, Messi's career looks less like a glorious story of triumph and more like a depressing tale of failure, punctuated by occasional outbreaks of success.

How does he possibly cope with such regular doses of misery? How do ruthlessly ambitious elite sportspeople deal with this constant enforced supply of grave disappointment, and somehow summon the strength to refuse to allow their repeated setbacks to distract them from their goals?

For starters, John Carlin believes the greatest athletes are able to use their painful experiences of defeat – in the pragmatic spirit of Mandela – in a positive and constructive manner by turning them into an inspiration and a motivation for the battles that lie ahead.

'All the really top sportspeople absolutely hate losing,' says Carlin. 'There are lots of stories about Messi being a terrible loser when he was a child, and Rafa Nadal was the same – even playing a card game he just hates losing.

'When they lose, these elite performers are absolutely devastated. They experience emotions not too dissimilar from those when you lose a close relative. For someone like Messi who is so terribly competitive, defeat really is like a death. It creates an unimaginable degree of resentment of the feeling of losing. That solidifies into an even harder desire not to lose next time, so it becomes a motivation on a very deep level.

'The autobiography I wrote with Nadal has as its backbone the famous Wimbledon Final against Roger Federer in 2008. The previous year he had also reached the final, also against Federer, and he spent half an hour crying in the locker room after he lost. What really killed him wasn't that he'd lost, but his perception that he hadn't played at his best. He was raging against himself because he felt he should have done better. That sense of disappointment with himself really killed him, and he was in floods of tears on his knees in the shower, absolutely despondent.

'But when the final came around the next year, it was part of his motivation: "For God's sake, I just felt so much pain and sorrow, and even an element of self-hatred; it's just lacerating, and I don't want to go through that again."

'These ultra-competitive athletes have to be like that. The desperate animal desire not to endure that degree of pain again becomes a motivating factor for next time around.'

Carlin's description of Nadal's pain in 2007 – his self-disgust at his failure to play at his best – helps to reveal a subtle but important distinction between two different varieties of sporting defeat.

The type of loss suffered by Nadal against Federer was, in Nadal's eyes at least, self-inflicted. He lost because he did not play at his best, full stop. He truly believed that if he had performed to his potential, he would have been the champion. Nobody but himself was to blame for the outcome. He had the situation under control, and he blew it.

Messi has experienced defeats of a similar nature. The 2012 Champions League semi-final exit to Chelsea, when he fired a penalty against the crossbar and squandered several clear goalscoring chances as the London club advanced 3-2 on aggregate after a late goal from Fernando Torres, was a prime example of a game when Messi let himself down by failing to reach his usual standards. Similarly, the 2014 World Cup Final against Germany is an extremely painful memory for his failure to take a very presentable chance in the second half, when he dragged a shot wide of the far post.

These are examples of what we could call 'internally imposed defeats' – losses caused by a failure to perform at one's best. But there is also another variety of loss: an 'externally imposed defeat', when you know that you have done everything you can, but still ended up being beaten. And, due to the differing natures of their respective professions, Messi has been forced to endure that external type of loss far more regularly than Nadal.

Tennis in the singles format is a relatively simple game, lacking the complexity of team sports. There are just two players, operating on a fairly small and well-defined playing surface, with little chance for peripheral forces to exert an impact upon the result – one of the few exceptions being a net cord shot, when the ball grazes against the top of the net and can then drop either way. If you lose a match point to a 'dead net', you can consider yourself to be very unlucky. Otherwise, nearly every point in tennis is won by the player who deserves to win it. Tennis is largely a meritocratic activity: you get what you deserve. In an ideal world, society would function in the same way.

When you start to include other factors, however, sport (and life) quickly becomes a lot more complicated. Add into the mix a few more players, whose behaviour is erratic, error-prone and largely beyond your control. Throw in a ball which spins and bounces around heavily congested areas and is always liable to take an unforeseeable deflection. Then consider marginal officiating decisions, subjective rulings which are open to human interpretation (unlike the simple 'in' or 'out' calls in tennis) but can still exert the single most significant influence upon the final outcome.

Now you're talking about an unpredictable environment, upon which one solitary human being – however good they are – can only exert a limited amount of control. Now you're talking about something close to chaos.

Now you're talking about a sport where, as we saw at the start of this chapter, Gonzalo Higuain misses an easy chance, Mario Gotze converts a more difficult one and, as a direct consequence, Lionel Messi loses a World Cup Final. Now you're talking about a scenario where Messi scores a title-winning goal but the linesman gets a split-second judgement call wrong, raises his flag for offside and, as a direct consequence, Atletico Madrid and not Barcelona are crowned La Liga champions.

Many of Messi's most significant defeats have come in that kind of situation, where events beyond his control have overwhelmed him – quite unlike Nadal's defeat to Federer in 2007 or Messi's penalty miss against Chelsea in 2012, where one man's failings can be said to have caused the loss. Mostly, when Messi loses the question of whether or not he 'deserves' to lose can be debated.

That's not particularly fair, but neither is life. Life is much more like football than tennis. Messi, or any other wronged footballer, can rage about the injustices they suffer as much as they want, but they cannot do anything to change the inherently haphazard nature of their sport. In the end, they just have to accept the vagaries of fortune and realise they can only attempt to, in a familiar phrase, 'control the controllables'. For everything else, what will be, will be. Que sera, sera.

Studying Messi's career makes it clear that, even though he is perhaps the best player in history, his ability to decide the outcome of matches and tournaments is sporadic and limited. Often, his goals or assists make all the difference. But on many other occasions the decisive factors lie beyond his control, irrespective of how well or badly he plays.

That realisation, in turn, can help us appreciate and come to terms with the unpredictable and often unwelcome vicissitudes of life itself.

'Messi is only one of 22 players on the pitch,' surmises Carlin. 'There are innumerable lucky bounces, refereeing decisions, team-mates making mistakes, and football contains particular lessons for life precisely because of all those variables. Precisely because it reminds us more than any other sport how little control we have over our fates.

'If you're a footballer, even if you're a serial winner like Messi who absolutely hates losing, you have to carry within you a reservoir of wisdom, to acknowledge there are some things you cannot control and cannot change. In order to avoid going completely mad, you have to possess that mental fortitude and acceptance of the inbuilt unfairness of football.

'It works both ways, of course. Even with the great Barcelona team managed by Guardiola that won six trophies in 2009, there were so many things that could have gone wrong, like the way they beat Chelsea in the Champions League semi-final [a last-gasp tie-clinching goal from Andres Iniesta amid several controversial refereeing decisions]. They could very easily have ended up winning only two or three of those trophies instead of all six, but there was a whole alignment of the stars in their favour, in the same way there was a very different alignment of stars against them when they lost against Inter Milan a year later.'

Having the ability to accept all this uncontrollable randomness is closely connected to Nelson Mandela's pragmatism: his incisive understanding of what was possible and what was not possible in the world. Making reasonable demands of reality. Playing the cards he had been dealt. Managing his emotions. Keeping his eye on the goal and not allowing himself to be deflated by factors beyond his influence.

'If you're involved in professional football, even if you're Messi, who has a greater control over his fate than any other player, you have to carry within you a mechanism of resilience, wisdom and a certain amount of resignation to the fates,' concludes Carlin.

'I think that lesson is particularly applicable in football, and Messi's story tells that lesson especially well. Because even someone like him, who has greater control over that ball and that game than any other player alive, is nevertheless subject to the capriciousness of fortune.

'He therefore offers an extreme metaphor for all of us, who are far more at the mercy of fortune than we would like to accept.'

In football, as in life, justice is not always served. We can do everything possible to give ourselves the best chance of succeeding, using our painful memories of past failures as a motivation to avoid future failures. Sometimes, that will be enough and we will succeed. But just as often, random events uncaringly conspire against us and there's absolutely nothing we can do about it – except accept those random events and come back for more.

Public enemy number one

One aspect of life that lies largely beyond the sphere of influence for footballers – and the rest of us – is the opinions of other people.

Having yourself and your work exposed to critical judgement can be a soul-destroying experience, especially if your detractors are ignorant of your circumstances, ill-informed or driven by powerful personal agendas. Being condemned by people who are biased or don't really know very much about what they are condemning is an infuriating experience for anyone, but it is part of day-to-day life for footballers.

Messi might be one of the most popular, admired and respected celebrities on the planet, but he has also been subjected to brutal levels of deeply personal and hurtful criticism throughout his career, including unfounded allegations that he is autistic or suffering from Asperger's syndrome.

He has fared particularly badly in his native Argentina, with his failure to win a trophy at senior level, his reserved personality and the fact that he moved away from home at such a young age resulting in vitriolic and downright nasty abuse, reaching its unpleasant peak after Argentina's quarter-final exit against Uruguay in the 2011 Copa America on home soil.

After that penalty shoot-out defeat, Messi was public enemy number one in the eyes of many Argentines, who accused him of lacking passion for his country. He was not a 'real Argentine', they said, because he left as a teenager and never returned. Millions of his own countrymen regarded him as distant, detached and disinterested in the fate of his nation, and he was routinely jeered by disgruntled fans during that disappointing Copa America campaign in 2011.

Imagine being Lionel Messi: you reject an offer to play for Spain, you give everything you've got for your country, you repeatedly suffer intense disappointments, and after all that you end up being 'rewarded' by whistles from your own fans and subjected to the publication of articles like this one, which appeared in the online magazine *minutouno.com*: 'Having left Argentina as a kid, psychologists believe he might feel a possible uprooting and resentment towards his country of origin. "Instead of getting upset with his parents, he takes the distress out on the nation," psychoanalyst Cristina Carrillo explains. "It is difficult for a child who grew up away from his country to connect amicably with it."'

Resentment towards his country? Taking out his distress on his nation? Failing to connect amicably with Argentina? Anyone who knows Messi, or has even studied him closely, would tell you those allegations are a million miles wide of the mark. But when you are a rich and famous footballer and you have failed to put the ball into the net in an important match, you are considered to be fair game for brutally vindictive insults – whether or not they are true is almost irrelevant.

John Carlin, who has an instinctive grasp of the Argentine psyche after spending most of his childhood in the country, believes Messi has not found it easy to rise above the hostility he has generated among his compatriots, noting: 'I'm sure the criticism Messi receives in Argentina affects him deeply, it really hurts him.

'He does feel utterly Argentine. The moment he leaves the Camp Nou or the Ciutat Esportiva [Barcelona's training ground] and goes back home, he goes back to [his place of birth] Rosario. By an accident of geography his house happens to be in Castelldefels [a beachside town near Barcelona], but his heart is still in Argentina.

'It's quite extraordinary how he's been in Spain for 18 years, has spent his whole adult life there, and there's not even one tiny hint of a Spanish accent. He lives in that closed Rosario family world, feels passionately, profoundly Argentine, and I'm sure there's absolutely nothing he would love more – nothing at all – than winning the World Cup for Argentina. So to hear those criticisms must be utterly irritating to say the least.'

Messi's shy, introverted personality does not help his cause. Playing up for the cameras and boisterously expressing feelings of patriotism do not come naturally, and Messi's discomfort in front of a microphone has swayed many Argentines against him, allowing them to believe he is aloof and arrogant.

'A significant sector of Argentines are anti-Messi and the problem is that he's not a populist,' says Carlin. 'We live in populist times now with Brexit and Trump, but Argentina as a country has succumbed to those charms for 60 or 70 years.

'There's a dichotomy between Messi and Diego Maradona, where Maradona is always reminding you what a great patriot he is, playing the role of defending the poor when actually he's not at all. There's this old joke from Mexico: the president is in his car, the chauffeur asks him which way to go, and he says: "Signal left but turn right." Maradona is a lot like that – there he is raking in the money, setting himself up as a working-class hero but in fact notorious for charging vast sums to everybody.

'Nevertheless, Maradona's story works and it sells, and Messi is the complete opposite – he's just not that type of person. He lets his deeds speak for themselves, and for a great percentage of the Argentine population the idea that actions speak louder than words is just not how it works. But that's all he can do.'

If Messi is to remain true to himself, that is indeed all he can do. Let his deeds speak for themselves and try not to worry too much about what people think about him, safe in the self-knowledge that the accusations being levelled against him are untrue.

And if we realise that even Lionel Messi, one of the highest-achieving people in contemporary life, regularly finds himself assailed by unfair insults and just has to take them on the chin, we might find it easier to handle the next time we are blamed for something we didn't do, or criticised by someone who doesn't really understand what they are criticising.

That, though, is far easier said than done, and in the summer of 2016 even Messi decided he'd just had enough. After losing the Copa America Final after a penalty shoot-out against Chile – his third defeat in a major final with Argentina in three consecutive years – he shocked the world by retiring from international football.

It was the first time in his career that Messi had ever given up. All the physical and mental anguish, the relentless pressure year after year, the routine incompetency within the Argentine FA and the sharp lack of appreciation from his homeland had eventually taken their toll. It was simply too much to bear, even for Messi, and he felt he had no choice other than quitting.

But he did have a choice, the only choice he has ever taken … the choice to crawl back up on to his feet and summon the energy to carry on. If at first you don't succeed, try again. And if after seven attempts you still haven't succeeded, still try again: within a few weeks of 'retiring', Messi reversed his decision to jump from Argentina's ship and apologetically resumed his international career, having missed a grand total of zero games.

Despite everything, he just couldn't bring himself to walk away. Despite all that abuse and all those disappointments, he was prepared to get back on to the same old treadmill and put himself through it all over again, in the forlorn hope that he would finally alter the course of Argentine football history and enjoy success on the senior international stage by leading his team to glory in the 2018 World Cup Finals.

And we all know how that turned out: another sorry failure to add to his long list of dispiriting failures in Argentina colours. Messi's international career is not a story with a happy ending, and it probably never will be.

Escaping the half-death

Perhaps Messi, Mandela and Nadal didn't simply decide to walk away from their ambitions despite suffering several serious setbacks for a straightforward reason: they couldn't. They couldn't just give up and decide it was no longer worth the effort, because human beings – especially the most competitive examples of our species – have evolved to become fighting machines of obstinate, stubborn and bloody-minded persistence in the face of adversity.

What's the alternative to getting back on our feet and coming back for more whenever we suffer a defeat? Just stopping? That's not how we live. That's not life. Life does not just stop. Life is a never-ending cycle of toil and struggle, effort and sacrifice. If we stop attempting to bounce back from losses, we stop living. And that's not how we are built.

Similarly, this also explains why elite athletes like Messi – or elite performers in any field – don't just quit while they are ahead. By his mid-twenties, Messi was already an extraordinarily wealthy man, who had already enjoyed incredible achievements and earned global admiration. Even at that young age, he didn't need to work again. He could have simply stopped, hanging up his boots knowing that he had achieved his ambition of winning major trophies and becoming the greatest player in the world.

But he didn't do that, and virtually no high achievers like Messi ever do that, because even a victory is a kind of defeat. The thrill is in the chase, and when the chase is completed – even if it has been successful – the entire point of existence has been eroded, just a little.

Many sportspeople report that some of their greatest triumphs have left them feeling strangely hollow and empty inside. They have achieved all their goals and seemingly reached their nirvana, but they feel low because the true meaning of their struggle was the journey itself. And so they set off on another journey, forcing themselves to start all over again in another cycle of striving.

One season finishes, and another begins. That's the way it has to be. Instead of living in the past, reflecting on former glories or dwelling on past failings, we continually set ourselves new challenges, new goals, new aspirations. We keep on coming back for more, because that's all we can do when the alternative is so unappealing.

When Messi won the Champions League for the first time, he wanted to win it again. When Nadal beat Federer for the first time, he wanted to beat him again. When Mandela was freed from jail, rather than settling down into a quiet life of well-earned liberty he forced himself to continue along the stressful and dangerous path of political activism. Because that was the only thing they could do.

John Carlin believes high achievers in any field are so immersed in their craft, and so focussed on their goals, that being forced to stop would be too painful to bear.

'They all have this fear of a half-death,' he observes. 'The horrifying fear that "When it's all over, that's half my life gone."

'For Messi it must be quite a terrible thought. Obviously he's deriving great delight from being a father, but his life is concentrated on football. He's got his family and football, and he doesn't really do anything else. The prospect of never playing football again must be absolutely terrifying for him. It's the same with Nadal – with a fraction less of that fear of stopping, he would have quit years ago.

'That's an even bigger incentive than winning. It goes way beyond saying that Messi "loves" to play football – he *needs* to play. It's his whole identity, his whole being on earth. I'd be willing to place a bet that he'll continue playing top level football until he's at least 36 or 38. He'll go on as long as he possibly can.'

Messi still playing at the age of 38? Let us hope he is able to delay the half-death for so long.

But if he does make it that far, can you imagine how many more losses he will have to suffer along the way?

From despair to joy

Less than 12 months after losing the 2014 World Cup Final, Lionel Messi was dancing around the pitch at the Olympic Stadium in Berlin.

It was the very same arena where his first World Cup had ended in the bitter disappointment of a non-playing penalty shoot-out defeat in 2006, but on this occasion Messi was in a celebratory mood, embracing his Barcelona colleagues and his family with a wide-eyed smile of total satisfaction after playing a central role in his team's successful quest to win the league, cup and European treble: the greatest possible achievement in club football.

Barcelona had just won the Champions League Final, beating Juventus 3-1, having already secured the La Liga crown and the Copa Del Rey in the previous few weeks. Messi had inspired those triumphs with a spectacular campaign, scoring 58 goals in 57 games and establishing a thrillingly fruitful connection with fellow forwards Neymar and Luis Suarez, putting the deep sadness of the previous year's loss at the Maracana well and truly behind him.

Less than 12 months after losing the World Cup Final, he had turned the crushing agony of devastating defeat into the overwhelming joy of glorious victory.

Messi had only been able to achieve such a dramatic turnaround for one simple reason: he had refused to allow failure to beat him.

Like Nelson Mandela, he had taken adversity on the chin, accepted that some things lie beyond his sphere of influence, kept on coming back for more, and eventually emerged from the depressing depths of his darkest hour into a bright and happy new beginning.

Maybe, even when everything looks lost beyond the point of repair, we can all try to do the same.

Chapter Three
The Brain Game

Barcelona 5-2 Getafe
Copa Del Rey semi-final, first leg
Wednesday 18 April 2007, Camp Nou, Barcelona

Lionel Messi receives a short pass from Xavi Hernandez, close to the right touchline about five yards from the halfway line.

He is immediately closed down by Getafe left-back Javier Paredes, but a quick flick of the ball and a lightning change of direction beats him. Then comes Nacho Perez, but he is also sent spinning off course by another rapid burst of acceleration and a nutmeg from Messi, who never seems to let the ball stray more than two inches from his foot.

Beating those two defenders has opened up space in front of Messi and now he sprints purposefully into the Getafe half, unopposed for 30 yards before the visiting back line advances to meet him just outside the penalty area. No problem. One change of direction with the outside of his left foot, then another immediately with his instep, and two more hapless defenders – Alexis Ruano and David Belenguer – are left meekly flailing in his wake.

Now there is only goalkeeper Luis Garcia to beat, and he comes out to the penalty spot in a hopeful attempt to smother the ball. But Messi produces another swivel of his hips to wrong-foot Garcia, steering the ball to the right. And finally, just before he reaches the byline, Messi stretches out his right foot to shoot from an ever-narrowing angle, putting just enough elevation on the ball to lift it over the despairing dive of a final defender, David Cortes, on the goal line.

The stadium rises as one to salute the scorer, who in the space of 11 seconds has completed a meandering, mesmerising run from the halfway line, dribbling past four defenders and the goalkeeper before finishing in style.

As Messi jogs away towards the corner flag, his team-mates converge en masse to join the celebrations: Samuel Eto'o instinctively puts both hands to the sides of his head in a sign of shock; Carles Puyol can only stand and applaud like an excited fan; Deco and Gianluca Zambrotta are just laughing.

Messi is only 19 years old, but already he has scored a goal which will be remembered forever.

Real Madrid 0-2 Barcelona
Champions League semi-final, first leg
Wednesday 27 April 2011, Estadio Santiago Bernabeu, Madrid

The atmosphere is decidedly tense.

The Champions League last four clash between bitter rivals Real Madrid and Barcelona has been simmering all night and threatened to violently boil over with the dismissal of home defender Pepe, who was swiftly followed down the tunnel by manager Jose Mourinho for his subsequent protestations.

That red card turned the tide of the tie in favour of Barcelona, who soon took advantage by going ahead as Lionel Messi converted a cross from winger Ibrahim Afellay. Now, with just three minutes remaining, it's clear that Madrid's only priority is keeping themselves afloat in the tie by preventing the visitors from doubling their lead. The home team are getting as many players as possible behind the ball to protect their goal, and Messi has nine defenders in front of him – and no team-mates – when he receives a short square pass from Sergio Busquets just outside the centre circle.

But Messi spots that the opposition have left a big gap between the two banks of four which comprise their defence and midfield – at least 20 yards of open green grass. So he signals Busquets forward, draws Madrid midfielder Lassana Diarra towards him, flicks the ball to Busquets and immediately runs past Diarra to regain possession from Busquets. Nobody else in the Madrid midfield has reacted quickly enough, so

Messi is away, streaking clear of Xabi Alonso and breaking between the lines as he gathers speed.

Diarra can't keep up with Messi, who now shifts the ball to the right to guide it away from the tentatively advancing centre-back Sergio Ramos, 30 yards from goal. The next obstacle is Raul Albiol, on the edge of the box, but the defender is on his heels and easily beaten by the now galloping Messi. Then he guides the ball gently back towards the centre of the pitch, protecting it from the rapidly retreating Marcelo, before another touch sets up a shot with his right foot which goes back across his body and low past Iker Casillas, whose attempts to narrow the angle have no effect as the ball rolls gently into the net.

After receiving possession from Busquets on the edge of the centre circle, seven touches were all Messi had needed to beat five defenders and the goalkeeper: one to control, another to accelerate past Diarra and Alonso, two more to beat Ramos and Albiol, another couple to hold off Marcelo and the last one to shoot.

Sometimes, genius can be bewilderingly simple.

Barcelona 3-0 Bayern Munich
Champions League semi-final, first leg
Wednesday 6 May 2015, Camp Nou, Barcelona

It is the game everyone has been waiting for. Three years after leaving Barcelona, legendary coach Pep Guardiola is returning to the Camp Nou as an opposing manager for the very first time, with the aim of leading his new club Bayern Munich past his former team and into the Champions League Final.

Ever since the draw for the last four was made, the prospect of Guardiola going up against the players he shaped into one of the greatest teams in history has been exciting eager anticipation – even persuading Messi to give a very rare pre-game press conference as the whole world waits to see who will come out on top: the master, or the pupil.

Bayern are under pressure in the opening stages as Messi creates a couple of early chances for Luis Suarez, but Guardiola's team then settle and are looking relatively comfortable as the game ticks deep into the second half with the deadlock still intact.

With 77 minutes played, though, Dani Alves does well on the right wing to find Messi in space, 25 yards from goal. The Argentine has no hesitation in setting himself up for a shot with his trusted left foot, and he makes no mistake with a fierce low strike which rockets past goalkeeper Manuel Neuer, who barely has time to dive before the ball crashes past him.

Advantage Barcelona – but Messi isn't finished yet. He's nowhere near finished yet.

Three minutes later, with Bayern's defence visibly tiring, Ivan Rakitic receives possession in midfield and threads a pass into the stride of Messi, who gathers the ball close to the edge of the penalty area, right of centre, with only visiting defender Jerome Boateng ahead of him. Messi immediately shapes to cut inside on to his left foot, a route which has seen him score hundreds of goals over the last decade. But then he swiftly turns back the other way, leaving Boateng off balance and clumsily falling to the floor, completely beaten by the nimble change in direction.

As Neuer races off his line to close down the angle, Messi has options: he could cut back inside on to his left foot, or take the ball around Neuer before shooting in the same way he had done for his memorable goal against Getafe eight years earlier, or he could deliver a square pass to Neymar or Suarez, who have made runs into the penalty area.

Instead, though, Messi doesn't even take another touch of the ball before delicately scooping it with his right foot, gently guiding it over the onrushing Neuer and giving sliding defenders Rafinha and Medhi Benatia no chance of making a goal-line clearance, sending the Camp Nou crowd into a frenzied delirium.

It's 2-0, but still the scoring isn't completed. In the last minute of stoppage time, Messi picks up a loose ball on the halfway line and instantly slices open the defence by caressing a low pass into the path of Neymar, allowing the Brazilian to run clear and slide a confident low shot past Neuer, who finds himself beaten for the third time in 17 minutes as Barça effectively book their passage into another Champions League Final.

With his late blitz of brilliance, Messi has succeeded in upstaging his mentor. Before the game, Guardiola's Camp

Nou return was the game's dominant narrative thread. By the end, everyone is only talking about Messi, and especially his bamboozlement of Boateng and brilliant finish for the second goal.

Messi 3, Guardiola 0.

The right decision

They are three of Lionel Messi's most famous goals. Three of his most magical moments, separated by almost exactly four years, with two of them scored in the high-pressure situation of momentous Champions League semi-finals and the other now remembered as his 'Maradona moment' as Messi emulated the former Argentina captain's iconic goal against England in the 1986 World Cup quarter-final.

Aside from being demonstrations of individual brilliance as Messi dribbled with dancing feet past helpless and hapless defenders before netting with a sharply taken finish from close range, have you spotted the common trait – and a highly unexpected one – shared by these unforgettable goals against Getafe, Real Madrid and Bayern Munich?

They were all scored with his *right* foot.

This is notable because Messi's right foot is by far his weaker. Frequently during games he will dance around the ball or take an extra touch to avoid using it, instead much preferring to get the ball on to the magical left foot which routinely mesmerises opponents, team-mates and fans alike. So the fact that three of his best goals – perhaps even the three very best of the 600-plus he has scored at professional level – were executed with his 'weaker' right foot comes as a rather considerable surprise.

What this tells us, in addition to his right foot being better than is generally appreciated, is that Messi is more than prepared, when circumstances dictate, to make a sharp deviation from his preferred method of playing almost exclusively with his left foot by applying the finishing touch with his right. Although he greatly prefers his left, he is also perfectly capable of solving the problems which present themselves over the course of a game – even at the most important moment of them all, attempting to score a goal – by taking the decision to use his right.

In this chapter we will see that solving problems and making decisions, sometimes in surprising ways, are absolutely fundamental aspects of football – and life.

In most sports, not only football, it can be argued that only four things are happening on a pitch at any given time: (1) technical ability is being displayed, (2) an appetite and aptitude for hard work is being tested, (3) problems are being set for the opposition, and (4) decisions are being made in an attempt to solve those problems. Football, at its core, is as simple as those four things. The rest is just detail.

Firstly, of course, it is a test of technical ability, which determines what a player can and cannot do. No matter how incisively you understand the game or how committed you are to your task, if you're not technically good enough to control the ball, deliver an accurate pass or make a dribble without losing possession, your capabilities will be limited.

In this respect, Messi has an inherent advantage over perhaps every other player on the planet thanks to his superior technical ability, which gives him an immediate edge because he can manipulate the ball in ways that others simply cannot.

But his peerless technical ability does not necessarily have to be a decisive advantage, because Messi also constantly finds himself challenged by opposing players and coaches who already know exactly what he can do: his adversaries are acutely aware that he is the biggest threat they will face and therefore do everything they can to nullify him, having studied his game for years and often played against him on many previous occasions. Messi's opponents are well armed to stop him: they challenge his technical superiority by setting problems for him and attempting to prevent him from solving them.

The attempt to inhibit highly skilled players from expressing their talents can often be successful, as evidenced by the regularity with which teams containing inferior players are able to beat their technical superiors. If a group of players are prepared to work hard, and make effective collective decisions to both set and solve the problems presented by the game, it is perfectly possible to compensate for technical deficiencies.

Technical qualities are clearly important, but on their own they are not enough. It is also indispensable to make the right decisions at the right time, both individually and collectively, in order for that technical ability to be employed in the most efficient manner.

How to control the ball; when and where to make the pass; how to create space for a team-mate or deny it to an opponent; what kind of shot to execute. The best players are generally those who, in addition to being technically adept, are also able to make good enough and quick enough decisions to solve problems and set problems. And the best teams are those who can work together to do those things in a seamless dance of coordinated collective movement.

Perhaps the best exhibitors of outstanding collective decision-making in modern football are Atletico Madrid, who have enjoyed remarkably consistent levels of overachievement since Diego Simeone took over as manager in December 2011: in the last seven years, the previously perennial underachievers have won La Liga, reached two Champions League finals, lifted the Europa League trophy twice and collected further silverware in the Copa Del Rey, the UEFA Super Cup and the Spanish Super Cup. And all of that despite operating on a fraction of the finances available to their rivals (when they won La Liga and were Champions League finalists in 2014, Atletico's budget was lower than that of Queens Park Rangers).

Due to monetary restrictions, whenever Atletico play against Barcelona or Real Madrid, they are confronted by an easily identifiable problem: they don't possess as much individual ability as their opponents. Simply put, their players are not as good. But Simeone ensures his team can attempt to solve that problem by employing better defensive organisation, by understanding their limitations and playing within them, and by preventing their opponents from playing to their strengths. This adds up to allow Atletico to shape the flow of the game to their liking, and forces their opponents into situations where they don't feel comfortable. In short, they attempt to make better decisions.

Simeone has freely admitted as much when he explains his team's strategy: they don't have any desire to control the ball, he says, but they do attempt to control the space. He knows his players don't possess enough technical talent to dominate possession when they play against a team like Barcelona, so they don't even try. But they do have the ability, thanks to the collective structures and disciplines he has instilled, to control the space. To make sure the game is played in areas of the pitch where they are less likely to be damaged, and to prevent their opponents from settling into their preferred method of playing.

That is how Atletico have competed on a more or less even footing with Barcelona and Real Madrid for the last few years. That is how they stopped Messi from scoring in six consecutive games during the 2013/14 season, which resulted in them beating Barça to the league title, knocking them out of the Champions League and then coming within one corner (converted by Madrid's Sergio Ramos for a dramatic equaliser in the last minute of injury time of the Champions League Final) of becoming European champions. Atletico Madrid have been football's biggest overachievers this decade, and good decision-making is the main reason why.

Every team, of course, attempts to make life uncomfortable for the opposition, not just Atletico. And Lionel Messi, by the nature of his technical excellence, is confronted by problems of a similar nature practically every time he plays: namely, the opposition have identified stopping him as their main priority and spend large chunks of the game positioning themselves between him and the goal, maintaining a rigorous focus on blocking his passing lanes and closing down his dribbling or shooting options. Opponents try to make Messi's life difficult; they try to give him a few problems to think about.

To solve those problems, Messi has to make a few decisions of his own. What are they?

Two systems of thought

Before we can understand how Lionel Messi makes decisions to solve problems, we should first consider how we all do so.

There is one obvious answer to that question: when we have a decision to make, we think about what our options might be, weigh up the evidence on all sides, and after careful consideration we take the choice we judge to be the most appropriate. We put to good use the special human quality that separates us from all other animals: our powers of reason.

In reality, though, we generally don't do that.

We make many thousands of decisions every day, but most of them are taken unconsciously, without us even being aware of it.

Consider, for example, just how many decisions we make every morning when we have breakfast. Shall I eat straight away after waking up, or have a shower and get dressed first? Tea, coffee, juice, water? Large mug or small cup? Toast or cereal? If toast, how many slices? White bread or brown? With margarine or butter? And jam, peanut butter, marmalade? Make the toast first or the hot drink first? Eat standing up or sitting down? Where? Which crockery to use? And cutlery? Wash the dishes immediately or leave them until later?

All these mundane questions and many more have to be answered even for a very simple breakfast of toast and coffee ... and the day hasn't even properly started yet.

When we make these choices – and the same applies to most of our other daily routines and simple physical actions – it doesn't feel like we are making any decisions at all. The mental processes involved have become so habitual through constant repetition that we can just glide through them on autopilot, not really thinking but still completing the task at hand with slick efficiency.

But they *are* decisions and at any stage we could opt, if we so wished, to take a different path: tea instead of coffee, and a glass of juice on the side; cereal instead of toast, followed by a piece of fruit; get up a little earlier to linger over breakfast and catch up on the news or social media rather than rushing through and leaving the house as soon as possible.

Endless possibilities of that nature are open to us at all times, and the fact that we mostly don't take them, instead sticking to our usual routines, is because we are creatures of habit, led by our unconscious, as much as – or more than – we are rational agents.

As human beings with complex brains, we are entirely capable of making informed, intelligent and carefully reasoned decisions in everything we do, but most of the time we don't. Instead, we allow our decision-making processes to remain hidden below the level of consciousness, trusting our unthinking, habit-based preferences to get the job done. The way we make decisions is examined in detail by the Nobel Prize-winning psychology professor Daniel Kahneman, whose 2011 book *Thinking, Fast and Slow* outlines a theory of thought developed over a lifetime of research and inquiry.

For the sake of simplicity, Kahneman labels our unconscious thought processes as 'System 1' (thinking fast), while our rational decisions are the result of 'System 2' (thinking slow). Mostly, he argues, System 1 is in charge: it is 'intuitive System 1' which allows us to prepare and eat breakfast without a moment of conscious thought; System 1 effortlessly recognises the voice of a friend; System 1 guides us to react to the greeting 'Good morning!' with a similarly cheery response.

System 1 does most of our thinking for us, keeping us blissfully unaware that we are actually thinking at all, and it does so in a highly effective manner because it has become so skilled at carrying out basic routine acts that they can be executed automatically. System 1 is an expert in making simple decisions, and there is no need for 'deliberate System 2' to complicate matters by getting involved.

The key asset of System 1 – alluded to in Kahneman's 'thinking fast' label – is speed. In the world of everyday thought, speed is necessary. In most situations, we don't have time to stop and think. Spending a couple of minutes calculating all the pros and cons before deciding whether it would be more beneficial to eat cereal or toast for breakfast would be, quite literally, a waste of time, and we would never get anything done if we employed our full powers of reason for every decision we have to make. So it's generally much better to take the quick, easy and efficient option, and allow System 1 to retain control.

Not always, though. Sometimes the impressive speed with which System 1 acts is a defect, preventing us from devoting the concentration necessary to efficiently execute a more complex task. On those occasions, the consciously aware processing faculties of System 2 have to step in.

A good example is the act of driving a car. On a sunny day along a familiar and smooth road with little traffic, an experienced driver can ease through a journey in autopilot, guided by System 1. The driver can safely and effortlessly hold a detailed conversation with a passenger, sing along to music, listen to a debate on the radio and enjoy the views of mountains in the distance. The actual process of driving the car is easy, and needs no active thought.

But now take that same driver and put him on a road he has never previously encountered, in a hire car, in a foreign country, in the rain, at dusk, on a pothole-filled road with lots of traffic erratically weaving from lane to lane. Now, fast-acting System 1 is ill-equipped to drive and the more deliberate processes of System 2 have to take over. Conversations end, the radio is switched off, scenery is ignored and the driver is forced to seriously concentrate on the road if he wishes to avoid an accident. The general action – driving a car – is exactly the same, but sometimes more brainpower is required than sprint-speed System 1 can provide.

In addition to its occasionally excessive speed of thought, another problem with unconscious thinking is that it makes mistakes. A lot of them.

System 1 is beset by biases – mental shortcuts which allow us, in the interests of quick thinking, to make snap decisions which are not always accurate and compel us, unknowingly, to arrive at many of our decisions and judgements the wrong way around: first we jump to an instinctive and intuitive conclusion which suits our pre-existing beliefs (Lionel Messi is better than Cristiano Ronaldo), and then we embark upon an act of mental self-justification by piecing together a convincing story to support the conclusion we had already made (Lionel Messi creates more chances for others, Cristiano Ronaldo only plays for himself, etc.).

Deep down, we know that System 1 is sometimes unreliable due to its occasionally reckless speed and its unavoidable inherent biases. So when important matters are at stake (such as driving a car in a dangerous situation), or if we are planning or developing strategies that are too complex to be made up as we go along, we choose to slow down and apply our conscious decision-making powers. We attempt to override our cognitive biases by making lists to carefully compare pros with cons. We undertake research to become better informed. We ponder the negatives and positives of all available options. We consult with experts who can provide insightful advice. We understand the limitations of System 1, and we instruct System 2 to take command. In short, we stop and think.

The extent to which System 1's weaknesses – excessive speed and cognitive biases – can be tamed and overcome is a matter of considerable debate. Kahneman, in contrast to some other cognitive scientists, generally has a pessimistic view of our ability to control our consciousness, believing we are largely at the mercy of our error-strewn intuitions.

He does concede, though, that two things can be done: firstly, we can give ourselves a better chance of correcting our faulty biases by making ourselves aware that they exist in the first place – if we know that our unconscious mental processes are liable to commit errors, we will be more likely to force ourselves to think a bit more carefully. In Kahneman's words, everyone can 'recognise the signs that you are in a cognitive minefield, slow down, and ask for reinforcement from System 2.'

Secondly, and more significantly, we can improve the decision-making abilities of our powerful unconscious System 1 and minimise the regularity of its errors by committing ourselves to the strenuous effort needed to become an expert. Through the power of practice, we can develop and refine our innate skills, allowing ourselves to become more capable of making great decisions – rather than faulty decisions – in the blink of an eye.

Kahneman writes: 'The acquisition of expertise in complex tasks such as high-level chess, professional basketball or firefighting is intricate and slow because expertise in a domain is not a single skill but rather a large collection of mini skills ... An expert [chess] player can understand a complex position at a glance, but it takes years to develop that level of ability ... During hours of intense concentration, a serious chess player becomes familiar with thousands of configurations.'

Applying ourselves carefully to hours of practice, with endless repetition of tasks such as studying a chess board or manipulating a football, allows us to develop 'muscle memory' – the ability to perform a complex physical task easily and without conscious thought: 'Memory holds the vast repertoire of skills we have acquired in a lifetime of practice, which automatically produce adequate solutions to challenges as they arise,' says Kahneman.

'The acquisition of skills requires a regular environment, an adequate opportunity to practise, and rapid and unequivocal feedback ... When these conditions are fulfilled, skill eventually develops and the intuitive judgements and choices that quickly come to mind will mostly be accurate.'

Controlling our mental lives isn't easy, but to an extent it can be done. And by now, your intuitive System 1 should be able to unconsciously guess to whom we will turn for an example.

The creative edge

Now we are armed with some knowledge about how people make decisions, we can address the more specific question of what might be going through Lionel Messi's brain when he is playing football.

As in life, most decisions in a fast-moving and dynamic sporting activity like football are taken by System 1. Most of the time, footballers are not thinking consciously – they are 'just playing', deciding what to do, where to run, how to pass and when to shoot by instinct rather than considered deliberation. They are thinking fast, not slow.

Again as in life, this is strictly necessary. It would be impossible for a player to give too much thought to every movement and every touch of the ball without becoming hopelessly ineffective – there simply isn't time, and the dangers of 'overthinking' technical aspects of performance are well known: if you think too hard about the specific physical acts required to kick a football in a straight line, you'll probably lose your natural rhythm and slice it straight out for a throw-in; if you receive a pass and spend too long deciding what to do next, all your options will be swiftly removed by a grateful opponent who takes advantage of your dopey dithering by nipping in to dispossess you. In football, thinking fast and playing fast is essential.

That's certainly the case *with* the ball, anyhow. Out of possession, it's a different matter – like driving a car in tricky conditions, organising a team's collective defensive shape and attempting to close down the space available to dangerous opponents like Lionel Messi is far too complicated and intricate to be left in the hands of the unconscious System 1.

This is where 'System 2' coaches like Diego Simeone come in, spending hour after hour on the training ground to drill their players into consciously understanding where they should stand and how they should move in unison in order to repel their opponents.

In general, it could be argued that the slower, more calculating and more deliberate mental powers of System 2 are employed when you don't have the ball, and the speedy and decisive action of System 1 takes over when possession is gained. (This is a gross simplification and there are many exceptions, such as a player receiving the ball in 20 yards of space and having time to carefully weigh up all the options, or a backtracking defender having to immediately and instinctively decide how to close down two onrushing opposition attackers on the edge of the box.)

But this is not a book about Diego Godin or Vincent Kompany. It is a book about Lionel Messi, so we are mostly concerned with attacking, not defending. We want to know what happens with the ball, not without it. We are interested in the magic Messi makes when he gains possession, rather than the dogged efforts of the unlucky defenders whose thankless task it is to stop him. We will therefore leave the premeditated and consciously conducted defensive organisational skills of System 2 to one side, and focus on how Messi does what he does – making chances and scoring goals in a split second thanks to the instinctively brilliant powers of his 'System 1' unconscious.

Messi, of course, possesses excellent technical abilities and tactical awareness. If anyone on a football field can be safely described as an expert, that man is Lionel Messi.

Those abilities were developed by the thousands of hours of practice undertaken by Messi during his childhood. Why is he better at kicking a football than anyone else? Because he has spent more time practising the art of kicking a football than anyone else. He was born with an aptitude for football and over time he developed, refined and perfected that natural ability – he became an expert – by devoting as much time as possible to practice. So now, when the ball lands at his feet, he is technically capable of controlling it, passing it, dribbling with it or shooting in the most appropriate way for the demands of that specific moment.

Similarly, those endless hours of practice have allowed him to develop great game awareness. Messi has been able to play in a variety of positions over the course of his career, always understanding his role in the team and how to fit his individual skills into the collective structure. He knows when to press, he knows how to close down space, he knows how to open up the pitch by spreading play from one wing to the other, and he knows how to break open opposition defences with short passing and quick movement.

Years of training and playing have allowed Messi to put his mental and physical faculties hand in hand to the extent that they can now be executed naturally, making his fast-thinking, instinctive System 1 a true expert in solving the problems presented over the course of a game. [1]

But there has to be more to it, because surely none of that – possessing great technical ability and the power to make good decisions – is really what makes Messi special. Most top-level players can do the same or at least similar; players with limited technique or tactical awareness don't get very far in elite football. Something is missing; there has to be something more.

Messi is more skilled than most other players, yes; that skill allows him to make better and faster decisions than most other

---

[1]   The extent to which 'talent' is present from birth or the result of deliberate practice has been the subject of fierce debate – the nature/nurture argument. Some believe that anyone could become as good at football as Messi if they devoted sufficient time to appropriate practice, while others argue that elite performers like Messi are born with a specific genius which could never be emulated by anyone else. Wherever the truth lies in this debate, for our current purposes it's sufficient to note that even if 'talent' is 'God-given', it will never be brought into fruition without practice. Even if we accept that Messi was blessed from birth with a natural genius for football, if he hadn't spent countless hours on the playing fields of Rosario during his youth, he could not have become the player he is today.

players, yes. But to really understand why he stands out, why he is one of the greatest players in history, we need to consider another aspect of his game which has been missing from our discussion so far: creativity.

One of the world's leading experts on the decision-making processes involved in elite sporting performance is Professor Daniel Memmert, Executive Head of the Institute of Exercise Training and Computer Science in Sport at the German Sport University in Cologne, and a consultant to many clubs and organisations including FC Barcelona.

Although Memmert broadly accepts Daniel Kahneman's 'fast and slow' theory of how decisions are made, he believes a further subtle but vital distinction is required within the 'System 1' unconscious framework in order to understand how top-level footballers like Messi decide to do what they decide to do when they have the ball at their feet.

In an interview for this book, Memmert outlined the concepts he detailed in his 2015 publication *Teaching Tactical Creativity in Sport: Research and Practice.*

'We distinguish between tactical intelligence and tactical creativity,' he begins.

'Normally when people talk about decision-making in sport they mean tactical intelligence. They mean the best option to complete a task, the best solution for a problem. However, decision-making is not only about finding the *best* solution, but also sometimes finding an *original* solution. A *seldom* solution which is very surprising for the opponent. This is tactical creativity.'

There is the key distinction: tactical intelligence is the ability to rapidly assess a situation, see the possibilities for action and then immediately select the best possible 'obvious' solution. Tactical creativity, on the other hand, is the ability to see all those possibilities but then decide to reject them and *do something different*. Something creative.

In the language of psychology, this is the difference between convergent and divergent thinking: in the former, thought processes assess all possible options and then zoom in (converge) on the most appropriate; in the latter, the brain acknowledges that solution but then expands outwards (diverges), scanning for another option which might be even more effective, if less obvious.

To understand the difference, here's a simple test to try at leisure: find a game to watch on demand or online, so you can pause the action. At any moment, it doesn't matter when, hit pause. Now look at the player in possession, think about his options, and guess what he will do next. More often than not, you will be able to narrow it down to two or three possibilities: running with the ball in a certain direction or passing to a certain team-mate. And more often than not, the player will indeed do one of those things (or at least attempt to). This, for Memmert, is tactical *intelligence*, recognising at speed (without the benefit of a pause button) the best option to take.

Sometimes, though, the player on the ball will surprise you, and the opposition, by doing something you could not have anticipated. Maybe a sharp turn to find space by beating his opponent; maybe a more difficult pass to a team-mate in a dangerous attacking position; maybe a snapshot from a narrow angle; maybe a change of pace to unbalance the defence. This is tactical *creativity*. Rejecting the options which appear to be obvious, and doing something *different*.

For a distinct example of the latter, look no further than Lionel Messi's goal against Real Madrid in 2011 which is detailed at the start of this chapter. Imagine you've never seen the goal before, and hit pause when Messi receives the ball just outside the centre circle.

Would you guess that his next move would be to exchange short passes with Sergio Busquets, dribble past the entire Real Madrid defence and score? No way.

Messi's decision-making in that passage of play was very far from obvious, and the course of action he decided upon definitely does not seem to be what you could ever describe as his 'best option'. In the last few minutes of a Champions League semi-final, with a 1-0 lead, away from home, against a deep-lying opponent, deciding to ignore a simple square or backwards pass to retain possession and instead attempting to dribble past an entire team from just outside the centre circle would appear to be extremely ill-advised to say the least – the kind of play to leave coaches in fits of fury.

Now watch the goal against Getafe in 2007, when Messi receives a pass from Xavi inside his own half, with three opposing players closing in, and opts to dribble with the ball for 50 yards, beat four defenders, go around the goalkeeper and shoot. And then the goal against Bayern in 2015, when he feints to go one way past Jerome Boateng on to his strong foot, then goes the other on to his weak foot, and then casually chips Manuel Neuer, the best goalkeeper in the world, who hadn't even gone to ground, with his right foot.

In those cases, what Messi chose to do was entirely unexpected. It was entirely original. It was entirely unusual. It was decidedly *not* the 'best possible option' from a conventional perspective – no coach would sensibly advocate doing what he did in those situations, instead inevitably advising the 'obvious' pass or run.

But by diverging from the norm and having the audacity to reject the predictable action in favour of something unexpected and unpredictable, Messi was able to score three spectacular goals which will never be forgotten by any fan who saw them. He didn't only score those goals because he's a great technician. He scored them because he is *creative*.

Adopting the description first applied by J.P. Guilford, one of the pioneers of modern cognitive science, Memmert defines creativity as an action which is 'original, seldom, flexible and useful', and cites Messi's dribbling skills as a key example of his creative capabilities being put into action.

'I was once at the Camp Nou and counted how many times Messi dribbled, how many times he attempted to set himself up for one-on-one situations against defenders,' he says. 'He attempted 35 dribbles, and an important point is that 30 times he failed to complete them. He failed so many times, a very high number, but he's so mentally strong he kept on trying. And on the five occasions he succeeded it led directly either to a shot or an assist.

'Every team in the world would love to have a player that completes five dribbles in a match, because the ability to create chances is obviously very important for the outcome of a game. Messi's quota of dribbles is unbelievable – so high that it doesn't even matter when he fails to complete 30 of them.'

The stats back up Memmert's analysis. Messi finished the 2017/18 season with the second-highest number of completed dribbles in Europe's major leagues, with his tally of 5.1 per game only behind former team-mate Neymar (7.1 per game) and just ahead of Chelsea's Eden Hazard (4.9 per game) – a trio of players who would be instantly recognised as being among the most creative, and most effective, attackers in the world (stats from WhoScored.com).

If we recall the three goals featured at the start of this chapter, the important role of creative dribbling in Messi's game is very striking – in each case, he weaved past a string of flummoxed opponents in an unpredictable manner to create a shooting opportunity.

Countless more examples could easily be offered – including, for starters, another of his all-time great goals in the Copa Del Rey Final against Athletic Bilbao in May 2015: receiving possession on the right wing, five yards inside the opposition half, he twisted and teased his way past four defenders, cutting inside into the penalty area in the process, before crunching a powerful low strike inside the bottom right corner. Like his goals against Getafe, Real Madrid and Bayern, one of the reasons that run was so unstoppable was that it was so unexpected: nobody could have anticipated what he would do next, not even Messi himself.

Not even Messi himself? Doesn't he know what he's doing? What exactly is going on inside Messi's head when he embarks upon these winding runs?

In short, nothing. Messi himself has stated that he is not thinking anything at all when he sets off on his dribbles, and Memmert concurs. 'He just does it,' nods the professor. 'We know from a lot of research that athletes don't have time to think too much. Football is so quick. It's not like chess, where you have time to consider what you're doing.'

Football really isn't like chess, much to the occasional frustration of coaches whose plans can only take their teams so far due to human imperfections (legendary Argentine coach Marcelo Bielsa, employed by Leeds United at the time of writing but quite possibly not by the time of publication, once lamented that if his players were robots, he would win every week).

In a slower sport, the most effective way to solve the consciously derived (System 2) problems set by opposition defences would be to respond with even better consciously derived attacking plans. Outsmarting defensive systems with even smarter offensive systems. And to an extent, cerebral coaches such as Bielsa and Pep Guardiola will do this by training their players to follow patterns – set plays in open play – which are designed to overcome even the most disciplined of defences.

But that's not enough. In the heat of the battle, there is rarely enough time for attacking players to consciously 'think' on the ball and follow rigid instructions. To overcome well-organised defences like Atletico Madrid, they have to react spontaneously and instinctively to the challenges in front of them, somehow finding a way through a brick wall of opponents when all roads appear to be blocked. And that requires instantaneous and unpredictable creativity.

'When Messi dribbles, there's no conscious thought,' Memmert continues. 'It's not deliberate because you have no time for that. It's just a feeling, which allows him to "drink" from the environment. The environment gives him stimuli and he just reacts to that in a way that is both smooth and smart. He feels and then he acts.'

A neat example of Messi's technical ability, decision-making powers and creativity all fusing together to conjure a split-second moment of magic – allowing him to 'feel and then act' – came in the 2018 World Cup finals against Nigeria, when Argentina needed a win to progress to the knockout stages after a dismal start to the competition.

Early in the game, Argentina midfielder Ever Banega gained possession near the halfway line. Sensing the opportunity to penetrate the opposition defence, Messi, 30 yards from goal, first darted inside to send his marker off balance, and then quickly straightened his run to attack the space near the edge of the box. Banega delivered a perfect lofted pass and Messi controlled in full stride, at full speed, in mid-air, on his thigh. Then, before the ball landed, another touch on the sole of his foot guided it further away from the defender and created the opening for a shot, which he dispatched clinically – with his right foot.

This was five seconds of perfection: the spatial awareness to make the run, the creative thinking to control the ball with two mid-air touches, the willingness to overcome his natural bias to shoot with his left foot, and the technical ability to execute the play all came together in a thrilling display of physical and mental excellence.

Seeing Messi score special goals like that is an exhilarating sight for football fans all over the world. For scientists like Memmert, though, it is far more than just a moment of sporting excitement. It is also a demonstration of ultimate high performance, attained through the capabilities of fast-thinking, unconscious, highly skilled System 1 in divergent creative mode. Lionel Messi isn't just a footballer ... he's also a case study.

Pass and shoot

Along with the dribbling highlighted by Memmert, another manifestation of Messi's creativity is the wide range of finishing he employs in front of goal, with the right-footed strikes we have already encountered by no means the only examples of his preparedness to respond to the situation at hand by overriding his natural preference to use his left foot and coming up with something more creative.

One of his most famous goals, against Manchester United in the 2009 Champions League Final in Rome, was a powerful and perfectly placed off-balance header; a few months later he netted another trophy winner by improvising a finish with his chest in the FIFA World Club Final against Estudiantes; his first World Cup goal for Argentina against Serbia in 2006 was a right-footed shot, and perhaps his most important ever assist – a square pass to Andres Iniesta in the dying seconds of the 2009 Champions League semi-final against Chelsea, leading directly to the tie-clinching goal – was also delivered with his right foot.

Messi regularly catches out goalkeepers by shooting at a time and towards a location they could not have predicted, perhaps best seen with a remarkable piece of improvisation during a torrential downpour at Sevilla in February 2014.

A counter-attack was launched down the left wing by Pedro, who reached the edge of the area and played a square pass to

Messi. Rather than taking one of the obvious options – shooting first time or controlling the ball before looking up and then shooting or playing a pass (finding the unmarked Alexis Sanchez on the right would have been a 'normal' decision) – Messi gently flicked up the ball with his first touch and then exploded a fierce half-volley which sent it arrowing into the bottom right corner, flying past home goalkeeper Beto before he had even properly begun to dive.

That kind of finish – of which there have been many from Messi over the years – is literally impossible to defend, firstly because his decision of how and where to shoot is so unexpected, and secondly because he executes it so quickly. Defenders and goalkeepers have no chance of anticipating what he is going to do, and not enough time to react when he does it.

A similar skill is exhibited with Messi's creative passing ability, an aspect of his game which is probably underestimated as a consequence of his outrageous goalscoring feats – when you're looking at a player who has scored at least 40 goals in nine consecutive seasons, who once set an all-time record with 91 goals in a calendar year and who has totalled well over 600 career goals, there's an understandable inclination to focus exclusively on his scoring and overlook everything else.

But despite our obsession with his goals, Messi is also one of the most incisive and audacious passers the game has ever seen. That skill derives from his mental ability to envision killer balls that few other players would perceive as possible – a creative talent poetically described by international team-mate Angel Di Maria as 'being able to see the world from above, like a bird'.

One of the best assists to illustrate his eagle-eyed vision came in a home league game against Celta Vigo in 2016, which became more famous for the 'indirect penalty' goal concocted between Messi and Luis Suarez (to be discussed in more detail in Chapter Five).

Before that penalty, Suarez had already got on to the scoresheet by running on to a lofted through ball from Messi and shooting home on the half-volley from ten yards. That makes it sound like quite a routine goal, but if you watch the video it's clear that Messi's pass was anything but routine.

When he received the ball a few yards outside the penalty area, with Suarez a couple of yards to his right, there were six Celta defenders between them and the goal. Three seconds later there were none, and Suarez was gleefully firing the ball on the bounce past helpless Celta keeper Sergio Alvarez. Find the video of that goal and hit pause when Messi takes possession. If you didn't already know what was coming next, you would not believe it was possible for the ball to be in the back of the net just three seconds later.

Messi was being closed down by one defender, with another five in good defensive positions, and Suarez was just starting his goalward burst. The 'best option', you would think (the convergent option), was for Messi to hold on 1to the ball and wait for Dani Alves, who was making an overlapping run to his right. Or he could have turned out to his left, where Andres Iniesta was moving into space and Neymar was lurking on the corner of the penalty area in anticipation of a diagonal cross.

Those were the normal and obvious options that most players would have taken, and the idea of gently floating a chance-creating pass straight over the top of the defence into the stride of Suarez doesn't even look feasible. Yet that was the creative decision – by far the most difficult of those open to him – taken by Messi, with the result that he instantly cut out six defenders and left the goalkeeper stranded.

Another example of a similar pass – although this time it did not lead to a goal – came in the first half of Barcelona's Clasico victory at Real Madrid in December 2017.

Receiving the ball just inside the right touchline, around 40 yards from goal, Messi spotted that Paulinho had just started to sprint towards the edge of the penalty area and perceived that one aerial ball could cut out the entire defence. So he bounced an implausible pass perfectly into the stride of the Brazilian midfielder, whose powerful first-time shot was brilliantly saved by Keylor Navas to deny Messi another highlight-reel assist.

The big difference between Messi's days in the false nine role under Guardiola and Barcelona's more recent set-up is that he now has a centre-forward ahead of him to fully profit from his freakish passing ability, and Suarez has been the happy beneficiary of many of those deliveries.

Messi celebrates his first major triumph: winning the World Youth Championship with Argentina in 2005.

Ronaldinho holds the young pretender aloft after setting up Messi's first league goal, against Albacete in May 2005. Together they were brilliant…but not for long.

Inauspicious beginnings – Messi is comforted by Argentina coach Jose Pekerman after being sent off just seconds into his international debut against Hungary in 2005.

His greatest goal? Emulating Maradona with a mesmerising solo effort against Getafe in 2007.

Netting a towering header against Manchester United in the 2009 Champions League Final.

Consolation from fellow legend and then-coach Diego Maradona after Argentina's World Cup finals exit against Germany in 2010.

*The co-architect…
celebrating with Xavi
as Barcelona deliver
arguably their greatest
performance to destroy
Jose Mourinho's Real
Madrid in November
2010.*

*Messi is
mobbed by his
team-mates
after scoring
against
Manchester
United in
the 2011
Champions
League Final.*

*Sports scientist
Daniel Memmert
(interviewed
in Chapter
3) pictured
with Messi at
Barcelona's
training ground
in 2011. [Photo
copyright Daniel
Memmert]*

Thank you. Sharing an embrace with Pep Guardiola after scoring against Espanyol in the coach's final game at the Camp Nou in May 2012.

Gratitude…Messi thanks Andres Iniesta for the assist after breaking Gerd Muller's record for goals scored in a calendar year at Real Betis in 2012.

Pablo Zabaleta has been a friend and team-mate of Messi's since 2005. Here they share a joke before a 2014 friendly against Brazil in Beijing.

Alone with his thoughts…Messi is beyond consolation after Argentina lose the World Cup Final to Germany in 2014.

The three amigos…Messi, Luis Suarez and Neymar celebrate the Argentine's goal against Atletico Madrid in January 2015 – the start of a beautiful relationship.

Messi lifts the ball over Bayern Munich goalkeeper Manuel Neuer – with his right foot – after leaving George Boateng on the floor in the 2015 Champions League semi-final.

Sharing a moment with Dani Alves, who has provided Messi with more assists than anyone else – and probably more laughs.

Messi and Luis Suarez celebrate their 'penalty assist' against Celta Vigo in 2016. Like the crowd, Jordi Alba can't believe what he has just seen.

Respect: a warm greeting for Cristiano Ronaldo – who is joined by his son – at a FIFA awards ceremony in 2017.

Remember the name…Messi taunts Real Madrid fans after scoring a last-minute Clasico winner at the Bernabeu in 2017.

The 2018 World Cup was a stressful headache for Messi – as vividly demonstrated before the group game with Croatia.

One of them came towards the end of the 2017/18 season, when Suarez netted in the Copa Del Rey Final against Sevilla. Messi received the ball a few yards inside Sevilla's half and ignored the obvious option of a simple pass to the unmarked Philippe Coutinho on the right wing – the pass which nearly every other player would have made – and instead threaded the needle to roll a perfectly directed and weighted first-time through ball to the seemingly well-covered Suarez, cutting out four defenders with one ridiculously ambitious pass and creating a clear path to goal.

Messi's threefold threat of dribbling, passing and shooting gives him more ability than perhaps any other player in history to solve the problems set by his opponents. The goals we have savoured in this chapter – and many more could have been cited – were all remarkable in their originality. Their likes are seldom seen. They arose from technical and mental flexibility. And they were most certainly useful.

They were the very definition of creativity.

Training creativity

The value of creativity in winning games of football is obvious. It's not a point that really needs to be backed up by stats but, just in case, Daniel Memmert's recent (2018) study of the 2010 and 2014 World Cup and the 2016 European Championships concluded that 46 per cent of the goals scored in those tournaments included at least one 'highly creative' action. Without creativity, you don't score goals and you don't win games.

Creativity is also an extremely important quality in many other aspects of life: the wheel, flushing toilets, light bulbs and the theories of gravity and relativity ... they all came about through creative thinking. A flash of inspiration, a spark of ingenuity, an ability to defy conventions and envisage something new, something different and something useful. Creativity, more than any other mental ability, changes the world.

As the population of the planet increases, the effects of global warming take hold and valuable resources become scarcer, the need for creative solutions to pressing problems (and not just Jurgen Klopp's gegenpressing) will become even more vital.

So what can we do about it? Can analysing the actions of a little bearded chap from Argentina as he runs around a field kicking a ball really save the planet? Can we learn to become more creative simply by watching Lionel Messi?

As silly as it sounds, maybe we really can.

Firstly, the bad news. The studies of elite sportspeople undertaken by Memmert and his colleagues conclude that creativity is mostly instilled during the early years of life, when the brain is still developing and therefore sufficiently pliable to be imbued with habits which will last a lifetime. Or, to employ more accurate scientific language, because children aged between zero and eight (take a deep breath) 'exhibit the greatest absolute number and density of synapses in the primary visual cortex as well as resting glucose uptake in the occipital cortex as measured by PET, indicators associated with creativity.' (Memmert, 2010).

However, those of us aged nine and above should not resign ourselves to a lifetime of tedious predictability, because Memmert (2017) also notes that: 'After childhood, the effect of training activities for tactical creativity probably becomes weaker and weaker, but is still possible.'

You heard the good professor: it is still possible. Hope for us all! And the way that we can improve our creativity, Memmert believes, is by following a programme he and his colleagues have devised – the Tactical Creativity Approach (TCA) – which allows us to develop (and here's another key scientific phrase) our focus of attention.

In psychology, the 'attention focus' refers to our ability to concentrate on something. And a wide attention focus, logically, means surveying a broad physical space and being capable of 'seeing' everything in the field of vision without focussing on one specific point.

Imagine sitting on a mountaintop, overlooking a lake: zooming in your vision to the exclusion of everything else on a small boat, bobbing up and down in the middle of the water, would be a narrow focus of attention; pulling back to perceive and retain awareness of the whole vista, from the hillsides on the left to the water in the middle and the forest on the right, without 'looking at' anything in particular, would be a wide focus of attention.

Or, alternatively, imagine being in possession of a football in the centre circle. If you are looking at your centre-forward and only your centre-forward, your focus of attention is narrow. If you are able see the centre-forward but also be aware of the left-winger making a diagonal burst inside, the left-back charging ahead on an overlapping run, the central midfielder showing for a short pass and the right-back calling for a square ball, then you can boast a wide focus of attention, dramatically increasing your chances of making a creative decision.

'When Messi receives the ball, he receives a lot of stimuli because he has a wide attention focus,' Memmert explains. 'With this, he can see a lot of possibilities. Through research we know this is linked to tactical creativity – people who have a wide attention window are more creative. And with training programmes you can develop the attention focus.'

To improve the focus of attention, and with it creativity, Memmert's TCA contains several different strands. In our interview, he particularly emphasised the importance of 'deliberate play', a rather counter-intuitive idea that people should be encouraged to develop their skills at their own pace and in their own way through trial and error rather than being force-fed technical advice from an authority figure like a coach, teacher or boss.

Memmert believes that deliberate play was a major factor in the development of Messi's creativity, explaining: 'Through a lot of research in a lot of sports, we know that many elite performers, like Messi, spent a lot of time "just playing" in unstructured environments when they were young. Without a coach, without feedback, without strict training programmes, and in lots of different scenarios rather than 11 versus 11 games.'

Sports science is a relatively young discipline with much more research still to be undertaken, but it is already a complex and sophisticated branch of learning and Memmert believes its insights – such as the importance of deliberate play – are currently underexploited.

'I think cognitive functioning is extremely important in football; for me it's much more important than physical endurance,' he says. 'Medical science is already integrated into the training of athletes, but there is a big gap in the integration of mental development.'

Memmert also believes the lessons gleaned from studying the mental abilities underpinning creativity in sportspeople like Messi can be easily applied in other domains of human activity.

'We work with businesses to see how they can change their environments to encourage more openness, more divergent thinking among their staff,' he says. 'Sport and business are both complex environments and much of the structural organisation is very similar, especially the interactions between coaches and players or bosses and employees. A lot of research is still being done but, for sure, sports science transfers into other areas.'

Will professional athletes of the future spend as much time carrying out mental training as they do physical training? Will they visit the lab as often as they currently visit the gym? And will 'divergence training' form a central part of personal career development plans in tomorrow's business world? We can't yet answer these questions, but sports science is making enormous strides and its potential appears to be enormous.

And if we ever need an example of how much can be attained by cognitive excellence, the central role played by mental gymnastics in Lionel Messi's dribbling, passing and shooting suggests we should not underestimate the importance of the brain.

The penalty problem

Here's a dramatic revelation which you may struggle to believe. Are you sitting down?

Lionel Messi is not perfect.

Yes, it's true. Lionel Messi is only a human being, and he is fallible. Especially when he is shooting towards goal from 12 yards with nobody around him, and the goalkeeper is forced to stay on his line. When he is taking penalties, Messi is very much a mere mortal.

His troubles from the spot have been well chronicled, with his miss in the 2018 World Cup opener against Iceland adding to further costly miscues in the 2016 Copa America Final shoot-out against Chile and the 2012 Champions League semi-final against Chelsea.

Overall, his record is not especially bad – by the end of the World Cup he had converted 82 of his 106 penalties, a conversion rate of 77.4 per cent. That's around average for a top-level player, but well short of the standard you would expect considering his ability and a long way behind, for example, Cristiano Ronaldo's record of 83.9 per cent (104 out of 124).

Considering Messi's technical expertise, his spot-kick problems make little sense. He is physically good enough, surely, to blast the ball unerringly into the corner every single time. His regular misses must, therefore, be a mental issue. Something inside his head is stopping Messi from being as deadly from 12 yards as he should be.

And perhaps that 'something' is the weight of expectation.

To seek the answer, Daniel Memmert points us in the direction of a study conducted by Geir Jordet from the Norwegian School of Sports Sciences: *When Superstars Flop: Public Status and Choking Under Pressure in International Soccer Penalty Shoot-outs.*

By studying 37 penalty shoot-outs from the World Cup, European Championships and Champions League, Jordet concluded that the biggest levels of underachievement were experienced by established superstars.

The findings of his study are striking, with 'current-status players' (established stars) scoring 65 per cent of their attempts, while 'future-status players' (stars in the making) succeeded with 88.9 per cent of their penalties, suggesting that the threat to the ego encountered by big-name players when they take crucial spot-kicks makes them much more likely to miss – whereas young and rising performers have less to lose in the eyes of the watching world.

A scientific explanation for why this might be the case has not yet been forthcoming. Jordet's analysis found little correlation between missed penalties and 'escapist self-regulatory behaviours' such as rushing through the spot-kick to get it out of the way, or avoiding eye contact with the goalkeeper. But the results, inexplicable as they might be, appear to be inconclusive.

Zico and Michel Platini in 1986; Diego Maradona in 1990; Roberto Baggio in 1994; Hernan Crespo in 1998; David Beckham in 2004; Frank Lampard and Steve Gerrard in 2006; Wesley Sneijder in 2014; Messi in 2016 and 2018; Ronaldo in 2016 and 2018. They and many more big-name stars have all missed crucial penalties in major international tournaments.

Whether those failures are really connected to a perceived ego threat remains to be seen – more research needs to be undertaken before a correlation can be proved. But due to some kind of mental lapse, it does seem clear that big penalties are missed by big names more often than they should be.

Even the gods, sometimes, are only men.

Standing still to move fast?

Before we leave the enthralling world of cognitive science, we need to briefly consider another striking element of Lionel Messi's game which is very easily evident whenever you closely watch him play. One surprising tendency immediately stands out: far more than any other player, he spends the majority of the time walking or standing still.

This obviously isn't because he's lazy, or because he can't be bothered to move with a bit more urgency. His lack of motion can hardly be caused by apathy – we know that he has an incredible competitive drive and that he is always looking for ways to win. So why does he spend so much time walking? What's going on here?

Firstly, and most obviously, he is conserving energy. According to his former personal physical trainer Juanjo Brau, as quoted in Guillem Balague's biography, Messi has an unusual 'muscular typology' which doesn't allow him to carry out the same number of high-intensity sprints as other players. This argument suggests he needs more rest than most, so it's even more important that he reserves his physical efforts for the moments that matter. The more energy he can save to create chances and score goals in the 90th minute, the better.

There are also benefits on a tactical level, because trying to mark a stationary forward is a surprisingly difficult task for a defender, who cannot know exactly when the opponent is going to start moving, or how quickly, or in which direction.

Motionlessness can have the effect of 'freezing' the defender and leaving him off balance or flat-footed when the injection of pace arrives – this is a common tactic of wide receivers in American football, who attempt to shrug off defensive coverage by slowing down before then bursting into space with an explosive acceleration in time with the quarterback's pass. In fact, moving from a standstill is mandatory in the sport, with every play – often consisting of no more than three or four seconds of action – preceded by all offensive players having to remain motionless at the line of scrimmage.

In basketball, point guards – the offensive playmakers – also regularly use changes of pace to attract defenders to the ball or lull them into a split-second false sense of security, creating space for a dribble or allowing a team-mate to dart uncovered towards the basket. Similarly, players off the ball will regularly walk slowly towards their defender before then exploding into space with a change of pace or rhythm.

Like many things in sports tactics, this is all about the creation and control of space: if you are playing football against a team lined up in a classic 4-4-2 formation, when you find space between the lines of their midfield and defence and then stand still, this presents them with a significant organisational problem.

Either they leave you alone in space, which nobody would ever want to do against a player like Messi, or they have to close you down by breaking their lines and losing their preferred shape. Neither option is a good one.

Standing still, then, has a physical explanation and a tactical explanation. But in the context of this chapter, it could be argued that there is also a mental explanation: when Messi is walking, he is slowing down the action in his mind, broadening his field of vision (widening his focus of attention) and allowing himself to decipher the structure of the game with greater powers of perception.

This idea can be supported with a simple experiment: try looking at a range of objects while you are running at full speed. Now stop, stand still, and look at the same things. The difference, both in the clarity of specific objects and general awareness of peripheral objects, is incredible.

Is this what Messi is doing? As well as saving physical energy, is he also unconsciously (or perhaps even consciously) saving mental energy?

By slowing down physically, is he also slowing down the pace of the game in his brain, making it easier for him to gain an overview of the opposition's alignment and understand how he can be most effective?

At the moment we simply don't know whether Messi derives such significant cognitive benefits from spending so much time standing still. 'It's a theory but we don't know whether it's the right theory or whether we can prove it!' laughs Daniel Memmert.

'Researchers are working in this area but they have not tested it so far. There's no study to show whether this silence, this calmness, is connected to creativity. But I think it's a good idea and I will have it in mind!'

And we can't ask for any more than that. Because that, after all, is where everything begins: in the mind.

Chapter Four
Strenuous Freedom

Barcelona 5-0 Real Madrid
La Liga
Monday 29 November 2010, Camp Nou, Barcelona

By the autumn of 2010, Lionel Messi is firmly established as the key player in Barcelona's all-star line-up.

He has, of course, been an important member of the side for several years already: as long ago as the 2006/07 season, he started 36 games and scored 17 goals in all competitions. But back then he was fitting into a team built around the mercurial talents of Ronaldinho, supported by the strong influence of experienced players like Deco and Samuel Eto'o. Messi wasn't exactly an afterthought in that line-up, but neither was it expressly constructed for him.

Then, in a hectic period in the summer of 2008, coach Frank Rijkaard was axed after a couple of below-par seasons, paving the way for the arrival of Pep Guardiola. He ruthlessly dispatched Ronaldinho, who was allowing his fun-loving, high-living lifestyle to affect his ability to deliver on the pitch, and Deco was also sent packing. The new coach immediately knew exactly how special Messi was and, before long, Guardiola instigated an innovative new playing system with the young Argentine as a 'false nine' deep-lying central striker. That bold approach enjoyed huge and immediate success as Barcelona claimed an unprecedented six titles at the end of Guardiola's first season, winning every competition they entered: La Liga, the Copa Del Rey, the Champions League, the UEFA and Spanish Super Cups and the Club World Cup.

But Guardiola was having to make compromises in his team's forward line, notably with Eto'o who did not appreciate being shoved out on to the right wing to accommodate Messi as a false nine, while veteran Thierry Henry was only ever going to be a short-term measure on the left flank.

In the summer of 2009, Henry left the club and Eto'o also departed in a partial swap deal with Inter Milan as Guardiola took an expensive gamble in the form of Zlatan Ibrahimovic. But the silky Swede also soon struggled with the need to allow Messi to occupy centre stage, and within a year he had been shipped out – after a bitter falling-out with his manager – on loan to AC Milan.

As a reinforcement, Guardiola recruited David Villa from Valencia, perhaps the most selfless, team-oriented superstar striker you could ever find, who was happy to change his position from centre-forward to left wing if it allowed him to play alongside Messi every week. The manager also decisively promoted former B team winger Pedro, who had gained an increasing amount of playing time in previous seasons and was now elevated to the role of certain starter.

And so, the 2010/11 campaign is the first time that Messi has been firmly installed as the overwhelming focal point of his team's attacking play, with no other stadium-sized egos getting in the way. Ronaldinho, Deco, Eto'o, Henry and Ibrahimovic have all been pushed aside, replaced by the more humble figures of Pedro and Villa, and the path is clear for Messi to assume the central role – literally and figuratively – that his talent and ambition demand.

Messi's first campaign in his new and elevated status is a particularly spicy one in Spanish football, thanks to Real Madrid's recruitment of pantomime villain coach Jose Mourinho from Inter – who beat Barça in the previous season's infamously bad-tempered Champions League semi-final – with the express intention of knocking the Catalan club off their lofty perch.

To emphasise their determination to restore ascendancy, Madrid made waves in the summer transfer market, recruiting German duo Mesut Ozil and Sami Khedira, experienced Portuguese defender and Mourinho favourite

Ricardo Carvalho and highly rated young winger Angel Di Maria. With a new manager, a new style and new personnel, Mourinho's men are ready to put up major resistance to Guardiola's dominance.

The two super-clubs go head to head with their new looks for the first time in a league clash at the Camp Nou on a cold and wet Monday night in November. Madrid are unbeaten, one point ahead of Barça at the top of the table and, even by the hype-overdrive standards of El Clasico, the game is hugely anticipated: will Mourinho again devise a plan to stop Barça in their tracks? Will the game signal a shift in the balance of power of Spanish and European football?

The answer could not be more emphatic.

In a mesmerising masterclass which rivals the 2011 Champions League Final victory over Manchester United as the most breathtaking demonstration of Guardiola's Barça at their absolute peak, the hosts destroy Mourinho's men.

It is the classic late-Guardiola-era Barcelona line-up, with Victor Valdes in goal behind a back four containing Dani Alves, skipper Carles Puyol, Gerard Pique and Eric Abidal. The midfield is anchored by Sergio Busquets and orchestrated by Xavi Hernandez and Andres Iniesta, behind the forward line of Pedro, Messi and Villa.

Although he does not score, Messi is at the heart of everything. From the moment he curls a sumptuous narrow-angled chip against the inside of Iker Casillas's post in the sixth minute, he spells danger for the visiting defence practically every time he touches the ball. The false nine role allows Messi to drift on to either wing, drop deep into midfield or lead the attacking line. He is able to go wherever he feels he can do damage, and he takes full advantage by twisting and turning the visiting defence into a bewildered daze.

Xavi opens the scoring in the tenth minute, dinking a close-range cushioned volley over Casillas after running into a space usually occupied by a striker to receive a pass from Iniesta, who had been found by a raking pass from Messi. A few minutes later it is 2-0, as Villa cuts inside from the left to cross and Pedro – exploiting space created by a run from Messi – converts a simple close-range finish.

The second half sees Barcelona really express their superiority, with Messi in particular running Madrid ragged as he takes advantage of the freedom delivered by Guardiola's tactical set-up to provide danger from all directions.

Six minutes after the break, he dribbles towards the edge of the box from midfield and delivers a delicately weighted reverse pass into the stride of Xavi, but the midfielder can only find the side netting. Just three minutes later Messi does it again, repeating almost exactly the same dribble and pass to release Villa, who shows his predatory instincts with a crisp finish into the bottom left corner – 3-0, and game over.

Game over, but the fun isn't over for Barcelona and their raucously celebrating fans. Within two minutes, Messi somehow manages to improve upon his previous assist by receiving the ball on the halfway line, dancing past Xabi Alonso and Carvalho and threading a glorious 40-yard pass between central defender Pepe and right-back Sergio Ramos, perfectly into the path of Villa who doesn't even need to break his stride before stabbing the ball past the onrushing Casillas.

The scoring is completed inside stoppage time when a long passing move, started by Abidal on his own byline, results in two substitutes combining as Bojan Krkic crosses for Jeffren Suarez to convert. The game then finishes amid ugly scenes as Ramos takes out his considerable frustrations by launching into an ugly swipe on Messi, nowhere near the ball, to earn a straight red card.

It is one of the few times a Madrid player has been able to get near him all night.

The relativity of freedom

Freedom!

Everybody wants their freedom. Wars have been waged and political movements launched in the name of freedom and its synonym liberty, with the importance of being free expressed in the very first sentence of the Universal Declaration of Human Rights: 'All human beings are born free and equal in dignity and rights.'

Liberty and justice for all; liberté, égalité, fraternité; freedom from tyranny; freedom from slavery; the freedom to vote; the freedom of choice; freedom of self-expression; freedom of speech.

We all want freedom, of course we do.

But freedom, in absolute terms, is a myth. It is an illusion, or at the very least it is relative and compromised. As humans are inherently social beings, freedom in the strict sense of the word is impossible. From the moment we begin to learn language, we surrender any claims for unrestricted liberty and are forced to submit to rules of communication which have been laid down by others, beyond our control. The English language word for affirmative agreement is 'yes' and, if we want anyone to understand us, we don't have the freedom to change it to 'snump'.

Philosophical analysis has identified two types of freedom: negative liberty (the freedom from oppression by others), and positive liberty (the freedom to self-expression). In an ideal world, conditions for both these forms of freedom would be met for every member of the community: laws and security measures would be strict enough to keep us safe (protecting our negative liberty), but not so strict that they prevent us from expressing our individuality (enjoying our positive liberty).

Even then, however, freedom still remains relative rather than absolute, forced to stay within the lines demarcated by the external forces which control cultural conventions and the law of the land, while economic realities ensure that many positive freedoms remain way out of reach for the vast majority of people.

The inevitable restrictions on our freedom mean that when we are children, we don't have the freedom to pick and choose when to go to school. When we grow up, we don't have the freedom to march into our boss's office and tell him what a terrible job he's doing. We don't have the freedom to wander into our nearest Italian designer fashion store and help ourselves to the latest top-name brands. You want the freedom to dine at The Shard and enjoy a filet mignon with a vintage Burgundy whilst taking in panoramic views of the London skyline? Great! You're perfectly free to do so ... if you can pay for it.

Some of us are afforded that kind of freedom and others are not, because the relativity of liberty is experienced by different people in very different ways. Human nature dictates that we are not born with equal talents or opportunities, and the existence of structured and competitive societies dictates that our innate differences quickly become further exaggerated. Some people, whether we like it or not, are blessed with more freedom than others.

Sportspeople certainly don't have much freedom – in either a positive or negative sense. All players in all sports are bound by a strict set of rules and traditions which explicitly forbid many forms of self-expression, and team sports entail a further denial of individual freedom by assigning specific oppressive tasks.

A center in American football doesn't have the freedom to pick up the ball and run with it if he becomes bored of passing it through his legs to the quarterback and then having to wrestle with a bunch of big guys. His only freedom is to snap the ball when he's told to and then attempt to protect his quarterback or make space for his running back. His opportunities for self-expression are limited to say the least.

Similarly, if you are playing as a central defender in football, you are not granted the liberty to stroll upfield whenever you feel like it and start playing as a striker simply because you fancy trying to score a goal. If you did that, you'd probably be substituted, dropped, and told to find another club. (Unless you are Gerard Pique in the last few minutes of a Clasico victory, in which case it's entirely expected.)

So much for freedom.

As freedom is experienced relatively, though, some players – as a consequence of their specific talents – benefit from more freedom than others. And in almost all cases, the greatest levels of freedom are given to the most technically gifted performers. For example, Lionel Messi.

During his childhood, Messi had freedom because he played in the position known in Argentine football as the 'enganche': the classic 'number ten', a free role (there's that word again) behind a centre-forward, tasked with getting on the ball in the attacking third, creating chances and taking shots.

But when he moved to Barcelona as a teenager, Messi found that his new club did not play with a system which accommodated the enganche – indeed, the word did not even exist in Spain. So his liberty was curtailed and he was shoved out to the right wing, where he was expected to maintain the team's width and help defend his flank, whilst also being given the licence – a limited kind of freedom – to cut inside and attack the opposition penalty area.

His first couple of years in the senior team were spent in that same position before Pep Guardiola decided to make Messi the centrepiece of his game-changing philosophy and placed him in the middle of the field – not strictly as an enganche, because there was no striker ahead of him, but as a 'false nine' where he could move freely around the pitch to get involved in the team's attacking play as much as possible, without having the same level of defensive commitment as his team-mates.

By releasing Messi from the shackles of playing on the right wing, and by purposely building the team around him with hard-working and humble players who were prepared to accept his primacy and privileges, Guardiola gave the young Argentine about as much liberty as any player could ever wish to receive on a football field.

Messi was granted both negative freedom from the oppression of being forced to maintain the team's shape by patrolling a specific area of the pitch, and the positive freedom to be as creative and expressive as he liked whenever he received possession.

Of course, his freedom was still relative: he was bound by the rules of the game and by the need to contribute to the team's wider structure, but Messi was afforded a rare abundance of positional flexibility and fluidity, encouraged to roam all over the pitch wherever he saw fit.

Pep gave Leo the gift of freedom.

The strenuous life

Before we further consider the nature of the liberty enjoyed by Messi on the football field, we will take a detour and confront a problem with freedom which is not always appreciated: it is very difficult.

The granting of liberty is unavoidably accompanied by personal responsibilities which can be hard to bear. If you are given the freedom to act as you choose, you necessarily become directly responsible for the consequences of those actions and should be held accountable for them, facing serious repercussions if you harm others. If you abuse your positive freedom (to self-expression) by impinging upon somebody else's negative freedom (from oppression), such as stabbing them to death, your freedom will be quickly taken away by something called prison.

In any social setting, the bestowal of liberty delivers a heavy burden and onerous personal responsibilities. This is why, for example, we don't give it to children – we believe they wouldn't be able to cope with too much freedom and would end up harming themselves and others.

On 10 April 1899, this inherent complication of freedom was articulated by Theodore Roosevelt, a respected statesman and soon-to-be President of the United States of America, in a speech at the Hamilton Club in Chicago concerning the state of the US military in the wake of the Spanish–American War (waged in 1898 over the issue of Cuban independence).

'I wish to preach, not the doctrine of ignoble ease, but the doctrine of the strenuous life, the life of toil and effort, of labour and strife,' Roosevelt begins. 'To preach that highest form of success which comes, not to the man who desires mere easy peace, but to the man who does not shrink from danger, from hardship, or from bitter toil, and who out of these wins the splendid ultimate triumph.'

Roosevelt is addressing the standing of his country within the world, and the duties – as he perceives it – of every American citizen to serve the greater good by supporting the state and its military forces. But at times it sounds as though he could be delivering a rousing pre-match dressing room speech before a Champions League semi-final.

'It is hard to fail, but it is worse never to have tried to succeed,' he thunders. 'Far better it is to dare mighty things, to win glorious triumphs, even though chequered by failure, than to take rank with those poor spirits who neither enjoy much nor suffer much, because they live in the grey twilight that knows not victory nor defeat.'

We should take the tough route to success, Roosevelt argues. If we want to be blessed with liberty, responsibilities cannot be shirked and duties cannot be dodged. Even when it is difficult or dangerous to take decisive action, facing up to the challenges of freedom is always preferable to a life of 'slothful ease and ignoble peace'.

'The work must be done; we cannot escape our responsibility. If we are such weaklings [to avoid responsibilities] ... then we are unworthy of freedom.

'Let us therefore boldly face the life of strife,' he concludes. 'Resolute to do our duty well ... resolute to be both honest and brave, to serve high ideals ... for it is only through strife, through hard and dangerous endeavour, that we shall ultimately win the goal.'

A century later, the same topic – the strenuous life of strife – was addressed in a very different context by the Buddhist monk Lama Yeshe Losal Rinpoche, the abbot of the Kagyu Samye Ling Monastery and Tibetan Centre in Scotland.

Despite occupying a rather contrasting ideological space to Roosevelt – as the peaceable spiritual guru of a Buddhist retreat rather than a warmongering future President of the United States – Yeshe Losal has similar things to say about the inextricably entwined relationship between freedom and responsibility.

'Many people in the West are very proud to say: "We live in a free world, we are free!" Whereas in fact – from my point of view – they are not,' he argues in his book *Living Dharma*.

'It is true that they are given permission to think, speak and act as they wish, but when such freedom is not supported by wisdom, human beings can behave worse than animals. When they lack wisdom, they often misuse their so-called freedom for the wrong purpose.'

Following Buddhist tradition, Yeshe Losal argues that inner peace and true contentment can only be attained through self-knowledge, and that an essential ingredient of self-knowledge is an uncomplaining acceptance of our moral duties towards both others and ourselves.

'Most people want to be free but don't want to take responsibilities,' he opines. 'But freedom is inseparable from responsibility! If I have the freedom to think, it is my responsibility to think positively. If I have the freedom to speak, it is my responsibility to speak properly and meaningfully. If I have the freedom to act, it is my responsibility to act correctly.'

There is a world of difference between an American presidential candidate campaigning for the strengthening of his country's military might and the serene ponderings of a Buddhist monk in rural Scotland promoting the benefits of meditation, but the basic idea of Roosevelt and Yeshe Losal is the same.

It has universal relevance which resonates with everyone from Lionel Messi on a football field to a high-powered CEO and a rebellious student: if you want freedom, you'd better be ready to face the consequences.

The paradox of freedom

Danny Kerry leans far back in his chair and gazes towards the ceiling, pausing to search for the right words to express himself clearly.

We are at the British National Sports Centre in Bisham Abbey, sitting in the Rio meeting room – named to commemorate the gold medal won by Kerry and his Great Britain female hockey team at the 2016 Olympic Games in Brazil.

That unexpected triumph cemented the status of Kerry – who was in charge of the female team for 13 years before being appointed to lead the men's sides in August 2018 – as one of sport's most progressive and insightful coaches, earning him the International Hockey Federation's coach of the year award and a trip to Buckingham Palace to receive an MBE.

His work has been also much admired and emulated by tacticians from other sports, with England's rugby union coach Eddie Jones inviting Kerry to spend time with his staff at RFU headquarters and observing that his 'ability to create such a dynamic and hard-working team is fascinating'.

And Kerry has firm views on the concept of 'freedom' on the field of play, which he believes is inherently paradoxical.

Still staring upwards to maintain his train of thought, he begins: 'I don't call it freedom. I would say that you can only have freedom if you also have a greater range of understanding about what your roles and responsibilities are, wherever you happen to be on the pitch.

'In the Rio Olympics we had a player in the free role, Helen Richardson-Walsh. But Helen knew that wherever she was on the field, she had to understand where she fitted in with our ability to outlet the ball, where she fitted into the team's pressing and so on.

'She was only able to have that freedom because she was also able to take on those roles and responsibilities.'

This is the paradox: the more freedom you have, the less freedom you have – because the very act of being granted freedom necessarily entails being saddled with responsibilities. The greater the freedom, the more burdensome the responsibilities. Eventually, those responsibilities can undermine and unravel your very freedom itself, because the expectation – or even the *demand* – of everyone around you is that you will fulfil your responsibilities time after time after time.

You will never hide. You will never take a day off and go through the motions. You will never pass the buck and expect somebody else to do your job for you. You will never make excuses. You will never be lazy. You will always be there, be available, completing the considerable demands which have been placed upon you. And then you will come back to do it all over again. So in the end, you're not really 'free' at all.

Kerry continues: 'If you are allowed to roam from left-back to centre-forward, you need to know all the roles and responsibilities that come with both those positions. If you're allowed to also drop across to the right wing, you need to know the roles and responsibilities there as well. The greater the amount of fluidity in your positioning, the greater amount of responsibility there is for you to understand and execute in all those different positions.

'If you call it a "free role" and somehow think you don't have responsibilities, that's missing the point. You actually have greater responsibility. You've got to understand where to go, when to go there, and what to do when you get there. The scoreline, the opposition, the conditions, the nature of the game, the substitutions which might have occurred or be about to occur ... you've got to be able to immediately compute all that information and have a tacit understanding of everything that's going on around you.'

Now think of Lionel Messi's role with both Barcelona and Argentina: he may have 'freedom' because he can move more or less wherever he wants on the pitch without being burdened by the same defensive tasks as his team-mates, but he also has huge levels of responsibility because he is *the* player, every single time, towards whom everyone looks in the expectation that he will create chances and score goals.

That doesn't only apply to his team-mates – fans and the media are the same: if Barcelona or Argentina are losing, nobody will expect Ivan Rakitic or Ever Banega to be the one who sparks a recovery. If his team loses, the headlines will be about Messi failing, not anyone else. All eyes will always fall upon him and, even though he knows he can't always succeed, he never refuses to live up to that expectation and constantly accepts the personal responsibility of carrying his team's efforts on his shoulders.

This is what Roosevelt was talking about with his advocacy of 'the strenuous life'. And it is what Yeshe Losal means by having 'the freedom to act' but also the 'responsibility to act correctly'.

Messi has a greater degree of freedom on a football field than perhaps any other player in the world. But he is also loaded with a greater burden of responsibility than any other player in the world. Ever since Guardiola converted him into a false nine and made him the centrepiece of his team, Messi has been granted an unusual amount of liberty. But that liberty comes at a cost – and the price he must pay is being relentlessly prepared to meet burdensome expectations and accept personal responsibilities.

Messi has freedom, but his life on a football field is also exceptionally strenuous.

Actively seeking opportunities

The personal responsibilities accepted by Messi whenever he plays football can be seen as a synthesis of everything we have seen in the previous three chapters: his commitment to improving his abilities through hard work, his determination to recover from setbacks and his creative decision-making skills allowed him to become the player that he is: a seamless fusion of mental and physical skills combining to form an awesome all-round package.

But that leads to another essential ingredient: Messi's willingness to be 'the man' – the player tasked with breaking open opposition defences and uncomplainingly shouldering the blame whenever things go wrong. His willingness to accept responsibility.

He does not, to use Roosevelt's phrase, take the option of 'easy peace' by settling for simple short passes just to keep possession ticking over. Instead, he opts for the 'strenuous life' of being the creator, the destabiliser, the destroyer, the penetrator, forever hunting down potential killer passes, chances to dribble one-on-one against a defender or opportunities to shoot, not allowing himself to be put off by the fact that they will be difficult to execute.

These factors are tightly bounded together. Firstly, he needs the mental powers required to make good decisions and solve problems, whether in a predictable or more creative manner. Then he needs the technical skills to make his visions a reality. But he also needs to have that unwavering sense of responsibility – a conscientious acceptance of what he is expected to do; a fully committed readiness to fulfil his duties rather than take the lazy option or pass the buck.

Danny Kerry believes this ambitious attitude – this determination to channel his talents in the most proactive and productive possible manner – is one of the main factors that allow elite players of Messi's calibre to stand out from the crowd.

'With truly world-class players in any sport,' says Kerry, 'I think there are small decisive moments within games that they actively find and seek.

'It's an attitude that expresses a desire for success rather than a fear of failure: "I need to use my abilities here, there is an expectation that I will use my abilities here. Somebody will give me the ball or I will go and find the space, create the space, and that will lead us to a winning opportunity. And I embrace that, I want to do those things."

'There are some players who you know will not go missing,' Kerry continues. 'It's almost the opposite – as soon as it becomes incredibly tough and competitive, that's precisely when they actively seek those opportunities. Not necessarily chasing the ball but always making themselves available.

'Essentially, they are taking that responsibility: "I know I can deliver here, and I relish that environment." Others might think: "If I don't succeed here, I have failed," or worry that if it doesn't work they might look stupid. The real world-class players are the ones who truly believe: "I am going to succeed. I have the skills and abilities needed here in this scenario. I am ready for this. I can do this."'

Kerry acknowledges that encouraging players to willingly embrace strenuous responsibilities is one of the major challenges he faces as a coach, saying: 'That attitudinal shift is a huge thing in coaching: how do you make athletes feel good about themselves in those situations?'

Ultimately, experience has told Kerry that everything comes down to the individual. Rather than trying to force players to perform in a certain way when that mode of thinking might run contrary to their natures, the best thing a coach can do is try to encourage players to undertake the necessary 'attitudinal shift' by themselves.

'When I was young and naïve,' he smiles, 'I would get very frustrated with players who wouldn't take responsibility. But the responsibility of the coach is to understand that people are in different places in their heads, with different influences and different environments. You have to work with individual players to understand how you can get them to a place to be mature enough to take ownership of their actions.

'You can offer responsibility to players but they have to be prepared to take it, and everyone is at a different level of emotional maturity. As a coach, rather than railing against players who don't necessarily want to take responsibility, you have to understand where they are in their personal journey and support them. You can't just tell them what to do, but help them achieve what they want to achieve.

'Coaches can fall into the trap of setting the coach's goals, where you're asking your players to take responsibility for something that isn't their own. If you're coaching well, you give your team an ability to set their goals so they are invested in them, and the taking of responsibility is ultimately going to be more effective – because they are the players' goals, not the coach's.

'If you understand your players on a collective and individual level, and they have an ownership in generating their goals, then you have fertile soil for people taking responsibility.'

Messi shapes his own journey

'Help people achieve what they want to achieve.'

If that is the key to encouraging people to accept responsibility, as Danny Kerry argues, we can certainly surmise that Lionel Messi was given every assistance right from the beginning of his own personal journey.

As we saw in the opening chapter, the only thing that Messi ever wanted was to become a top-class professional footballer, and he was prepared to make deep sacrifices to achieve that aim.

But his own unbounded ambition wasn't enough. He also needed the love, encouragement and support of his family to play football at every opportunity during his childhood. Then he needed expensive medical treatment to overcome his hormone deficiency, which was only forthcoming after his family took the extreme step of moving thousands of miles overseas.

When the Messis headed to Barcelona, young Lionel, despite being aged just 13, was old enough to know that he was personally responsible for breaking up his family, who were taking a huge risk in the hope that their son would make a living in the unpredictable, unforgiving and ruthlessly unsentimental world of football.

Messi knew how much his family was sacrificing in order to give him the best possible chance of succeeding. This quiet and sensitive young boy saw how much his sister was suffering in her new surroundings, with her failure to settle in Barcelona eventually compelling her to move back to Argentina with her mother, splitting the family in two across separate continents. He saw how his father had quit his job and thrown himself into an uncertain future in a new country. He saw the emotional turmoil suffered by his mother and his brothers as they were forced to leave home and then live apart.

He was old enough to see all the difficulties his family was facing, and to understand that everything they were going through was because of him. He knew that without his ambition to become an elite footballer, none of the turbulence and unrest would have happened. And he knew that to repay the enormous moral debt he owed to his family for their faith and commitment, he was obliged to do whatever it took to forge a successful career.

That is an incredible amount of pressure and responsibility to place upon the slender shoulders of a shy and physically underdeveloped 13-year-old, but it is also an incredible amount of trust for parents to place in their son – and an incredible amount of freedom to be granted to a young teenager. Messi's parents indisputably gave their son every last ounce of help to achieve what he wanted to achieve, and they also gave him the freedom to pursue his own goals, rather than telling him what to do.

And that, perhaps, is why he was able to take such an extraordinarily challenging situation in his stride, and why he has always been so willing to accept his responsibilities – because those responsibilities have been in line with the goals he set for himself.

When he took responsibility for injecting himself with growth hormones every day, it was because those injections were helping him to achieve his goal of becoming the best possible footballer.

When he took responsibility for moving his family to another continent, it was because that move was his best chance of enjoying the career he wanted and eventually being able to return the support his family had given to him.

When he took responsibility for becoming the focal point of the attack at one of the most demanding football clubs in the world, it was because the false nine role given to him by Guardiola corresponded with the way he wanted to play.

Messi, to use Danny Kerry's phrase, has nearly always been granted 'ownership in the generation of his goals' – going right back to his grandmother taking him to football practice every night and his family being prepared to uproot their entire lives in order to pursue his dreams, through to Guardiola and subsequent managers creating a team structure purposely created to maximise his talents.

Those factors created the 'fertile soil' for Messi to take responsibility on the field of play, because he had been given every piece of assistance that he could ever have asked for. The rest was down to him, and he knew it.

The lesson from the story of Messi's freedom, it could be argued, is that if we want people to feel genuinely invested in and personally committed to their responsibilities, they should be given the freedom to shape those responsibilities in the first place. And this idea has repercussions not only in the coaching of sports teams but in many aspects of normal life.

If the best way to entice people to accept responsibility is giving them ownership of their goal generation, perhaps the most effective way of educating children is the 'student-centred learning' approach which was pioneered by Maria Montessori and is now being increasingly integrated into mainstream schooling. Don't just stand a teacher at the front of a room full of children and lecture them; give those children the freedom to shape what and how they are learning.

If the best way for business leaders to develop efficiently functioning teams and maximise individual talent is supporting people on their personal journeys rather than forcing them to accept authority, that implies a thorough transformation in the traditional workplace relationship between boss and employee. Maybe even the entire concept of 'bosses' is misplaced, and all operations in the workplace should be the result of collaborative decision-making rather than authoritarian orders handed down from above.

The suggestion that Lionel Messi's willingness to accept huge levels of responsibility on a football field results from those responsibilities coinciding with his own self-generated ambitions is, if nothing else, thought-provoking. And although we can't pretend that thinking about Messi's career provides all the answers to life's great questions, at least it might help us ask a few more pertinent questions.

2017/18: Messi's greatest responsibilities

Lionel Messi has never been given more freedom or forced to carry a greater share of responsibility than he experienced in the 2017/18 season – both for club and country.

When Messi started his career at Barcelona he was surrounded by world-class attacking talent in the form of Ronaldinho, Deco and Samuel Eto'o, soon to be joined by Thierry Henry. Then came the Pep Guardiola era and the passing carousel orchestrated by Xavi and Andres Iniesta, before a different approach under Luis Enrique with the spectacular 'trident' forward line of Messi, Luis Suarez and Neymar.

Throughout that period, Messi was able to share responsibility for the team's attacking efforts with a group of world-class stars, whose work was further supplemented by a succession of highly talented, hard-working and team-oriented forwards such as Eidur Gudjohnsen, Pedro, Alexis Sanchez and David Villa.

By the time of the opening league game of the 2017/18 season against Real Betis, however, Messi was partnered in attack by Paco Alcacer and Gerard Deulofeu, who were substituted by Aleix Vidal and Denis Suarez.

Talk about a fall in standards.

In fairness, that's a distorted picture of the support structure around Messi: Alcacer only played because Suarez was injured, while Deulofeu was soon replaced by newly signed Brazilian midfielder Paulinho, with whom Messi struck up a surprisingly good relationship.

Nevertheless, the 2017/18 campaign saw Messi forced to personally carry his team more than ever: Suarez was injured and out of form until November; Iniesta was a fading force; new signing Ousmane Dembele suffered a poor first season; Philippe Coutinho didn't join until January, was cup-tied in the Champions League and flitted in and out of the league eleven. And the remaining attacking players in the squad – like Andre Gomes, Alcacer, Deulofeu, Vidal, Denis and Paulinho – were, to be frank, sub-standard for a club of Barça's stature.

So how did Messi respond to this marked increase in pressure and expectation, labelled as 'Messidependencia' by the Spanish media? The same way he always responds: by accepting his responsibilities, rolling up his sleeves and getting on with the task in hand.

It helped greatly that new manager Ernesto Valverde was able to erect a strong defensive structure behind him, but

Messi's success in leading a relatively limited team to an easily gained league title, secured with four games to spare, still ranks among the greatest achievements of his career.

This really was Messi's league, 'La Liga de Messi', with his all-round splendour evidenced by the fact that he finished the season leading the competition in a remarkable number of performance metrics including goals, assists, shots, chances created, pre-assists (the pass leading to an assist), passes in the opposition half, touches in the opposition box and completed dribbles. Very rarely if ever before, surely, has a single player dominated a major league to such an extent.

If Messi was being forced to create a one-man band at club level, however, on the international stage the scale of responsibilities being placed upon his shoulders at the same time were somehow even greater.

Argentina were in a mess, with a flurry of managerial changes and random team selections creating an unstable environment which badly affected results and performances, leaving the team more reliant upon Messi than ever before.

By the time of the final World Cup qualifier, against Ecuador in October 2017, Argentina had won just one of their eight games without Messi but won five of nine with him in the team – they averaged 0.875 points per game when he was absent, and 2.0 points per game when he played.

Those poor results had left Argentina deep down in a dark hole, needing to win that last qualifier away to Ecuador to secure qualification. To make it worse, the game was being played in Quito, a notoriously difficult venue for opposition teams due to the Olimpico Atahualpa Stadium being located in the Andes mountain range, 2,782 metres above sea level – nearly two miles up in the sky.

And when the contest opened with Ecuador scoring after just 37 seconds, Argentina's most dreaded nightmare – failing to qualify for the World Cup finals for the first time since 1970 – was looking very much as though it would come true.

Who was going to step up?

Who else but Messi, of course. The captain kick-started his rescue act by levelling after 12 minutes, finishing decisively after linking neatly with Angel Di Maria. Then he made it 2-1 midway through the first half, dispossessing a defender to fire home, and finally he wrapped up a qualifying-securing victory by completing his hat-trick just after the hour mark with another thumping strike.

Messi's hat-trick display in Ecuador was a truly heroic performance of comic-book proportions, and the disparity between Argentina's results with and without their skipper made it very plain just how much responsibility he was being forced to carry for his national team.

That became even more obvious with the pre-World Cup friendlies, which included shockingly heavy losses against Nigeria (2-4) and Spain (1-6) while Messi sat on the sidelines. And so Argentina headed to Russia in June with the whole world voicing one opinion: they've only got any chance of success because they've got Messi, an opinion even acknowledged by his coach Jorge Sampaoli, who piled on yet more pressure by saying: 'This is Messi's team more than it is my team.'

This is Messi's team? By admitting that, Sampaoli was showing nothing but respect and support for his key man, with the consequence that perhaps no player in the history of football has ever been given so much freedom to mould a major international side, supposedly one of the leading candidates for the World Cup title, as Messi was apparently granted in 2018. And as we have seen, the greater your freedom, the greater your responsibilities.

World Cup 2018: negative liberty undermined

The expectation facing Messi ahead of the 2018 World Cup finals was captured by an emotive video put together by ESPN – and shown to Messi during an interview – where a succession of teenage Argentine footballers were filmed close up, looking straight at the camera to deliver messages of motivation to their hero. One after another they came, beaming down the lens and asserting their faith in the captain.

'Every Argentine trusts you!' 'We trust you completely!' 'Every time I see you play there's hope in me.' 'Go on to the pitch and show them your magic!' 'Come on Leo, let's go to Russia and win the World Cup!' 'Leo, you're the best player of all time, this will be your World Cup!' 'This will be your World

Cup!' 'I see you lifting the trophy.' 'You will take us to the World
Cup and win it for us!'

No pressure, then?

To understand just how much mental strain Messi was
being subjected to before and during the World Cup finals, it is
worth considering the different shades of pressure confronting
him:

— Internal pressure: the expectations he placed upon
   himself to succeed and satisfy his own personal
   desire to become a world champion. This variety of
   pressure was entirely self-generated (his own goals)
   and had nothing to do with anyone else, compelling
   him to live up to the immaculate standards he sets
   for himself even in the toughest of circumstances.

— Local external pressure: the burden of realising
   the dreams of his team-mates and coaching staff
   – his friends and colleagues within the immediate
   environment of the Argentine national team, who
   surrounded Messi day after day and knew that their
   chances of success rested on the achievements of
   their captain. If he didn't succeed, neither would they,
   and everyone knew it.

— Wider external pressure: the knowledge that tens
   of millions of his fellow Argentines, as shown by
   ESPN's frightening 'motivational' video, were pinning
   their hopes fairly and squarely on him and him alone.
   He was carrying the unrealistically lofty dreams of
   an entire nation, and nobody was ever reluctant to
   remind him of that enormous expectation.

When, then, the opening group game in Russia saw Argentina
drop valuable points against the minnows of Iceland with a 1-1
draw after Messi missed a penalty midway through the second
half, not only did Messi let down himself – he also let down his
team-mates and coaches, and he let down his country.

It was an extraordinary amount of pressure to bear and
many would have buckled under such strain, going into hiding
to avoid the burden. But Messi's immediate response to missing

the penalty again showed that he was more than willing to take responsibility for leading his team's efforts: in the remaining half-hour after his spot-kick failure, Messi insistently and persistently went in search of the ball, demanding as much possession as possible in a furious frenzy of attacking endeavour to give himself a chance to make up for his penalty miss.

In that half-hour alone, Messi sent two free kicks into the wall, another over the bar, fired a 20-yard curling shot narrowly past the left-hand post, miscued an ambitious right-footed shot well wide and – in a moment which served to encapsulate his misfortune on the day – saw a powerfully struck goalbound effort deflect off the back of his unsuspecting team-mate Ever Banega and apologetically dribble out of play for a goal kick.

After the game reached its dispiriting conclusion, legendary former captain Diego Maradona – who had been watching from the stands, casually breaking FIFA regulations by chomping on a fat cigar – attempted to lessen the load on Messi by saying the poor result was not his fault. But Messi was in no mood to accept such charity. The phrase 'It's not my fault' does not exist in his vocabulary and so, rather than making excuses or attempting to shift the blame on to his team-mates, the referee or the opposition, he faced the music and accepted his leading part in his team's failure, admitting: 'I feel responsible for not having been able to take the three points. A goal from the penalty would have changed everything. It hurts that I missed.'

Always leading from the front. Always facing up to the strenuous life. Always relishing his 'freedom to act' whilst also acknowledging his 'responsibility to act correctly'. Always trying to do the right thing.

Nearly always. But not this time. This time it all became too much.

Five days after that draw with Iceland and his penalty miss, Messi and his team-mates had a chance to make amends in the second game against Croatia, who had taken early command of the group by downing Nigeria 2-0 in their opener. The scrutiny being faced by Messi was savage in its intensity and, for once, the pressure got to him.

The pre-game formalities ahead of the meeting with Croatia delivered one of the iconic images of the World Cup, with Messi captured on camera during the Argentine national anthem furiously rubbing his forehead in an excruciating gesture which appeared to betray intolerable emotional pain. 'My head is hurting, it's going to explode,' he seemed to be saying to the outside world. 'I just can't deal with this any longer.'

Perhaps, recalling the ideas explored earlier in the chapter, Messi was in such a bad state because although he theoretically had the positive freedom to act however he wanted, his negative freedom – the protection from external oppression – was not secured. The oppression, in this case, was twofold: the oppressive demands of his nation to satisfy their ambitions for the title, and the oppressive threat of the opposition. And the second of those was something he rarely experiences.

With Barcelona, especially during the Guardiola era, Messi's negative freedom has always been protected by his team-mates. They have been the heavily armed security guards on the border, giving Messi the peace of mind to sleep safely at night. The club sides he has represented have been always good enough, both individually and collectively, to at least give him a chance of flourishing. Even in the 2017/18 season under Valverde, probably the most limited Barcelona team he has played for, there was sufficient strength to ensure that Messi's team-mates would nearly always dominate their opponents both in terms of possession and territory, laying firm foundations for Messi to do the rest. His negative freedom – freedom from oppression – was protected in two senses: the opposition would not be able to dominate him, and his personal role in the team would not limit him.

At the World Cup in Russia, however, Argentina were just not in a realistic position to succeed. The team was weak and underprepared, and it was inevitable that they would be dominated by any decent opposing side. Messi would therefore be oppressed by his opponents, undermining his negative freedom and making it much more difficult for him to express his positive freedom. And, judging by the way he was frantically rubbing his forehead before the game against Croatia, he knew it.

Sure enough, the game unfolded into a disaster for Messi and his team-mates as Croatia romped to a comfortable 3-0 victory, with the Argentine skipper barely making any impact as he registered only one shot and had just 49 touches of the ball – 17 less than inexperienced team-mate Maxi Meza and less than half the total of his team's left-back Nicolas Tagliafico (99).

Nevertheless, Argentina's World Cup still wasn't over because victory in the final group game, against Nigeria, would be enough to secure second place in the group. This time, Messi was able to respond to his responsibilities by scoring a brilliant opener as he ran on to Banega's lofted through ball and took two deft touches to control before firing home an unstoppable right-footed shot.

Marcos Rojo subsequently converted a dramatic late winner to send Argentina through to the knockout rounds, but the post-match analysis was dominated by claims that Messi – with the assistance of his old ally Javier Mascherano – had started to take on an unprecedented level of responsibility and was now effectively coaching the team, with under-fire manager Sampaoli reportedly relegated to the role of an administrator rather than tactician.

The heavy loss to Croatia in the previous game had led to a series of wild rumours, including reports that Messi had been personally paying the wages of the Argentina FA's staff for the last six months, along with claims that Argentina's players had demanded Sampaoli's immediate sacking en masse and, when that failed to transpire, elected to take over the running of the team for themselves.

During the game against Nigeria, Messi was seen delivering a team talk to the players in the tunnel at half-time, and later appeared to personally authorise the introduction of Sergio Aguero from the bench, talking past Sampaoli rather than to him. Had he become a player-coach as well as captain? The level of speculation, rumour and misinformation coming out of the Argentina camp makes it impossible to know what was really going on, but it does seem unquestionable that senior players – Messi and Mascherano in particular – were exerting an unusual level of influence over their team's strategy.

Amid the mayhem, it was no surprise when the last-16 meeting with France proved to be the end of the road. However much Messi tried to get on the ball, his team was inferior in every department as the lightning-fast French attack predictably took full advantage of the lack of pace in Argentina's defence. Teen sensation Kylian Mbappe enjoyed a particularly fruitful afternoon, scoring twice and winning a penalty, and the gulf between the teams was in no way reflected by the apparent closeness of the 4-3 final scoreline.

Messi didn't get on the scoresheet but he did register two assists – the first fortunate as his mishit shot was deflected home by Gabriel Mercado, and the other a superbly angled cross straight on to the head of Aguero. He had done everything he could in the circumstances. He had given every fibre of his soul, dreaming against all realistic evidence that maybe this would be Argentina's year. He had given his all, and more. But it wasn't enough because the team was just not ready to be competitive.

And maybe, as he attempted to make sense of the chaos on Argentina's sinking ship, part of the problem was that Messi had felt compelled to take on *too* much responsibility.

The end of responsibility

The last thing we need to consider about meeting responsibilities is knowing where responsibilities end.

Argentina's desperate struggles in the 2018 World Cup finals made it painfully obvious that one player, even when he is Lionel Messi, can only do so much.

A football pitch is a vast area – the Camp Nou playing surface covers 7,140 square metres (105m x 68m) – and the laws of physics dictate that it's impossible to be in more than one place at a time (unless Messi is somehow able, over the remainder of his career, to apply the theories of quantum physics and allow himself to literally appear in midfield, on the right wing and up front all at the same time ... a possibility we perhaps should not completely rule out).

We saw in Russia that Messi, like any other player, needs his team-mates. He can't go chasing all over the pitch to receive and play every pass; he can't score every goal; he can't win every header; he can't make every tackle; he can't be responsible for team selection and tactics. What he *can* do is very considerable indeed, and often proves to be decisive, but it has limits.

Messi understands this. Watch him closely, and you will see that occasionally he goes two or three minutes without touching the ball, but doesn't become frustrated and go hunting for possession. He watches and waits, continues to look for the right positions to create space for himself and others, and trusts that eventually his team-mates will bring him into the action. Invariably, of course, they do – except when they are so badly structured, like the Argentina team of 2018, that they have no idea how they can properly utilise his talents. And then he has a problem.

When he plays for a properly organised team, though, Messi accepts that he can't do his team-mates' jobs for them. Everybody has a task to fulfil and sometimes he just needs to leave them alone. As well as taking responsibility for his actions, he also has to know where he is not responsible at all.

England hockey boss Danny Kerry stresses this can be a difficult thing to do for a coach like himself or an elite player like Messi. The thirst to control everything and everyone is not easy to quench, especially for a deeply insightful performer with such a strong 'game sense', such an intricate and instinctive understanding of the game's patterns and rhythms, as Messi. But letting go – allowing others to shape the development of the game and the team – can also be liberating. For everybody.

'It becomes particularly interesting when you're willing to allow others to take responsibility,' says Kerry.

'That can be scary because you are ceding control, but actually it's a higher order of responsibility because you are saying that you believe in the process, you believe it is the right thing to do for the long-term good of the team, and you are willing to take the risk.

'That's when you're at a higher order of understanding players and roles. It's a different type of responsibility – by ceding responsibility, you're actually taking responsibility for the development of the team.'

If you are Lionel Messi, by not expecting yourself to be able to do absolutely everything, you encourage your team-mates to increase their own contribution. They know that they can continue to rely on you to do everything that you reasonably can, but they also learn to trust themselves to embrace the responsibility for the things you cannot.

With Argentina in the last World Cup, that wasn't possible because the team simply wasn't in any kind of position to perform well, but for Barcelona it has been a different matter and Messi has been afforded the occasional luxury of sitting back and letting others take control.

A memorable example came with 'La Remontada' on Wednesday 8 March 2017, one of the most spectacular comebacks in recent football history and one of the most famous nights in Messi's career, when Barcelona overturned a 4-0 first leg Champions League deficit against Paris St Germain by winning 6-1, scoring three goals in the final seven minutes.

Messi did not exactly have a poor game on that incredible, spine-tingling night at the Camp Nou, but neither was he the decisive character. Instead, the architect of the comeback was, without any doubt, Neymar.

Having excelled throughout the game, it was Neymar who sparked late hope when Barça still needed to score three more goals with only two minutes of normal time remaining, winning a free kick 22 yards from goal and then arrowing it into the top left corner. It was Neymar who scored a penalty two minutes later. It was Neymar who took the final free kick in the final minute of added time. And when that set piece was cleared, it was Neymar who picked up the loose ball and delivered it again into the box for Sergi Roberto to convert the tie-winning goal and prompt scenes of mayhem.

The whole thing was Neymar's doing far more than anyone else, and Messi's only direct contribution during that frenetic, scarcely believable passage of play was to release a long ball through the middle for Luis Suarez to run on to and fall under the challenge of PSG defender Marquinhos, winning the penalty which Neymar converted to make it 5-1 on the night.

Other than that, Messi had a secondary role as Neymar came to the fore. And sensing that Neymar was 'in the zone', that Neymar was the best person to lead the challenge, that Neymar was ready to seize the initiative and take the responsibility, Messi just stood back and let it happen.

When the free kick was awarded just outside the penalty area with three minutes of normal time remaining, Messi could have pulled rank and insisted that he took it. When Suarez won the penalty a couple of minutes later, he could have grabbed the ball and taken it himself. When goalkeeper Marc-Andre ter Stegen, playing as a midfielder in desperation, was fouled to win the last-gasp free kick, he could have taken responsibility for delivering it into the penalty area himself.

In normal circumstances, that's exactly what he would have done. All three of those set pieces would usually be Messi's domain. But on this occasion, sensing that this was Neymar's moment, not his own, Messi handed over the responsibility for deciding the outcome to his team-mate.

That certainly didn't mean Messi didn't care, as his frenzied, delirious celebrations after Sergi Roberto's dramatic strike – climbing on to the advertising boards to unleash a primal scream of joy towards adoring fans – made abundantly clear. He cared very much indeed. At that moment, he cared about nothing more.

But the interesting thing about Messi during those few minutes of unforgettable action was that, despite caring so much, he was still able, somehow, to let go. To let Neymar have his moment, to let Neymar take centre stage and to let Neymar be the difference-maker. To take responsibility by ceding responsibility, showing that he had attained, to use Danny Kerry's phrase, a higher order understanding of his team-mates and the game.

Sometimes, even when you're as good as Lionel Messi, that's what you have to do. Because ultimately, however much freedom you might have been granted and however much personal responsibility you might be prepared to take, you are only one member of a team.

And, however much of a cliché it might sound, if you really want to be successful, the team truly does have to come above everything else.

Chapter Five
The Reciprocal Altruist

Barcelona 6-1 Celta Vigo
La Liga
Sunday 14 February 2016, Camp Nou, Barcelona

With ten minutes remaining in Barcelona's home league game against Celta Vigo and his team leading 3-1, Lionel Messi receives the ball on the right corner of the penalty area.

He embarks upon one of his trademark dribbles, shifting the ball past Celta defender Jonny Castro and sprinting towards the byline. Jonny briefly recovers his position, but is then left stranded again as Messi adroitly stops the ball with his right foot, promptly flicks it past Jonny with his left, and immediately runs the other way around the defender to meet the ball on the other side.

Dazed and confused, Jonny instinctively backs into Messi and scrappily flings out his arms and legs to impede the run, sending his opponent tumbling to the ground. There was nothing else he could do, but he has given referee Alejandro Hernandez a simple decision ... penalty!

And not just any penalty. This is a milestone moment, because Messi's opening goal of the game during the first half – a brilliantly struck 25-yard free kick into the top right corner – took him to the grand total of 299 goals in La Liga, so this spot kick gives him the chance to become the first player in Spanish football history to reach the triple century. History beckons.

As Messi places the ball on the penalty spot, the fans inside the vast stadium catch their collective breath in anticipation. Thousands of bright lights twinkle in the darkness of the night sky as supporters hold up their mobile phones to record the moment for posterity. A moment to be shown to friends, shared on social media and preserved with a warm glow of reflection, pride and a touch of smugness: 'When Messi scored his 300th league goal, I was there! And I've got the video to prove it!'

Leo stands rigid still a yard inside the penalty area, hands casually placed on hips, waiting for referee Hernandez to blow his whistle and stoically ignoring the attempts of Celta goalkeeper Sergio Alvarez to intimidate him by 'making himself big', standing tall on his tiptoes, stretching his arms high towards the crossbar.

The whistle is blown, and Messi nonchalantly commences his run-up. A few short stutter steps. One, two, three, four, five little paces. As Messi's right foot is placed next to the ball and his left foot is pulled back in preparation to shoot, Alvarez starts his dive to his left – attempting to move early enough to give himself a better chance of making a save, but not so early that Hernandez orders a retake.

With his body perfectly balanced and his eyes firmly fixed on Alvarez's movement, Messi is ready to shoot.

But he doesn't shoot.

In the last split second, Messi's leg speed subtly slows – too subtle for the naked eye to detect – and he pulls out of the shot, instead gently rolling the ball at an angle of 45 degrees a couple of yards to his right, perfectly into the path of Luis Suarez, who knows exactly what is happening and comes steaming through, unopposed by defenders, to emphatically blast an easy right-footed finish past the bewildered Alvarez.

The stadium erupts with a noise quite unlike the roar that greets most goals: a glorious combination of amazement and delight. Did I really see that? Did they really do that? Is that allowed? Was that for real?!

Yes it was for real, yes it was legal, and now Messi and Suarez are running away together in fits of laughter, embracing to celebrate their moment of impudent brilliance.

Jordi Alba joins them, wide-eyed in shock and rapidly shaking his right hand at the wrist in the Spanish way which signifies that something really cool has just happened. Then

Sergio Busquets, with a more understated grin that seems to be saying: 'You crazy kids!' Then Neymar, Arda Turan, Ivan Rakitic, Aleix Vidal, Gerard Pique. They all join the celebrations, all of them revelling in the moment with the same emotions as 72,580 spectators in the Camp Nou crowd ... astonishment, amusement, admiration.

Commentating for American television network beIN, the never-knowingly-understated Ray Hudson is going into overdrive, even by his own delirious standards.

'What we have seen here is absolutely Shakespearean!' Hudson roars. 'But Shakespeare got it wrong: it wasn't King Lear. It's King Leo! The assist from the penalty kick recalls the great days of Johan Cruyff. Amazing, beautiful, magisterial Barcelona! The audacity of Messi!'

It should have been Messi's goal. What's more, it should have been his 300th league goal, yet another historical personal landmark to further emphasise his greatness. But instead he actively chose not to score. He chose to sacrifice 'his' moment and to gift the goal to Suarez.

He did it for the sake of creative enjoyment with his teammate – the conspiratorial sense of fun derived from conniving to pull off an almost unheard-of stunt, the likes of which might sometimes be light-heartedly rehearsed on the training field but which is virtually never carried out on the serious stage of a competitive fixture in front of tens of thousands of people.

He also did it for the sake of victory – confidently (and correctly) believing that Celta would be totally unprepared for the move, and that it would therefore increase the team's chances of scoring a goal.

And he also did it because, alongside Suarez and Neymar, he was inhabiting that rarely discovered footballing nirvana where a group of people 'click' and everything comes together. The chemistry is right, mutual understanding and trust is reached, and everything just flows, effortlessly, gloriously. The perfect environment for Messi to strike the rare balance between the deeply felt personal need to express his individual talents and still servicing the collective demands of the group.

He did it for the sake of teamwork.

Messi: natural-born reciprocal altruist

Are human beings inherently selfish? Or do we possess natural instincts for empathy and generosity towards fellow members of our species? And, to facilitate the smooth functioning of society without undermining individual freedom, should we allow our behaviour to be driven by personal desires, or by the demands of our community?

As we have seen with the previous chapter's discussion of liberty, these questions have been endlessly explored for millennia, yielding differing answers depending upon the prevailing cultural norms of the day.

As long ago as the height of classical Greek civilisation 2,500 years ago, philosophers and politicians were passionately debating exactly how the balance should be struck between the rights of individual human beings and the wider needs of society.

In one of the most influential social treatises ever written, *The Republic*, Plato argued in favour of measures that would seem exceptionally drastic to modern sensitivities. He advocated the concept of 'philosopher kings', who would upon birth be immediately separated from their parents and reared communally, with everything in their upbringing geared towards shaping them into future leaders. They would have no say in the matter, and neither would the people they ended up ruling. A few years later, Plato's most celebrated student, Aristotle, captured the general feelings of the age by writing in his *Nicomachean Ethics*: 'No citizen belongs just to himself ... he must regard all citizens as belonging to the state. While it is desirable to secure what is good in the case of an individual, to do so in the case of a people or a state is something finer and more sublime.'

This subjugation of the individual to the collective was perfectly normal to the ancient Greeks, who also casually accepted slavery and admired the social principles of Sparta, a ferociously disciplined and warlike city state where deformed or undeveloped babies were murdered and compulsory military training began at the age of seven.

Our outlooks have changed considerably since then, and most contemporary cultures place a much greater emphasis on individual rights – the kind of freedom discussed in the last chapter. But the conflict between individual liberty and collective duties has never subsided, reflected by the ongoing ideological struggle between socialism (emphasising collective duties ahead of individual liberty) and liberalism (emphasising individual liberty ahead of collective duties).

No matter how far to the left or to the right your personal politics happen to lie, though, very few people would disagree with the suggestion that humans are inherently social beings, and that our lives can only find meaning and purpose through our interactions with others.

Nobody can exist in a vacuum, and from the day we are born we are physically and emotionally reliant upon the support of other people. As the contemporary writer Kenan Malik puts it, even if you believe in extreme individualism it is hard to escape the conclusion that humans are unavoidably 'social beings whose individuality emerges through the bonds they create with others.'

A popular current theory to describe the balance between individual selfishness and the needs of the group – the way we create bonds with others – is *reciprocal altruism*, a phrase coined by biologist Robert Trivers in the 1970s and now widely regarded as an enlightening explanation for our inbuilt social instincts.

The concept is intuitive and easy to grasp: I will be altruistic to you (I will be selfless, generous and compassionate without thinking directly of myself) if I know that you will reciprocate (you will show the same kind of selflessness, generosity and compassion to me in return). You scratch my back, and I'll scratch yours. But if you won't scratch my back, I won't have anything to do with you.

For high achievers like Lionel Messi, it is not always easy to be a reciprocal altruist. As we have already seen, Messi's intense determination to make the most of himself, his unwavering belief in his own ability and his strong character have allowed him to bear an extraordinary amount of pressure and expectation. When crunch time comes, he always wants to be there, taking personal responsibility for deciding the outcome.

This is admirable, of course, but it also presents a potential problem when it comes to working alongside other people and giving them the freedom to express themselves. For elite performers in the mould of Messi, it can be very easy for a sense of megalomaniacal selfishness to take over.

There have been occasional glimpses of this during the course of Messi's career. In his biography of the player, for instance, Guillem Balague relates how his first youth team coach at Barcelona, Rodolfo Borrell – who now works at Manchester City – would desperately struggle to coax little Leo to play the club's trademark one- and two-touch football during his early days in Spain. The youngster, eager to impress his new coaches, often preferred to endlessly dribble with the ball until he was either tackled or could shoot. He wanted to do it all by himself, because he wanted everyone to see how good he was.

Later, as discussed in Chapter Two, Messi's initial refusal to celebrate the success of his team-mates when injury forced him to miss the 2006 Champions League Final victory over Arsenal – an act of self-centred youthful immaturity – was another early instance of placing personal interests before those of his team.

Those are exceptions, however, and generally speaking one of the reasons that Messi is admired by many neutral fans is that he plays for the team rather than for himself – illustrated by his regular habit of turning down shooting opportunities and instead passing if he can see that a team-mate is in a better position, exemplified most clearly (and most unusually) with the famous 'penalty assist' to Suarez at the start of this chapter.

Perhaps the best example of Messi's natural selflessness, even more than his tendency to look for passes to team-mates, is something that can be seen on an almost game-by-game basis: the way he celebrates goals.

While many players – Cristiano Ronaldo being the most obvious example – instinctively regard the act of scoring as an opportunity to grab as much of the spotlight as possible by indulging in an ostentatious and self-glorifying celebration, Messi's immediate reaction is to think of others.

Nearly every time he scores, Messi's response is to run straight towards whichever team-mate delivered the assist, thanking them for the pass by joining them in a group celebration. A recent demonstration came in the Copa Del Rey Final in April 2018, when he fired home his team's second goal and turned immediately to Jordi Alba, who set up the chance with a clever back-heel.

Messi even does this in moments which would be ideally suited to a spot of narcissistic muscle-flexing. In an away game at Real Betis in December 2012, for example, he set an all-time world record by scoring twice to take his tally for the calendar year to 86 goals, surpassing the previous high of 85 set by German striker Gerd Muller four decades earlier (Messi eventually finished the year with 91).

This was an entirely personal milestone, which had been heavily hyped by the media but, coming midway through the season, it had little direct correlation to his team's quest for trophies – this was very much Messi's record, not Barcelona's, and it also came at a time when he was at the peak of his personal rivalry with Ronaldo, whose free-flowing scoring exploits had helped Real Madrid beat Barça to the league title a few months earlier.

If ever Messi was going to turn the spotlight on himself rather than his team-mates, this was the time. But when he broke Muller's record by exchanging passes with Andres Iniesta and rifling a first-time strike into the bottom right corner, rather than heading directly to the nearest television camera he instead turned straight to Iniesta, pointing at him with an expression of gratitude. As the two players embraced you wouldn't even be able to tell which one of them had scored, never mind that one of them had just broken an all-time individual record.

Messi's instinctive impulse to think of others is also shown in his famous 'pointing to the sky' gesture after he scores, in memory of his grandmother Celia who gave him so much encouragement as a child.

And another instance of this sharing attitude came in the 2005 World Youth Championship, when he celebrated his goals in the final against Nigeria by declining the opportunity for a spot of self-aggrandisement and instead lifted his jersey to reveal a T-shirt bearing the names of his sister, nephews and cousin.

Even in the immediate aftermath of his greatest glories, Messi is thinking of others. For him, reciprocal altruism comes naturally.

Generous ... but demanding

One of Messi's longest-standing team-mates – and one of the earliest high-profile beneficiaries of his unselfishness on the pitch – was Pablo Zabaleta.

They first played together in 2005, when the latter captained Argentina's Under-20s to victory in the World Youth Championships. As you may recall from Chapter Two, Zabaleta netted an injury-time winner against Brazil in the semi-final when Messi broke inside from the left wing and, rather than attempting to find space to unleash a shot, delivered a low cross which eluded Sergio Aguero but was forced home by Zabaleta.

The pair have remained close friends ever since, helped by them becoming near-neighbours when Zabaleta kick-started his senior career immediately after that youth title triumph by joining Barcelona-based Espanyol, and they continued to play regularly together at international level for more than a decade – including heart-breaking losses in the 2014 World Cup Final and 2015 Copa America Final.

A couple of days after Zabaleta finished his stint as a BBC television pundit for the World Cup finals in Russia, we sat down at a café near the beachside apartment he still owns in Barcelona as a remnant of his playing spell with Espanyol.

Between sips of espresso, Zabaleta – who knows Messi better than nearly anyone else in football – explained how such a gifted performer is able to express his individual talents within the context of a group activity, which is not always an easy balance to reach.

'Leo is just a very nice and generous person,' begins the full-back. 'I met him more than 13 years ago, when he was not a big superstar, and he's still the same person now that he was then. For the people who know him well, he hasn't really changed. He's a humble guy, and even though he knows he's the best he also knows that he needs every player to succeed.'

That humble nature, Zabaleta believes, explains Messi's willingness to fully engage with his team-mates on the field of play rather than trying to do everything by himself.

'Leo has always known when to pass and when to shoot,' he says. 'He's not a selfish player. Now he's in his thirties, the way he's playing he looks even more for passes from a deep position, looking for someone like Jordi Alba making a run from left-back and then getting into the box for a cross. In the last few years we've seen Messi look for the pass more often if he thinks it's the best option, but really he's always had that ability.'

In this respect, Messi is very easy to play alongside because he is unselfish, he reads the game so well and he has such great technical ability: if you move off the ball, he will see your run and he will deliver the pass exactly where you need it. That point was elegantly observed by Angel Di Maria, who recalls that when he first started playing for Argentina alongside Messi 'all I had to do was run into space. I would start running, and the ball would arrive at my feet. Like magic.'

None of this means, however, that playing alongside Lionel Messi is a bed of roses, because he is also exceptionally demanding.

He has extremely high standards and expects everybody around him to come as close as possible to matching them. Many Barcelona players over the years have encountered the wrath of Messi for failing to do so, with young wingers Isaac Cuenca, Cristian Tello and Gerard Deulofeu perhaps the most notable among those who have been on the receiving end of withering stares or sharp rebukes after failing to deliver the right pass at the right time.

Elite sport is an unforgiving, unsentimental environment, where people are judged on what they do rather than who they are. None of those home-reared players survived very long in the Barcelona team due to a simple, brutal truth: they were not good enough. And Messi, however much a team player he might be, made it clear that he didn't regard them as good enough by routinely turning down the option of making passes to them that he wouldn't have hesitated to release if they had the ability of Iniesta or Neymar.

'Leo is demanding because he wants to win,' explains Zabaleta. 'He's a winner and he feels that in Barcelona he needs to succeed every single time, and win trophies every single season.

'He also knows that at some point in every game he can make the difference, because he has so much talent. So when the wingers get to the byline, the cross has to be perfect. He doesn't want to make a 30-yard sprint into the box and not get the ball because of a bad cross or a bad decision.

'That doesn't mean he's the type of person who always wants to score himself – he also wants the rest of the team to play a part in the attacking. If the best thing for his team-mate to do is shoot or cross to another player, that doesn't upset him. It's not like you always have to play the ball to him. But he's got so much ambition, so he always demands the perfect pass, the perfect cross. He does everything perfectly himself, so of course he always wants the best from his team-mates.'

Messi demands the best from himself, and he demands the best from his team-mates. And if they can't reach those standards, his natural instincts for collective cooperation face a major challenge because he cannot trust that his altruism will be reciprocated.

First among equals

Playing alongside Lionel Messi is a unique benefit, of course, but in another way it is also difficult. Firstly because, as we have seen, he does not tolerate sub-par performers, but also because he is granted special privileges in terms of his roles and responsibilities in the team.

Ever since he was put into the centre of the field by Pep Guardiola, Messi has never been expected to track back in defence. He doesn't have to contest loose balls, and he doesn't have to cover the runs of the opposition full-back – his team-mates are expected to do his running and carry out extra defensive work for him, meaning they often have to supress their own talents to compensate for Messi's privileges.

The best example in recent years is Barcelona midfielder Ivan Rakitic, a gifted and versatile performer who – to retain his place in the team – has been obliged to play within himself to ensure he covers the tasks Messi will not even attempt to complete. Rakitic was particularly restricted during Messi's stint as a right-winger in a 4-3-3 formation, with the Croatian international expected to shuttle between the centre of midfield and the right flank to offer defensive support to his full-back, with Messi more or less relieved of defensive obligations.

For people like Rakitic, Messi can even be, at times, an oppressive presence – just ask Tello, Cuenca or Deulofeu. It is very much *his* team, playing the way *he* wants to play, and everybody else is there first and foremost to serve *him*. If Barcelona are a team of equals, some of them are certainly more equal than others – and that starts with Messi. It's the same off the pitch in matters such as media duties, with Messi last holding an open press conference in 2015, almost never attending post-game mixed zones to face questioning from reporters, and only very rarely conducting interviews with the club's in-house TV channel. None of his team-mates are given that dispensation.

Taking the situation to a fanciful extreme, if Barcelona's players decided to follow the exhortations of Karl Marx, as asserted at the end of the *Communist Manifesto* ('Workers of the world, unite! You have nothing to lose but your chains!'), and seek equality within their little community, Messi would be the first to find himself overthrown.

This is the main reason Pep Guardiola jettisoned players like Ronaldinho, Samuel Eto'o and Zlatan Ibrahimovic, who were unwilling or unable to accept Messi's primacy. It is why Neymar left to join Paris St Germain, and why Alexis Sanchez departed for Arsenal: as long as they stayed at Barcelona, they knew they were condemned to remain in Messi's shadow.

And that matters. For highly competitive and richly talented elite athletes, who have been relentlessly striving all their lives to make themselves the best and most influential players possible, it's not easy to become reconciled with the idea that somebody else is more important.

As noted by Zabaleta: 'Strikers always want to feel they are the main man, the star of the team. But at Barça you know that has to be Leo. He's the best and he's been in Barcelona since he was 13 ... he's like a god in Barcelona. For some players, being in Leo's shadow is hard, so they prefer to go somewhere else where they can be the star and stay in the spotlight.'

Within any sports team, there is always that strong sense of competition *within* the group, as well as externally. Of course, the main purpose of the squad is to come together in pursuit of shared ambitions: winning games and trophies. But there is always a delicate and fragile internal tension as well: contracts, livelihoods and individual pride and honour are at stake.

There can, self-evidently, only be one goalkeeper in a football team, and when, to use an example from the summer of 2016, Marc-Andre ter Stegen was ready to claim ownership of that position for Barcelona, Claudio Bravo knew that he wasn't going to get many games and had little real option but to accept an offer from Manchester City – in turn abruptly displacing England international Joe Hart from the role he had filled for the previous nine years.

This brutal, unforgiving and intense sense of internal competition is even evident when everything is working perfectly well. For instance, the famous indirect penalty routine against Celta Vigo, initiated by Messi and converted by Suarez, was actually designed to be scored by Neymar. But Suarez was quicker off the mark, beat the Brazilian to the ball and had no hesitation in taking the goal away from his team-mate. If you watch the footage after the goal it's noticeable that although Neymar does all the right things and joins in with the group celebrations, he then makes a point of complaining to Suarez – looking distinctly irritated – that it should have been *his* goal.

All of this creates an awkward and potentially extremely disruptive dynamic within the group, meaning that relationships are never too far from being broken or damaged, however productive they might have been in the past. It's very easy to offer platitudes about the importance of teamwork and everyone sticking together, but actually achieving and then maintaining those qualities within an ego-filled dressing room can be a considerable challenge.

Witness, for example, how quickly and ruthlessly Sir Alex Ferguson always used to break up his Manchester United teams if he felt a change in the internal atmosphere was necessary, and how Neymar decided with similar swiftness to abandon the glorious MSN trident when he concluded it was in his personal interests to head to Paris.

Considering all the personal agendas at play and the substantial egos involved, it is not always easy for Barcelona players – all of whom are world-class talents in their own right, or they wouldn't be playing for Barcelona – to accept the preeminence of Messi. But mostly they do, for a very simple reason: his presence in an overwhelmingly influential role makes it much more likely that they will win.

If Messi was an office worker, he would be that infuriating guy who shows up an hour late, leaves an hour early, violates dress codes, never washes up his coffee mugs and gets paid much more than everyone else but is still accepted by his co-workers because he's so good at his job. And, to make it more palatable, he also has the uncanny ability to make everyone else better at their jobs. So he is tolerated, or even admired, and everyone expects the big bosses upstairs to do whatever it takes to retain his services and keep him happy.

There is also the expectation, naturally, that he will consistently fulfil his side of the bargain – that he will reciprocate – by continuing to do his job so well that he remains worthy of receiving all these special privileges. And, of course, that's what he does. Messi's incredibly consistent record shows that he can always be relied upon to apply his personal freedoms – which, as we learned in the last chapter, also inevitably brings personal responsibilities – in the right way for the good of the team, and he therefore continues to be indulged.

Pablo Zabaleta, Messi's team-mate of more than a decade, insists there have never been any problems in any of the dressing rooms they have shared as a result of the privileges Messi is given. Any potential jealousies or resentments are swept away simply because Messi is so good, and so consistent. His team-mates know that Messi will always fill his side of the bargain, so they accept the special treatment he receives. They scratch Messi's back by doing his defensive work; he scratches theirs by scoring and creating goals to win games.

'When you have a player as good as Messi, you know he's different to the rest,' begins Zabaleta.

'He's the best player in the team, and sometimes if he feels he has to take some rest or not train as much, or not train at 100 per cent, but then in the game he makes the difference for the team, the other players will accept this. Only if he does make the difference. If you see that he's lazy in training and then in the game he doesn't work much either, that would create a bad atmosphere in the dressing room. But we have seen Messi for the last 13 years always making the difference for his team.

'And anyway, he's a humble guy and he trains well. He's good in training. Maybe not exactly the same as someone like [Carles] Puyol or [Javier] Mascherano, because everyone's different and players like them need to train at 100 per cent to prepare themselves. They don't have the same quality as Messi, so for players like that it's all about intensity, desire, winning duels, and they have to train like that too. They have to be prepared physically and mentally to play like this. Messi doesn't really need to train at 100 per cent because he knows that in the game he will still make the difference.

'Players are different and football has always been like that. As a player you accept it, and it's not hard because you don't want your best player to waste his energy. When you're playing with Messi, you've always got the feeling something will happen if you can give him the ball. So if I'm playing behind him on the right wing, I don't want him to spend his energy tracking back with the opposition full-back.

'Having him there also helps me, because I know their full-back is thinking he can't get forward too much because then Messi will be standing in behind him, so he can't leave himself exposed. If you give space to Messi, you'll be in trouble and concede goals because he's so good. So of course when you play against Messi you don't try to go forward so much, and that makes everything easier for his team-mates.'

However, Zabaleta does admit that playing alongside Messi comes with strings attached, and that he was forced to modify his style of play when he headed away from club football to join up with Messi and his Argentine team-mates.

'With Man City, I was always pushing forward, because the way we played we used the full-backs a lot,' he recalls.

'But in the national team, we had Aguero, Higuain, Di Maria, Messi ... I couldn't expect them to track back all the time, so I couldn't push forward as much. I had to keep my eye on the opponent on my side and be more defensive.

'I didn't mind, because I needed to do what was best for the team, but it meant I had to be more defensive. I always really enjoy getting forward, trying to have an assist or a shot, but

I also know that's not my main job as a defender – the first thing is to defend. I enjoy playing at both ends of the pitch, but sometimes everyone has to change and make a compromise.'

Despite the need to make those compromises, though, Barcelona and Argentina players, however much they might sometimes be tempted, would never seriously think about rebelling against Messi. They would never really unite, throw off their chains and attempt to carry out a revolution to unseat their benevolent oppressor. They accept inequality because they know what we all know: Messi should be pampered and looked after, because you will win more games with him than without him. And if that means other players have to accept a smaller share of the limelight or subdue their preferred playing methods, it's a price worth paying.

As Zabaleta notes, not every player is created equal. They have different characteristics and different capabilities, and should therefore place different demands upon each other while still working together in pursuit of a common goal.

'You will not find another Messi out there, so when you have him in the team, you always try to get the best out of him,' says his former international team-mate.

'It's not like I will *always* pass the ball to him. If he's not in the right position or if someone else is free, of course I will pass the ball to another player. But when he's in the starting eleven it's such a relief for everyone because we know that when he's in the team, we have more chance to win the game. Every player has their own responsibilities, but we don't all have the same qualities.'

These delicate dynamics within a sports team are a revealing living example of how reciprocal altruism works in practice as well as in theory, striking the precarious balance between individuals and the collective as each member of the group accepts the necessity of making certain concessions to their colleagues on the shared understanding that they will all benefit in the long run.

And there has never been a more vivid demonstration of reciprocal altruism on a football field, with all its advantages and complications, than MSN.

The greatest forward line in history

For 15 months, the MSN trident – Messi, Suarez, Neymar – was simply glorious.

Watching Barcelona during the period from January 2015 until March 2016 was a thrilling, exhilarating experience, with the front three working together in perfect synchronicity while the rest of the team selflessly but effectively backed them up, creating an almost unstoppable unit which just worked perfectly on every level.

It worked for Suarez because the Uruguayan knew that he was coming towards the end of his career, because he knew that he'd never find better team-mates to service his goalscoring needs than Messi and Neymar, because Barcelona was the club he had always wanted to play for, and because it was the city where his family had always wanted to live and already owned a house.

It worked for Neymar because he had arrived in Barcelona as a young and inexperienced player who was taking his first steps in Europe and who knew that, for all his undoubted potential, he still had a lot to learn and a lot to prove. Playing alongside the more experienced Messi and Suarez, he was aware, would give him the opportunity to grow and develop as part of his longer-term quest to become the greatest player in the world.

It worked positionally, with each player able to occupy a space on the field which allowed them to showcase their talents: Messi cutting in from the right wing, Neymar doing the same from the left, and Suarez running riot through the middle. They complemented each other, rather than getting in each other's way.

It worked collectively, because coach Luis Enrique (after an initially difficult few months) established a solid supporting structure consisting of selfless, team-oriented players like the regular midfield starting trio of Sergio Busquets, Ivan Rakitic and Andres Iniesta, who did not mind subduing their attacking instincts and allowing their heralded front three to bask in most of the glory.

And of course it worked for Messi, because he was able to perform with a pair of attacking team-mates who were very close to his own extraordinary level of ability but who were also unquestioningly accepting of his position of supremacy within the group. The 'MSN' acronym was appropriate not only because it recalled the tech giant, but also because it placed Messi at the front. He came first, everyone else followed, and nobody had a problem with that.

With all those factors falling into place, Barcelona were ready to take on the world – and they did exactly that, beating all-comers and beating them in style to finish the 2014/15 season by claiming a spectacular treble: La Liga, the Copa Del Rey and the Champions League.

Barcelona's success on the European stage that season was especially notable for the arduous route they were forced to take by a series of unfriendly draws: during the knockout stages they defeated the reigning champions of England (Pablo Zabaleta's Manchester City, 3-1 on aggregate), France (Paris St Germain, 5-1 on aggregate), Germany (Bayern Munich, 5-3 on aggregate) and Italy (Juventus, 3-1 in the final).

That Champions League campaign ended with Neymar and Messi both scoring ten goals, while Suarez netted seven. Messi also topped the assists chart (with six), just ahead of team-mates Iniesta (five) and Dani Alves (four), with the appearance of the latter two players on the list showing that the rest of the team – not just MSN – was also contributing in a secondary but still significant manner.

That point was further emphasised by the opening goal in the final against Juventus, which saw Iniesta burst into the area and lay a square pass for Rakitic to convert from close range – it was the most important goal of the season, and neither M nor S nor N were directly involved.

Rakitic also scored the only goal in Barça's second leg victory over Manchester City that season, and Zabaleta – who played in that and several more games against MSN – believes the ability of the forward trio to focus their efforts within the framework of a collective effort was the biggest key to their success.

'As a City player, we were always very worried about playing against those three,' Zabaleta recalls with a rueful smile.

'Apart from their quality, they had such a great connection. There was no selfishness, they were always trying to play between themselves and they created so many chances for each other. They could do everything – they knew how to dribble, how to play one-twos, how to create chances and how to score goals.

'But they also worked well for the whole team. The three of them are such great individual players but they knew they had the best midfield in football with Rakitic, Iniesta and Busquets, and Xavi was still there as well. Then they had Alba and Alves at full-back, so there was a lot of quality in that team and they used everyone. You can be one of the best but you still need great players around you to make you better.'

The stats compiled in that triumphant 2014/15 campaign by MSN, thanks to the backing of their team-mates, were outrageous. Messi led the way by scoring 58 goals, followed by Neymar with 39 and then Suarez with 25. That made an astonishing combined total of 122 goals in just one season, the highest tally registered by three players on the same team in football history – but not for long, because the following year saw them break their own record as Suarez took over as the main scorer with 59 goals, while Messi registered 41 and Neymar added 31 for a total of 131.

But far more than just impressing with stratospheric, record-breaking numbers, the Barça team of early 2015 to spring 2016 were a dazzling delight for the senses. Their mutual understanding and selfless generosity – their reciprocal altruism – allied with their individual ability created a stunning cocktail of scintillating attacking play, and it was hard to argue against the assertion of coach Luis Enrique, among many others, that his prized trident was the greatest forward line ever.

A large part of their greatness was that elusive but vital quality often described as 'chemistry'. Each member of the MSN trio trusted the other two, genuinely wanted them to succeed and, judging by the smiles and laughter on their faces, they clearly very much enjoyed playing together. With Messi, Suarez and Neymar together, football was fun – as long as you weren't playing against them.

Their willingness to create chances for each other was particularly notable. Watching back through the goals they scored during that period, it's amazing how many of MSN's conversions were simple tap-ins after one of the trio declined the chance to shoot in favour of setting up an easier chance for his amigo.

Examples of their stunning collective play are too numerous to mention more than just a small fraction, but perhaps the greatest encapsulation of their shared success was a stunning goal against Roma in the Champions League in November 2015.

The play started with Neymar receiving the ball in midfield and instigating a dazzling one-touch passing move which followed the sequence Neymar-Messi-Neymar-Messi-Suarez-Messi, culminating in the latter chipping the ball over the advancing goalkeeper to score an astonishing goal which was made even more remarkable for the fact that Dani Alves, who could have netted a simple tap-in after following in Messi's shot, instead actively got out of the way so the goal would belong to his team-mate.

In comfortable wins against outclassed opposition, MSN often went to extremes to ensure that all three of them scored. If Messi and Suarez had already netted, they would spend the rest of the game desperately attempting to fashion chances for Neymar to join them on the scoresheet, with one occasion coming in an 8-0 victory at Cordoba (yes, 8-0 ... that's the kind of thing they did) where Messi and Suarez had both already scored twice when the team won a penalty and, rather than one of them completing their hat-trick, they just handed over the ball to Neymar.

This reciprocal altruism was not only on display in comfortable strolls against vastly inferior sides like Cordoba, but also on the biggest of stages such as the 2015 Champions League semi-final second leg at Bayern Munich, where they helped secure their passage to the final with a superb connection as Messi cut open the defence with a through ball to Suarez, who rejected the chance to shoot by rolling a square pass to give Neymar an easy finish.

Watching Messi, Suarez and Neymar in full flow during that period was simply one of the best viewing experiences a football fan could ever hope to enjoy. But it was also short-lived. The success of MSN was built upon specific circumstances, and before long those circumstances changed and the environment which had allowed reciprocal altruism to flourish disappeared.

Starting with a 2-1 home loss to Real Madrid in April 2016 – the worst possible way to commemorate club legend Johan Cruyff, who had passed away a few days earlier – the previously unbeatable team just lost their way.

That Clasico upset was the first of four defeats in five games, including a Champions League quarter-final exit against Atletico Madrid. Suddenly, there was a big disconnect between MSN and everyone else, with Barça at times looking like two teams within a team: eight players standing around at the back in the hope that the three magicians up front would win them the game.

Although they held on to take the 2015/16 league title, the beginning of the end had set in. The next campaign was a major disappointment as Real Madrid won La Liga, while a convincing 3-0 aggregate defeat against Juventus condemned Barcelona to their second consecutive quarter-final exit on the European stage.

The productivity of MSN dipped to 111 goals (compared to 131 and 122 in the previous two seasons), and although there were still moments of magic they were less frequent, and more reliant upon individual brilliance rather than collective play. And at the end of the season, Neymar – like many before him – decided he'd had enough of living in Messi's shadow.

As forewarned by his slightly peeved reaction to Suarez's 'indirect penalty' goal against Celta Vigo, the terms of the deal drawn up between MSN were no longer mutually acceptable. Neymar had served his apprenticeship, he was ready to advance into the next stage of his career and he was no longer getting what he wanted out of his reciprocal altruism with Messi – as far as the Brazilian was concerned, it had become too altruistic and not reciprocal enough.

Follow the leader
The example of MSN shows just how difficult it is to achieve genuine reciprocal altruism – selfless teamwork – within the highly competitive, pressured and dynamic environment of elite sports. But it also shows just how important it is.

When MSN were truly playing together, and they had the properly integrated backing of the eight other members of the team who genuinely connected with them rather than feeling like unnecessary appendages, everyone benefitted.

During that period from January 2015 to spring 2016, Messi was able to give full expression to all his talents. He scored goals, created goals, received as much possession as he could possibly ask for, and had the pleasure of playing alongside a pair of team-mates who would never let him down when he gave them the ball and who would always, in due course, return the favour.

Suarez and Neymar excelled in a similar fashion, each knowing that the other would always repay any assists provided to them, while the rest of the team was still given plenty of opportunity to contribute in a meaningful manner – most notably with that opening goal in the 2015 Champions League Final, fashioned between Rakitic and Iniesta.

Before long, though, it all started to go wrong. Nobody could really say why, but the group just was not working properly together anymore. The teamwork had gone, and results deteriorated accordingly.

It had only been when Barcelona found a method of play which encouraged reciprocal altruism rather than isolated outbreaks of individualism that they really enjoyed success. With smoothly functioning teamwork, they won every competition available in 2015; without it, a couple of years later almost exactly the same group of players had to settle for only the least significant title available to them, the Copa Del Rey.

That disappointing season wasn't the first time Messi experienced how a lack of teamwork limits his ability to excel and win trophies. In 2013/14 the situation was even worse, with short-lived manager Tata Martino failing to find a formula that worked and seeing his team often reduced – without much exaggeration – to ten players standing around in the hope that Messi, with little assistance, would somehow find a way to score. It sometimes looked like a playground kick-about where the best kid attempts to dribble past everyone and shoot, and it was no surprise that Barça finished the season trophy-less.

The tendency of Messi's teams to rely heavily upon him has recurred frequently enough to have been given a specific label, usually applied with negative connotations, by the Spanish media: *Messidependencia*. Dependence upon Messi. And, if anything, there's an even greater case of Messidependencia when he pulls on his national team shirt, with the painful and damaging extent of Argentina's over-reliance upon him during the 2018 World Cup finals described in the previous chapter.

Messi's presence in a football team is a blessing but also a delicate balance. When you have a player with his ability, of course you want to depend upon him – it would be absolutely crazy not to. Simply having him alongside you virtually guarantees victory in most games. But against opponents of a similar strength, a real problem arises when that dependence becomes an over-dependence, and staying on the right side of the boundary between those two states is not easy.

In football, as with many other aspects of life, ultimate responsibility for striking the necessary but elusive balance between individual expression and collective coherence is placed in the hands of one person: the manager. The boss.

Messi, for all his brilliance, is only one member of a team – in the oft-repeated Spanish phrase, 'soy uno mas'. I'm just one more. Ten other players have to fit in alongside him, and the manager is the one who has to command how all those disparate strands should move together, and stop them from moving apart.

At various times during his career, such as the 2018 World Cup finals, allegations have been cast that Messi sometimes oversteps the mark and attempts to seize some of the responsibilities which should belong to his manager: in 2012, he was forced to deny reports that he had been nicknamed 'the little dictator' by some of his Barcelona team-mates, while over the years there have been constant claims that he controls Argentina's selection policy, with only members of his inner circle supposedly given any chance of being picked for big international games.

Those rumours have never been substantiated by any of his current or former team-mates or coaches, but it certainly is true that Messi has always been at his best when he has played under strong leaders and has been prepared to place himself under their authority rather than – as dismally demonstrated during the 2018 World Cup finals – attempting (or feeling obliged) to take on too many responsibilities for himself.

At club level, during Guardiola's reign at Barcelona there was never any doubt whatsoever about who was in charge, and that was the most successful spell of Messi's career; conversely, the least convincing leader on the Barcelona bench in the last 15 years was Martino, whose trophy-less year in charge coincided with the least spectacular season of Messi's career.

Messi, like any other player, needs to be guided by strong leadership to fit into a solid team framework; without that leadership and that collective structure, he is nowhere near as effective.

Zabaleta, who also played under Guardiola for a year at Manchester City, believes it's no surprise that Messi was perfectly happy to accept the authority of Guardiola during their time together, because the coach was able to give him clear and confident direction.

'The thing with Pep was that he really understood what Messi needed when he played him in that central false nine role,' begins Zabaleta, who then launches into a fascinating explanation of the understanding that flourished between the iconic coach and his star player.

'Pep was really good for Leo. Pep told him: "I need you to play here because I prefer to have players on the wings like Pedro, Alves, Abidal – players who can really work up and down the pitch, and I can demand that from them. They will do the job I need from the players on the outside.

'"I want you to be ready to receive the ball close to the 18-yard box. I will make sure that everyone will press high, because you will make the difference for the team. I will make sure everyone else will do the running and pressing. It's not like you don't have to do anything without the ball – you will also need to add some pressing, but only five metres, two-metre sprints.

'"I want you to stand here, get into space, and by pressing high we will win the ball back and play in the half-pitch, and in that way we will create more chances and you will score more goals."

'Pep convinced all his players why they should play in that way, why they had to press high up the pitch. They were already doing this with Frank Rijkaard before, but Pep was another level, very clear on every single detail. And Leo enjoyed it. He saw there was a clear idea which would benefit him, so he trusted Pep. The rest of the players also had the same idea, and everyone did what Pep asked from them. That's why his Barcelona team was unstoppable.'

That Barcelona team was unstoppable because they had great players, of course. But also because – like the team led by Luis Enrique during the treble-winning season a few years later – those great players were all following the same game plan in the same way. They had a mutual understanding, or reciprocal altruism, and were happy to walk along the path towards perfection that had been plotted by their trusted leader Guardiola – which, as described by Danny Kerry in the last chapter, also coincided with the goals of each individual player.

In a complex team environment like football, it is extremely rare, if not impossible, to achieve that kind of shared vision without the guidance of a strong leader to keep everyone moving along in the right direction. The same, surely, is true for other fields of human endeavour. The ethos of teamwork is important; but so too is the role of the leader who creates and sustains that ethos in the first place.

The quiet leader

In addition to knowing how to submit to authority when that authority is expressed in the right way, one unavoidable aspect of being a team player, especially as Messi has become older, is that he also assumes a leadership role himself.

On the face of it, there might appear to be a problem with this idea because he does not look anything like what we might regard as a 'natural leader'.

In football, we often think of leaders as big, tough and loud warriors – someone like John Terry, Carles Puyol or Sergio Ramos. Someone who will be strong and commanding; someone powerful and intimidating; someone who will give sweat, blood and tears for their team's cause, exemplified by the famous image of England captain Terry Butcher with blood pouring down his face and staining his shirt after a draw against Sweden in 1989.

Lionel Messi, it's clear, will never be that kind of leader.

The other stereotypical form of leadership is not the warrior but the authoritative general: the calm and composed orchestrator and organiser, the perceptive soothsayer who directs the traffic and has a hypnotic ability to tell everyone where to go and when to go there. Xavi, Andrea Pirlo, Socrates, Bobby Moore and Franz Beckenbauer are among those who fit the bill for this other traditional form of leadership.

Messi, though, doesn't really fall into that category either.

Maybe, one might wonder, he's just too quiet and unassuming to fill the role of a motivational and inspiring leader of men at all? He's not a shouter, and he's not a pointer, so perhaps he's just not really cut out to be a leader – and this was the view taken by former Argentina World Cup-winning skipper Daniel Passarella, who argued in 2016 that Messi should not be the national team's captain due to his reserved personality.

But irrespective of whether or not Messi is formally named as a captain, he is still expected to perform leadership duties due to his seniority and his status. And despite his apparent temperamental unsuitability to that kind of demand, he does fulfil the task because leadership takes many forms and Messi is perhaps the ultimate personification of one of them: leading by example.

Pablo Zabaleta – who initially captained Messi in the Argentine youth team and was later captained by him for five years in the senior side – notes that the experience of simply playing alongside Messi is motivational in itself, saying: 'If I'm at Barcelona or playing for Argentina and I see that Leo Messi is showing me his ambition to win, that's inspiring! If the best player in the world is producing his best in every game, then every single player needs to do the same. You follow people like that.'

Talk is cheap, and we can always see through duplicitous politicians who say one thing but mean another. It's easy to say the right things, but what matters much more are your actions, what you actually *do*. Anyone can thump their chest and shout inspiring words about bravery and character, but when your team is losing in the last minute and you're still prepared to get on the ball and take responsibility for trying to find an equaliser, that's *real* bravery and character, and real leadership – even if you don't make a song and dance about it.

Messi, as we have seen, is always prepared to take on that kind of responsibility, and a powerful recent case of his leadership through example came towards the end of the 2017/18 season in the Clasico clash against Real Madrid at the Camp Nou.

At half-time, Barcelona were in trouble. The game was tied at one apiece but Madrid had dominated the latter stages of the first half, looking by far the more likely team to go ahead, and also had the additional advantage of an extra man after home team right-back Sergi Roberto was sent off for retaliating against Marcelo just before the break.

Messi had endured, by his standards, a poor first half. With his team disconnected and disjointed, he had rarely been able to get on the ball and found his attacking efforts well controlled by the visiting defence whenever he got within sight of goal. In the second period, though, he exploded into action, appearing determined to compensate for the loss of red-carded Roberto all by himself. He charged around the pitch displaying levels of energy and defensive commitment rarely shown in recent years, constantly looking for the ball, constantly giving his team-mates a passing option.

His efforts bore fruit when he scored a superb goal to make it 2-1, receiving a pass from Suarez and jinking past two defenders to rifle an unstoppable low drive into the bottom left corner. And although Madrid fought back to level through Gareth Bale, Messi did not stop running until the final whistle was blown to signify a 2-2 draw.

That second-half performance was an instance of Messi accepting personal responsibility, as discussed in the previous chapter, and also a great illustration of leadership: he knew that his team-mates were struggling and needed a lift, so he provided it – not by shouting at them or flying into tough tackles (although he did earn a yellow card for a crunching foul on Ramos in a telling indication that he was not prepared to lose a physical battle), but by giving a personal demonstration of what his team-mates had to do and showing that he was prepared to do it himself.

Over time, Messi has also started to embrace a more active role in mentoring his younger team-mates. This was not really the case during the early stages of his career, when he really was a man of few words – although he always led by example, he appeared to be so focussed on his own game that he didn't have any headspace for proactively helping his team-mates, leaving the likes of Xavi and Puyol to administer words of advice or encouragement.

Now, though, Messi has reached elder statesman status – he is the third oldest member of the regular Barcelona starting eleven, and was the oldest of all the attacking players in Argentina's 2018 World Cup squad. And perhaps as a result of the greater sense of maturity that comes naturally with age, he has recently started to live up to his status as a role model to his younger team-mates in a more direct manner.

A particular example has been evident at Barcelona, where the almost impossible task of replacing Neymar was handed to young Frenchman Ousmane Dembele, signed from Borussia Dortmund in the summer of 2017 for an eye-watering sum of €105 million – a colossal fee for a 20-year-old with only two seasons of senior football under his belt.

At first, Dembele struggled desperately with the triple demand of being 'the new Neymar', living up to his price tag and adjusting to his new team's style of play. After a patchy start to the season, he overstretched his hamstring attempting a back-heel and was out of action for more than three months, and upon finally returning to fitness he often looked lost, appearing to have little idea of how he could fit into the team.

It was the kind of situation where Messi, in the past, might have rapidly grown frustrated and made plain his contempt at the under-performing newcomer. Instead, though, he became a model of cajoling patience and understanding with his nervous young colleague, appearing determined to build Dembele's confidence and make him feel like a proper part of the group.

That softly-softly approach was rewarded in a Champions League last-16 meeting with Chelsea, when Messi finished a trademark dribble by squaring a sumptuous pass into the stride of Dembele, who took one touch to control before blasting a powerful rising drive high into the net. There was a look of paternal pride on Messi's face as the two celebrated together, and Dembele's strong subsequent finish to the season reignited hopes that he could, after all, prove value for money by flourishing into a top-level performer under Messi's wing.

Zabaleta has not been surprised to see his friend accepting a greater leadership role in recent times, explaining: 'Some of the big players in Barcelona have left in the last few years – Valdes, Puyol, Xavi, Abidal, Alves, and now Iniesta, so Leo has taken on that responsibility.

'There were some leaders before who knew the club and who were always talking in the dressing room. But now none of them are there, Leo is the captain and anyone who comes to Barcelona will see he's the main man.

'When you are a captain, you also have responsibilities to welcome everyone to the club, make them feel this is a great place to be, make them realise they have to work hard and win trophies. Leo does that kind of thing more naturally now because he is more mature – he's not a kid anymore, in fact he's the father of his own three kids! He's grown up, he's a proper man now. He's also a family man and he knows how to treat people like a family.'

In one sense, Messi's proactive mentoring of young players like Dembele is a new development and it will be interesting to see whether he continues to take on a more overt leadership role over the remainder of his career, perhaps even moving into coaching when his playing days end (something he has previously said would not interest him).

But in another way, his enhanced role within the dressing room is also unsurprising because it is symptomatic of a trait he has displayed throughout his career: no matter how successful he has been, Messi has never been frightened by the prospect of change.

Chapter Six
A Different River

Barcelona 3-1 Atletico Madrid
La Liga
Sunday 11 January 2015, Camp Nou, Barcelona
Is it really happening? Is Lionel Messi leaving Barcelona?

That is the question on everyone's lips in the build-up to the Camp Nou clash between Barça and reigning Spanish champions Atletico Madrid, whose last visit to the stadium saw them clinch the title on the final day of the 2013/14 season.

And now, ahead of the latest visit from Diego Simeone's powerful team, there seems to be a genuine danger that Messi is seriously considering dramatically quitting his only professional club – perhaps even as early as this month's transfer window.

On the face of it, the crisis point came in the previous weekend's 1-0 defeat at Real Sociedad. It was the first game of the new year and Messi and fellow superstar Neymar were both left on the bench by manager Luis Enrique after returning from their respective Christmas breaks in South America with little preparation time. Predictably, Barça conceded an early goal and the coach was forced to introduce his 'rested' star duo at half-time, but it made little difference as they delivered lifeless displays and the team failed to rescue a point.

The following day, Barça held their annual open training session at the Mini Estadi, the club's reserve team stadium, next to the Camp Nou, to celebrate Three Kings Day, the most important date in the annual festive calendar in Spain – especially for children who relish the visit of the gift-bearing three wise men on their camels. But on this occasion there was a big disappointment for those young fans: Messi was not there, officially laid low by a sudden case of 'gastroenteritis', an illness generally regarded in Spanish football as shorthand for 'having a strop and refusing to train'.

Messi's obvious disgruntlement at being left out of the team against Real Sociedad and his subsequent failure to attend the Three Kings celebrations sparked serious speculation over his future, further intensified when he mischievously took to Instagram and started following the official account of Chelsea, a club which had been linked with his signature.

So now, ahead of the meeting with Atletico, according to widespread media reports the events of the past week have resulted in Messi and Luis Enrique suffering a total breakdown in their relationship, with the player consequently delivering an ultimatum to the board: either he leaves, or I leave.

Rather than being a sudden explosion, this crisis has been developing for a long time. Neither the club nor the team have ever really recovered from the departure of Pep Guardiola in 2012, not helped by his replacement Tito Vilanova being forced to resign after suffering a relapse in his fight against cancer. He was replaced by Argentine coach Tata Martino, who always looked out of his depth and suffered a season of abject failure as the 2013/14 campaign finished – shortly after the tragic death of Vilanova – with the team failing to win a major trophy for the first time since 2008.

The club is also in trouble off the pitch, being handed a transfer ban by FIFA after breaking regulations on the signing of young players from overseas, while club president Sandro Rosell has been forced to resign in the wake of allegations that the club committed tax-dodging offences during the purchase of Neymar in the summer of 2013.

Sailing right into the middle of this playing and institutional crisis came the aggressive figure of Luis Enrique, the volatile former Barça forward who was appointed to take over from Martino and inherited a team which was looking stale, bored and desperately in need of a new direction.

The first few months of the season have been predictably difficult as the new coach experimented with a series of different formations and strategies, including a bold and bizarre line-up for a Champions League meeting with Paris St Germain containing four central defenders, no full-backs, two midfielders and four forwards – one of whom was Luis Suarez, controversially signed from Liverpool in the summer whilst serving a four-month ban for biting Italy defender Giorgio Chiellini during the World Cup finals.

The whole sorry situation has been inevitably building towards a breaking point for a long time, and the crescendo came with the loss at Real Sociedad and the reported bust-up between the coach and his star man Messi, who is therefore finding himself at the centre of the global media's attention – even more than usual – as he prepares to face an Atletico team which held him scoreless in their seven previous encounters.

When the opening whistle blows, there is a surprise: Messi has abandoned the false nine deep-lying forward role he has famously occupied for the previous five and a half years, and is playing instead on the right wing with Suarez in the middle and Neymar on the left flank.

This isn't entirely new – Messi started his career on the right, and also spent a few games there under both Martino and Luis Enrique. But it is an unexpected move for a game of such importance, immediately sparking a lively debate about whether he has decided upon the new playing position for himself or whether the coach has placed Messi out wide in a provocative attempt to assert his authority.

Either way, the question of Messi's state of mind is soon answered. From the opening minute, he is alert, alive, engaged and completely committed, looking like a totally different player from the apathetic figure who has drifted half-heartedly through much of the previous few weeks.

After just 12 minutes, Messi tricks his way past Diego Godin on the right of the penalty area and delivers a low cross to Suarez, and although he can't control Neymar is there, reacting quickest to stab home the loose ball for the opener.

The danger continues to flow: Messi releases Suarez and his cross is headed narrowly wide by Neymar; soon after Neymar breaks to find Messi, whose delivery forces Godin into a desperate clearance. Then, ten minutes before the break, Messi receives possession on the right wing, sneakily using his upper arm to control the ball, and drives inside, releasing a perfectly timed pass to allow Suarez to sweep home the second goal.

After a week dominated by reports of vindictive and bitter in-fighting, this is more like it. This is the football we want to see from Barcelona, and especially from Messi. But it's not all over yet, because now there's an unexpected twist as Messi challenges visiting full-back Jesus Gamez inside the penalty area – a part of the pitch rarely visited by the Argentine in previous weeks – and referee Alberto Undiano whistles for a controversial penalty which is converted by Atletico forward Mario Mandzukic. 2-1 and game on.

But the final word, with a sense of inevitability at the end of a harrowing week, belongs to Messi. With three minutes remaining and the result still in the balance, he receives a crossfield ball from Suarez, exchanges passes with Ivan Rakitic and stabs home for a goal which settles the outcome and joyously launches a new era: it's the first league game in which Messi, Suarez and Neymar have all scored, and comes at the end of Messi's first game back on the right wing.

After years of playing as a false nine in a passing game based on midfield dominance, it is time for Messi to embrace a new style of play under a new coach with a new position and new strike force partners.

It's time to change.

The relentlessness of change

The original philosopher of change was Heraclitus.

Born in 535 BC in the ancient city of Ephesus, near Selcuk in modern-day Turkey but then part of the Persian Empire, many of his ideas were complex and cryptic, leading to him being bestowed with the nickname 'The Obscure'.

Our understanding of his thought is further clouded by the fact that only fragmented records of his work have survived, but Heraclitus did leave the world with one incisively futuristic and prophetic insight: the concept of constant change. Everything in the world, in every instant of existence, is in a ceaseless state of flux, summed up by a simple phrase: you can never step in the same river twice.

If you set foot in a river, step out, and then return again a few seconds later, it might look like the same river and it might feel like the same river. But that is an illusion. In reality, the water flowing through your toes is different; the banks are different; the riverbed is different.

Natural forces are constantly moving the mud and stones and eroding the rocks, subjecting the river to relentless and inevitable change, even if those changes are taking place far too slowly for the naked eye to detect.

By further extending Heraclitus's insight, it follows that everything else is also changing. However solid and permanent they may appear, all the objects around you are changing, all the time. With every passing millisecond, nothing remains the same. The table you are sitting at might look strong and sturdy, but in fact it is being endlessly subjected to a perpetual battering from invisible and uncaring forces on a sub-microscopic scale, and eventually it will crumble into nothing.

The human body is part of the same process. Over the course of a couple of decades it's easy to see how our physical states change – we lose hair, gain wrinkles, add weight in some places and lose it in others. But those long-term and noticeable changes in appearance are nothing more than the gradual accumulation of a constant process of small-scale decay and renewal which is taking place inside our bodies, unseen, from day to day, minute to minute, and second to second: in the time it takes for you to read this sentence, around ten million of your blood cells will die (but, much more happily, another ten million will be born).

Like everything around us, our physical beings are part of the ever-changing river of life, and the only thing that ever stays the same is that nothing ever stays the same.

When we consider the trajectories of our lives, Heraclitus's insight is simultaneously a rather disturbing and comforting idea. Our instinct is often to resist change, fearful of what the unknown might bring – and there are good evolutionary reasons for avoiding potential threats and preferring to stick with what we know. But we should also be cognisant of the law of the different river, which dictates that it is futile to fight against change. Whether we like it or not, change will happen anyway.

Rather than resisting, it's wiser to accept the inevitability of change and be ready to adapt to new circumstances.

Even if you're Lionel Messi.

Messi's phases one to four

Football's different rivers come in many shapes and sizes: new clubs; new managers; new team-mates; new opposition. And Messi's turning-point occasion against Atletico Madrid in January 2015, which introduced this chapter, was by no means the first or last time that he has been forced to reinvent himself.

Of course, his first major change came as a teenager when he left Argentina to move to Spain, but even if we restrict ourselves to only studying his senior career at Barcelona we can divide it into four distinct and separate phases.

In the first, between his initial emergence into the team in 2004 and the arrival of Pep Guardiola in 2008, he played on the right wing, generally with Samuel Eto'o as the centre-forward and Ronaldinho cutting in from the left, an exciting three-pronged attack which provided the launching pad for his career as Messi dazzled opposition defenders with his dizzying dribbling ability.

Then came phase two, when Guardiola moved him into the centre of the field as the focal point of his bold tactical masterpiece, ushering in the era of Messi playing as a false nine deep-lying forward with the task of joining in the team's associative play in midfield before springing into space when the opposition became pulled out of position (as described by Pablo Zabaleta in the last chapter).

The next distinct period of Messi's career started that night against Atletico in early 2015 with the birth of the MSN strike partnership – another new way of playing, yielding some of the most spectacular attacking football ever seen, with Messi positioned as a narrow right-winger and mostly looking to attack the opposition penalty area as quickly as possible, rather than building from deep in midfield as he had during the previous few years.

Finally, the shock departure of Neymar and the arrival of conservative coach Ernesto Valverde in the summer of 2017 ushered in phase four, with Messi now appearing for the first time in his club career in the 'enganche' position he had occupied during his childhood in Argentina – a centrally positioned attacking midfielder, the traditional number ten, tucking in behind a centre-forward (Luis Suarez).

Right wing to false nine to inside-right to attacking midfielder ... Messi has fulfilled so many different roles over the course of his career, often appearing in all of them in the same game, that it's not very easy to define his playing position with any precision: you wouldn't really say that he's a striker, even though he has been one of the most prolific goalscorers in the history of the game; he's definitely not a winger, despite spending long periods of many games on or near the right touchline; calling him a midfielder would be far too restrictive, notwithstanding the fact that he has always been comfortable dropping into the centre circle to spark attacking moves by exchanging passes with the likes of Xavi Hernandez, Andres Iniesta or Sergio Busquets, especially during this latest incarnation of his career.

So, Messi is not a striker, he's not a winger and he's not a midfielder ... what can we call him, then? A forward, perhaps, is the best loose description, but even that feels inadequate when you consider how much time he spends being positionally more backward than forward. In the end, we probably should be prepared to settle for an even greater generalisation: Lionel Messi is just, well, a footballer.

This difficulty in pigeonholing Messi is a tribute to the way he has always been capable of evolving his game by adapting to the changes that have unfurled around him.

His willingness to change is really quite noteworthy. If there was one person on the planet, after all, who could have been forgiven for believing he'd be able to continue doing the same thing forever, it would surely have been Messi at the end of 2012, when he had just set an all-time world record by scoring 91 goals in a calendar year on top of a new Spanish league record with 50 goals in the 2011/12 campaign.

He was achieving an outrageous and unprecedented level of goalscoring, so why on earth would he possibly need to change anything at all? He would simply keep on doing, surely, what he was already doing. But no: Messi was forced to change –

within a few months he was scoring at his slowest rate for years, and it was only when the initially painfully conceived MSN partnership took off in 2015 that he was able to return to his best.

And if even Lionel Messi had to change, shortly after scoring 91 goals in a year, what does that say about the rest of us? Nothing stays the same; life is change.

The burning platform and better never stops

'When I think back on my career, there were three significant periods of change. The first was a change after a failure, the second was a change after a success, and the last one was a change in career when I left the sport. So there was one at the beginning, one in the middle and one at the end.'

Adrian Moorhouse was a towering figure in British sport during the 1980s, maintaining his status as one of the world's top swimmers for nearly a decade. The height of his achievements came when he won the gold medal in the 100 metres breaststroke at the 1988 Olympic Games in Seoul, adding to a glittering collection which also included four European Championship golds and three more in the Commonwealth Games.

Now Moorhouse is a successful businessman – more of which later – but as he reflects on his sporting glories, he readily admits none of them would have been possible if he hadn't been willing to embrace change.

'My first major transition was immediately after my first Olympics, in Los Angeles in 1984,' he reflects when we meet on a sunny summer afternoon at his company's brand-new offices in Maidenhead, Berkshire.

'I was 20 years old and I came fourth, which is the worst position you can finish in the Olympics. Until then, I had been running my career in a very self-oriented way. Swimming has to be naturally that way to an extent because you're on your own in the pool, but I was really trying to do it all myself. I didn't know how to work with team principles in the way that a tour cyclist or a Formula One driver might manage the people around them – all the specialists who create your performance. I didn't get that idea at all.

'But after LA, I realised that I really needed to understand how other people could contribute. That failure made me see that I actually needed other people: I needed to share the goals, share the pressures, share the inputs. For example, I didn't need to learn everything about nutrition myself – I just needed to find a bloody good nutritionist.

'I was thinking: "This is pretty bad, I might quit swimming. And if I'm going to carry on, I have to do it differently." So really it was a forced change. It was hard to cede control in that way, but I had no choice. And big changes like that often come from trauma – the "burning platform" syndrome. If you're standing on a burning platform, you've got to do something to get off it.'

The changes Moorhouse implemented after his disappointment in Los Angeles took effect. Four years later, at the 1988 Olympics in Seoul, he not only climbed into the medal places but took gold, holding off the challenge of Karoly Guttler from Hungary by one hundredth of a second. The new, inclusive approach to managing his career had allowed Moorhouse to achieve the tiny improvements he needed, making all the difference from deflating fourth place to triumphant first.

But then he changed again.

'I didn't break the world record!' he laughs. 'So I was slightly disappointed when I'd just won the Olympics, which is weird but I was this uber-achiever who just wanted to keep on achieving greater heights.

'I was thinking: "OK, what do I need to do to improve my time? I've got the medal but now I need to get 0.2 seconds off my time."

'I sat down with my coach and we recognised that my dive was an area of weakness. My dive was the fifth or sixth best in the world but it wasn't the best – so that was the component of my race that could be improved. We spent three months picking apart my dive and putting it back together again. We went to Switzerland for video analysis, did some wacky things, and in the end I shaved 0.4 seconds off my dive. A year later I broke the world record by 0.3, and that had been a successful change in the mentality of "better never stops" [the motto adopted by the British Olympics team in 2012].'

During the peak years of his career, then, after already establishing himself as one of the world's top swimmers, Moorhouse had firstly changed his approach towards working with others and then changed a fundamental technical aspect of his performance. But none of that was enough to fully prepare him for an even bigger and more unsettling change: retirement.

'I retired from swimming after the Barcelona Olympics in 1992, and the change I went through then was about my whole identity. It was much more fundamental,' he recalls.

'In the two previous changes, I still saw myself as an Olympic swimmer. But when I let go of my career, I didn't even know who I was anymore. The phrase "Who am I?" was very valid. The day after I quit the sport, I couldn't say "I am a swimmer." Because I wasn't a swimmer any more. So what am I? Who am I? I found that really hard, and for about a year I don't think I was clinically depressed but I was very low. The change in 1984 was "Am I good enough?" and in 1988 it was "How can I get better?" But 1992 was "Who am I?" and I found that very difficult.'

In time, Moorhouse came through his identity crisis by carving out a new career, having embarked upon a voyage of self-discovery – his biggest change yet – and asking himself with painful honesty which skills that he already possessed could be transferred into a different field of work, and what that different field might be.

'I went through my skills and attributes,' he recalls. 'And it took me several months to work out my strengths: I was goal-oriented, I worked hard, I was coachable, could work in a team, I accepted feedback. That was interesting, realising that I had those qualities, and that process allowed me to start rebuilding my self-belief and self-esteem, reminding myself that I was good.'

And so, three years after retiring, having briefly worked as Head of Talent Development for British Swimming, Moorhouse made another change: he teamed up with a couple of friends to start his own business, using the skills he developed in his sporting career in a new context with the intention of giving business leaders the 'tools of performance' which can breed success.

A couple of decades later, that company, Lane4, employs more than 200 people and consults for several major international corporations including Jaguar Land Rover and Coca-Cola. By accepting the need for change after change after change, Moorhouse had been able to move from success to success to success.

False nine: from good to great

The first, biggest and most profound change experienced by Lionel Messi during his professional career came in 2009, when he moved from the right wing position he had occupied since his youth team days to the false nine role at the behest of Pep Guardiola towards the end of the coach's first season in charge. And, in the light of what we've just heard from Adrian Moorhouse, the circumstances surrounding that transition make it worthy of a more detailed examination.

Guardiola could not have chosen a more dramatic stage to unleash his masterplan: a trip to face Real Madrid at the Bernabeu in May 2009, with the league title in the balance. The home team were in great form, having won 17 of their last 18 games, and a victory would have left them just one point behind the first-placed Catalan club with four games still remaining. The perfect time, then, for Guardiola to come up with a tactical tweak which was unlike anything seen in elite football for years.

Until then, Messi had been playing on the right wing with Samuel Eto'o as a traditional centre-forward and new recruit Thierry Henry in Ronaldinho's old slot on the left. The system had worked well enough to take Barcelona to the top of the table and the Champions League semi-finals, with all three forwards scoring at a rate of nearly a goal per game. But Guardiola still felt there was room for improvement, and decided this was the right game to try something different. Something very different.

Gonzalo Higuain opened the scoring for Madrid after 14 minutes, but even by that stage Messi was already baffling the home team by lining up as a striker rather than in his usual right wing berth, with the added twist of continually dropping deep into midfield to leave home team central defenders Fabio Cannavaro and Christoph Metzelder with nobody to mark while the man they expected to be guarding, Eto'o, restricted himself to the right wing.

Barça soon exploited their confusion to level as Messi, given space in the centre of midfield, floated a pass into the stride of the onrushing Henry, who was being marked neither by centre-back Cannavaro nor right-back Sergio Ramos and had a simple task in sliding the ball past Iker Casillas.

The same pattern continued throughout the game, as Madrid's central defence remained in a desperate quandary. With nobody to mark, should they follow Messi into midfield and leave a big hole behind them, or should they hold their line and allow him to turn and run at them? The approach they were facing, with no centre-forward in the opposition line-up, was so unusual they just didn't know what to do, and the visitors exploited their collective confusion to run riot.

Two minutes after Henry's leveller Barcelona went ahead when the Frenchman again raced down the left and was desperately fouled by Cannavaro, allowing Xavi to deliver a free kick which Carles Puyol thundered home. Then Lassana Diarra dwelled in possession, Xavi nudged the ball away and Messi pounced, surging clear to score with ease. Ramos pulled one back, but 3-2 rapidly became 6-2 as Henry ran on to a Xavi through ball to net again, Messi ghosted forward from midfield to receive Xavi's pass and fire home, and Gerard Pique completed the rout by charging into attack and converting a cross from Eto'o.

6-2 at the Bernabeu? Without a centre-forward? Outrageous.

It was fair to conclude that Guardiola's audacious plan had worked, and his revolutionary repositioning of Messi had been fundamental to the ground-breaking demolition job which sent shockwaves through the footballing world. With two strikers – Henry and Eto'o – playing as wingers, and a winger – Messi – playing neither as a striker nor a midfielder, the Madrid defence was totally perplexed. Barça had discovered a new style of play which would deeply influence the global game over the next few years: out of nowhere, the false nine became the height of fashion, all because of Guardiola's willingness to take a risk and innovate, and because of Messi's willingness and ability to change his role in the team for the sake of improvement.

The all-conquering side moulded by Guardiola, starting with the onset of the false nine system that famous night in Madrid and concluding with their second Champions League triumph two years later, offers a great example of the power of change effected through the 'better never stops' mentality adopted by British Olympians and referenced by Adrian Moorhouse.

Before that game at the Bernabeu, Barcelona were already a good team. A very good team. But becoming a truly great team – one which would define a generation and make a legitimate entrance into the conversation about the greatest football team of all time – was only able to happen because the coach and his players were willing to embrace change even though it wasn't really needed.

On the face of it, this looked like a case of change for the sake of change. There was no 'burning platform' underneath the feet of Guardiola and his players, who were already top of the table and into the last four of the Champions League. They didn't have to change but – led by their coach – they collectively elected to seek further improvement. Guardiola analysed the resources at his disposal, contemplated how he could allow his players to become even more effective than they already were, and devised a plan which would maximise their strengths by persuading them to do something drastically new.

It was a big risk. If moving Eto'o to the wing and Messi to the false nine role had backfired and Madrid had won the game, thereby claiming enough momentum to eventually overhaul Barça in the title race, Guardiola would have been pilloried.

It was also a risk for Messi. Although the chance to play in the centre of the pitch rather than being stuck out on the flank was a prospect he relished, the positional switch also entailed accepting a set of mental and physical demands and expectations which were very different from everything he had become accustomed to.

Messi hadn't played in the middle since his youth team days, and he had enjoyed a huge amount of success from his starting slot on the flank, scoring at a rapid rate and becoming lauded as one of the world's greatest players. The right-sided role was not broken, there was nothing to fix, and many players would have been very reluctant to be plucked out of their comfort zone and plunged into an experimental new position – especially for such a high-profile and important fixture.

But Messi was prepared to make the change because Guardiola convinced him that it would allow him to hit even greater heights. He was already a hugely influential player in an elite team, but he wanted to become an even better player and have an even bigger role to help make the team even more successful. Just like Adrian Moorhouse being prepared to alter his dive in pursuit of the world record when he had already won an Olympic gold, Messi was the relentlessly ambitious uber-achiever who was determined to pile improvement upon improvement.

So he accepted Guardiola's tactical proposal, and started occupying a strange playing position he had never previously filled in his professional career.

A few weeks later, he was celebrating a La Liga, Copa Del Rey and Champions League treble. Seven months later, he won his first Ballon d'Or award.

The risk had been worth taking. The change had paid off.

Crossing the mountain

Picture the scene.

You are transported back to prehistoric times, and are living in a small and peaceful community in a river valley. The fertile soil and good irrigation allow you and your fellow villagers to be entirely self-sufficient, easily catering for all your basic needs, and the steep mountains on all sides provide protection from marauders. Life is easy and life is good, but in such a small and isolated community there are few opportunities for progress.

One day, a friend approaches you. Pointing to the mountain in the distance, she says: 'Look over there. They say that on the other side of that mountain there's a big city filled with riches and exciting things to do. I want to go and find out for myself. I'm going to find a path and cross the mountain. Are you coming with me?'

What do you do? Do you turn your back on your settled life and peaceful existence and go in search of new adventures, or do you politely decline your friend's invitation for fear of the unknown dangers which may lie in wait? Do you cross the mountain?

Lionel Messi and Adrian Moorhouse would have crossed the mountain. But not everybody would. In that situation – and in the varied situations encountered by the two sportsmen during the course of their careers – many people would prefer to stay right where they were, in the safe confines of their comfortable valley.

After all, when Moorhouse finished just outside the medals in the Olympic Games at the age of 20, many people would have rejected the idea of changing an approach that had already taken him so far; having won gold four years later, many people would have rejected the idea of changing an aspect of his performance (the dive) that had helped make him the best swimmer in the world; having retired from his sport, many people would have rejected the idea of transferring his sporting skills into a completely different environment, swapping trunks and pool for suit and desk.

When Messi was diagnosed with a growth deficiency as a ten-year-old, many people would have been too afraid of the unknown to agree to a course of injections every day for three years; when he was offered a contract by Barcelona, many people would have been too nervous of the risks to move his whole family to a new continent; when Pep Guardiola wanted him to adapt to a new and bold playing position in 2009, many people would have been reluctant to abandon a role which had already allowed him to become a superstar.

Our automatic, instinctive reaction to the idea of change is often a cautious and nervous rejection. Change makes us uneasy. Change makes us uncomfortable. Change is scary.

Or, on the other hand, change is an opportunity. Change should be embraced and actively sought. Change is exciting.

What causes those two distinct mentalities? What makes some people believe that 'better never stops', whereas others in the same situation would say: 'OK, this is enough. I'll stop right here'?

The difference between the two attitudes is the contrast between a growth and fixed mindset, as described by American psychologist Carol Dweck, who spent more than a decade developing a theory with the aim, in her words, of discovering 'how people cope with failure or obstacles. I was curious about why some students love challenge and others, who may be equally talented, shy away from challenges – play it safe. I just wanted to figure that out.'

Dweck's theory is widely accepted, and Moorhouse's experiences in both sport and business have allowed him to conclude that it is essential in determining how successfully people are able to anticipate and respond to changes in circumstance: if you have a fixed mindset, you stay in the valley; if you have a growth mindset, you cross that mountain.

'High-level performers have the growth mindset, it's very obvious,' asserts Moorhouse.

'All the elite athletes I've ever met – people like David Beckham and Jonny Wilkinson – are always out there, asking: "Where will I get a bit extra? How can I improve?" They are the ones who stay on the training pitch a little longer than everyone else, or talk to different people, or read something new, because that just might give them an edge.

'I genuinely believe that everyone has a talent for something, but the question is how that talent can be unlocked. The ability to shift and be open and progress is fundamental. If you've got that mentality, it's a natural habit to always be looking for the next new thing. If you haven't got it, you'll struggle.'

However, it's not as simple as some people being born with a growth mindset and others being fixed with nothing in between. There are many shades of grey, and we are all liable to fluctuate between the two attitudes in different aspects of our lives or even on different days of the week depending on our mood – and we can all develop methods of making ourselves better at dealing with change.

Moorhouse, for example, admits that his mind was initially closed to the idea of modifying his dive after he won the Olympic gold in 1988: 'When my coach said to me "You need to change your dive to get better", I said: "Don't be stupid, I've just won the Olympics!"' he laughs. 'But I trusted him and soon after that I moved from denial to resistance, then acceptance.'

Allowing ourselves to follow this process – from denial to resistance and finally to acceptance – is the way we can all steer ourselves away from a fixed mindset and towards personal growth.

'The key is getting people to reflect and realise when they are being fixed,' says Moorhouse. 'Even for people with an open mindset, the initial reaction to change is often denial, when you point-blank insist there isn't even an issue to address. Then, when evidence to support the need for change is presented, that leads from denial to resistance, an emotional response which can carry a lot of anger.'

This, perhaps, is what was going on with Lionel Messi at the start of 2015 and over the preceding months.

For a long time, it had been apparent that his false nine position was no longer working. Opposing teams had worked out ways to minimise its effectiveness, sitting deep and narrow on the edge of their penalty area and 'giving' Barça the wide areas, safe in the knowledge they were unlikely to score from those positions due to their lack of dangerous targets for crosses.

Messi was being defended in a 'staggered' approach – rather than man-marking him or even surrounding him with three players at the same time, opponents would close him down with one defender, but with another and then another close behind, lying in wait to snuff out his attempted dribbles. Also decisive was the age-related decline of Xavi, who was no longer able to run the midfield with the same magnificence of the glory years. Potential heirs to his role, including Thiago Alcantara and Cesc Fabregas, did not work out, and the engine room of the team's success was stalling.

All told, Barça were simply not supplying Messi with the ammunition he needed, and his league goal tally dipped substantially from a record 50 in the 2011/12 campaign to just 28 two years later. Change was required.

For a long time, though, Messi and his team-mates continued to attempt to dip their toes into the same old river, persisting with the false nine formation long after it stopped functioning well. And that's understandable: Messi had enjoyed an unprecedented amount of success as a false nine, and he was reluctant to return to a more restricted right wing role. He was, it seems, denying the need for change and showing resistance to working with Luis Enrique – culminating in the dramatic events of the first week in January 2015, perhaps the closest he has ever come to leaving the club.

Overcoming this kind of emotional rejection of change can only be achieved through a similarly emotion-led approach, Moorhouse believes.

'Change and transition are psychological,' he states. 'If you are taking an organisation or an individual through change, such as integrating a new methodology or buying a new business, you can't just tell people: "Now you must do this." The worst changes are always when they are imposed upon people who are not involved and simply told what to do.

'In the end you have to manage emotions, and that usually involves a process of "letting go". [American writer and consultant] William Bridges did some fantastic research in this area and he used the metaphor of a trapeze artist: when you're holding on to the bar, flying through the air, what can encourage you to let go? What makes a change less scary?

'[To let go] people have to go through a psychological process, and ultimately it has to be an emotional commitment. It never works unless you can make that emotional connection, which comes through dialogue. You have to challenge people to change but also show them that you care, put your arm around them and help them accept the change. Few leaders do that well.'

One leader who does that well, as we saw in Chapter Four, is Danny Kerry, who appreciates the need for his hockey players to be emotionally invested in the generation of their goals rather than having them handed down from above.

Another who does it well is Pep Guardiola. In 2009, the Barça coach succeeded in winning over Messi to the idea of the false nine role by convincing him that it would serve him for the best, and the Argentine's open outlook – his growth mindset – allowed him to immediately buy into the idea.

Luis Enrique, though, with his more confrontational approach, appears to have initially struggled to make the necessary emotional connection with Messi to convince him that change was needed, and the first six months of his reign inhabited dangerous terrain. But eventually, after going through the process of denial and anger-fuelled resistance – skipping the club's open training session on Three Kings Day; following Chelsea on Instagram – Messi came through the crisis, relented in his opposition to change and made the emotional commitment to repositioning himself on the right wing for that epoch-changing game against Atletico. And the rest is history.

Jumping off the platform

Messi, of course, had been forced to 'let go of the bar' at a very early age.

He let go of his whole childhood, in fact, when he decided to break up his family and move to Barcelona at the age of 13. In doing so, at the risk of mixing metaphors, Messi was crossing the mountain and immersing himself in a different river – he was making an emotional commitment to the idea that a new life lay ahead of him, which involved turning his back on everything he had ever known. He was accepting the need to make a profound and dramatic change which few teenagers would be willing to undertake.

By then, he had already showed himself to be in possession of a growth mindset – quite literally – by accepting the need to administer himself with growth hormone injections on a daily basis.

There is a great deal of power in the 'better never stops' mentality which seeks continual personal improvement, and this is clearly an attitude Messi has embodied throughout his career, playing a key part in his acceptance of the move to Barcelona and his many positional changes. But his story also shows that many changes – probably the majority in Messi's case – are enforced by external pressures: the burning platform syndrome described by Adrian Moorhouse when he realised he needed to fundamentally alter his approach to managing his career.

The painful process of Messi's hormone injections, stabbing himself in the leg every day for three years, was something that nobody would ever actively *choose* to do. But it was the first of many turning points in Messi's career which were forced upon him. That and many other things all just sort of happened, in the natural but unpredictable course of events which are bound to rudely intrude upon a long playing career in the dynamic environment of competitive team sport.

By agreeing to have those hormone injections, by leaving Argentina, by adjusting to new coaches and new team-mates and new playing styles, by moving from one position to another and then another and then another, Messi and the people around him were really just doing what they had to do in response to changes in their environment, and changing their approach accordingly. Because Messi (and, we can assume, his family) possessed the 'growth mindset', a willingness to be taken out of his comfort zone, he was open to those changes and was prepared to meet them with emotional acceptance rather than resistance. The platform might have been burning, but he had no hesitation in jumping off.

However, every time he landed on a new platform, there was no way of knowing how long it would be before the flames started to surround him once again. Before long, another change would be necessary but it was impossible to pre-judge how or why, and Messi's career has been a series of unexpected and unplanned improvisations rather than a pre-determined plot line.

When he broke into the Barcelona first team, Messi didn't sit down with a team of power-dressed strategists armed with a bunch of slick PowerPoint presentations and concoct a five-year plan to take on the world. His advisors didn't conduct extensive industry research and hold a series of blue-sky brainstorming sessions to devise the best way for this precocious young talent to become the greatest player in the world. Instead, to a great extent, he was making it up as he went along.

That's not to say he was wandering aimlessly through his career without any particular aspirations in mind. Of course, he knew that he was heading for the top and that he was prepared to work very hard to get there. He knew the 'where', the end destination, but the direction he would take – the 'how' – was left open. He had a plan – being the best possible footballer he could be – but the details of the plan hadn't been filled in, and could only be sketched out at a later date depending upon the particular needs of the moment.

This illustrates the two different but connected abilities required to effectively deal with change: firstly, the ability to recognise when the platform is burning and to be willing to jump off without delay or regret (when he left Argentina), and secondly, the ability to occasionally leave the platform even when it is not burning (when he moved to the false nine role).

Sometimes we have no choice but to step into a different river. At other times, the waterways of the world are just waiting to be explored.

Planning to change

The story of the changes undertaken by Lionel Messi throughout his career suggests another question which applies in many other walks of life: how much should we plan?

As we've seen, Messi could never have planned his regular transitions from one position to another, and even if he'd tried, he would have failed because the situations in which they arose were unpredictable. Rather than precise planning, he has been much better served responding to unforeseeable changes in circumstances by making appropriate changes to himself and the way he plays.

Would the original forward line of Ronaldinho, Eto'o and Messi (thankfully before the days of forward line acronyms, or we'd have been forced to endure countless bad REM puns) have broken up so quickly if the Brazilian had maintained a higher level of professionalism rather than allowing himself to enter into decline? Probably not. Would Messi have ever played as a false nine if Barça had appointed a less visionary coach than Guardiola? Probably not. Would he have abandoned that role in 2015 if opposition teams hadn't worked out how to stop him, or if Xavi was five years younger and could have maintained his mastery of the midfield? Probably not. Would the MSN partnership have ended in 2017 if Neymar had patiently turned down his mega-bucks offer from Paris St Germain? Probably not.

But all those things, unpredictable factors beyond his control, did happen, so Messi had to change and any plans that he had laid down in advance would have been left in shreds, suddenly irrelevant to his ongoing development as a player.

This conundrum – how much should we plan against how much should we improvise as we go along – is grappled with on a daily basis by Adrian Moorhouse.

'There's a famous military phrase: no plan survives first contact with the enemy,' he observes. In business, if you're working with a four-year plan but the customers don't want what you are providing, you have to change that plan. You won't even last four years if you don't. If all your customers have started to buy everything digitally on Amazon and all you've got is bricks and mortar shops, you're dead – and that's something we've seen a lot in the last few years.

'It doesn't matter if your plan says "we'll get to digital in four years" when your sales are falling off a cliff. You might have a great strategy and a great product, but when you take it to the marketplace the customer might not want it, or they might want it packaged in a different way. And then you just have to change your plan.'

Similarly, on the level of individuals rather than organisations, Moorhouse believes we should all be prepared to make deviations from our career plans in the same way that he accepted the need to modify his dive, and in the same way that Messi was prepared to move from the right wing to the false nine and back to the right wing before ending up in the position he wanted to play all along, the 'enganche' (and who knows what his next move will be?).

'A career is less likely to be a straight line than a jagged one,' says Moorhouse. 'There are usually some sideways moves in order to eventually move forward. The opportunities that come along might not be the obvious ones you had initially expected, and at every stage of a career development, there is always some kind of transition.

'Most people start off their working lives being an individual performer who just comes in and "does stuff". Then you might get promoted to be a team leader, supervisor or manager. It will be the first time you've ever managed anybody, and they are often your friends or people you've been working with in a team. So that's an interesting transition, and involves letting go of the things you used to do. Then there's another transition when you get promoted again to become a manager of managers – those guys are already managers themselves, so they don't need you to tell them what to do and you have to manage differently again.

'Each new level brings a new challenge.'

One of the most regular criticisms of Messi – especially from the Anglocentric world – is that he has shied away from those kind of challenges by staying with the same club throughout his whole career. This is the 'cold and wet Tuesday night at Stoke' brigade, who defiantly argue that until Messi takes himself out of his comfort zone by playing in the Premier League, he will always be somewhat unproven and should therefore be regarded as a lesser player than others, like Cristiano Ronaldo, who have excelled for clubs in different countries.

This argument overlooks the fact that Messi has scored nearly 200 goals in the Champions League, the UEFA Super Cup, FIFA Club World Cup and international football, suggesting that he is more than capable of finding the net against a wide range of opposition (including 20 goals in his last 18 games against elite Premier League teams in the Champions League ... so perhaps Stoke wouldn't fare that well, after all).

It also omits to recall the regularity with which Messi has been forced to adapt and evolve as his career has progressed: new playing positions; new team-mates; new coaches.

And perhaps most importantly, in the same way that businesses are forced to constantly adapt to new technology-led advances such as the recent replacement of physical shops with online commerce, the passage of time and the emergence of younger and quicker rivals has also forced Messi to submit to change.

Remember the famous goal he scored against Getafe in 2007, detailed at the start of Chapter Three, when he ran with the ball from the halfway line and dribbled past the entire opposition team? He could not score that goal now, because he has lost his electric pace. The natural effects of ageing dictate that Messi is not as quick in his thirties as he was in his teens, and many defenders can now catch up with him even when he has a head start.

Conversely, however, some of the passes that Messi plays now were not part of his arsenal in the early days of his career. His instinct for moving the ball from the halfway line to the penalty area by dribbling with it has been replaced by a different method: he can't *run* the ball through the entire opposition from the halfway line anymore, but he can *pass* it through them.

In addition to Luis Suarez, the most frequent beneficiary of that ability these days is Jordi Alba, Barcelona's marauding left-back, who used Neymar's departure as an opportunity to exploit the suddenly available space on the left wing by establishing a clinical relationship with Messi – most vividly demonstrated in a Copa Del Rey meeting with Celta Vigo in early 2018, when Barça's 5-0 victory was sparked by three goals in the opening half-hour: the first two scored by Messi and assisted by Alba, and the third scored by Alba and assisted by Messi.

Again, this demonstrates Messi's ability to embrace change. Neymar isn't there anymore? OK, I'll use Alba instead. However great it was while it lasted, the reality is that the connection between Messi and Neymar is now a thing of the past. It has gone. And regrettable as this might be for those of us who enjoyed the magic they created together, including the players themselves, the dissolution of their partnership was just one of those things.

There would be no point in Messi crying about it – in the style of the pragmatist described by John Carlin in Chapter Two, he got on with it and found another solution, accepting that even the best ideas can eventually stop working, for no particular reason other than the normal flux of life.

The false nine position didn't become a bad idea when it stopped working in 2013/14; it had just passed its use-by date because other teams had worked out how to nullify it and Messi's supporting cast was different. Similarly, MSN was perfect for its time, but that time soon passed. And although Messi is still a great dribbler, he has lost some of his pace and therefore has to use his dribbling in a slightly different way, opening up space in compact areas rather than as a prelude to an unstoppable 50-yard slalom towards goal.

Lionel Messi's career has been one long story of evolution and development, and – just like one of his famous dribbles – it has not always followed a straight line.

Barça's stable foundations vs Argentina's chaos

Despite the over-simplicity of the 'Tuesday night in Stoke' argument, the fact that Messi has always played for Barcelona is certainly not irrelevant. In fact, it is an extremely significant aspect to the other side of change's coin: the need for stability.

Change for the sake of change can be disruptive and destructive in sport, business and life alike, and in addition to being open to new environments and new opportunities it is also vital to be able to operate from a firm foundation of stability.

Earlier in this chapter, Adrian Moorhouse talked about the depressing alienation he felt when he retired from swimming. His foundations as a human being had been swept away, and he was forced to re-examine the meaning of his life in the most fundamental terms – he had lost the personal internal stability which, for more than a decade, came from his knowledge that 'I am a swimmer.'

Eventually, he was able to rebuild his self-esteem and sense of identity by reflecting upon the human qualities he possessed that transcended swimming – the underlying aspects of his personality that made him 'Adrian Moorhouse' rather than 'Adrian Moorhouse, the Olympic swimmer'.

After embarking upon his voyage of self-discovery and finding those attributes, which had been there all along but which he had mistakenly only linked to his sporting career, he was able to once again answer that most basic question: who am I? No matter how open his mind had always been to the idea of growth and change, without those solid foundations of knowing who he was – without that stability – he had been unable to move on with his post-swimming life.

So if there's one important balance to strike between change and planning, there is another to be found between change and stability.

'There's a common phrase I use: freedom within a framework,' says Moorhouse as he considers this latest balancing act.

'You have a framework and you're putting scaffolding around it, but then – in a business context – you are letting people have the freedom to be aware of the marketplace, and they have a chance to move that framework and the scaffolding around a bit. But you have to have the framework in the first place. You have to put a platform in place. You have to create some stability.'

Whether you are a business or a football team or just an individual human being navigating the different rivers of life, just because your plans need to be flexible and open to change, that doesn't mean you don't need to plan at all. Without any kind of plan, without stability, the sense of identity provided by Moorhouse's knowledge that 'I am a swimmer' vanishes and leaves a void of uncertainty and insecurity.

Lionel Messi's career illustrates this point well.

At Barcelona, as we have seen, he has undergone several significant changes. Throughout that period, however, those changes have been balanced by key consistent elements, underpinning his endless evolution with a bedrock of stability.

Many of his team-mates, for starters, have remained the same: Dani Alves, Sergio Busquets, Xavi Hernandez, Andres Iniesta and Gerard Pique have all been there alongside him for nearly the entirety of his club career, while many others have shared several years with him in the dressing room.

The team has also always played in roughly the same way: a possession-based game with an emphasis on short passing along the ground, creating chances with quick interchanges around the opposition's penalty area, and defending by pressing high up the pitch to smother the opponent's attempts to establish possession.

These were the principles espoused by Pep Guardiola, but they were already in place during the reign of his predecessor Frank Rijkaard, who in turn was carrying the mantle handed down by his fellow Dutchman and former Barça player and coach, Johan Cruyff. It is now more than six years since Guardiola left the Camp Nou, but the Cruyffian methods both he and Rijkaard championed were also followed – to a greater or lesser degree – by each of their successors.

To be sure, there have been tweaks here and there: Luis Enrique's spell in charge saw the adoption of a more direct style, focussing on getting the ball to the 'MSN' front three as quickly as possible rather than playing through midfield, while his replacement Ernesto Valverde has been more cautious and pragmatic, relying on defensive discipline and even reverting to a most un-Cruyff-like 4-4-2 formation. However, the core principles underlying Barcelona's play have remained unchanged throughout Messi's career: keep the ball, pass the ball, create chances through rapid movement and press the opposition.

And that sense of identity, that sense of 'who we are' has been a fundamental part of Barcelona's success, allowing a series of players and managers to come and go without the basic approach of playing football being significantly altered. Players who are brought into the system know exactly what is expected of them, because the continuity of the team's playing style makes it obvious.

If you want to be a Barcelona goalkeeper, you'd better be able to play with your feet. If you want to be a Barcelona full-back, you'd better be athletic and capable of pressing high but also able to contribute in attack. If you want to be a Barcelona midfielder, you'd better know how to keep the ball and service the team's creative players (especially Messi). That is all obvious, and imbues a sense of confidence which runs throughout the squad, each of whom implicitly understands what he is supposed to do. When you can take that kind of deep mutual understanding as a basic starting point, the task of winning becomes a lot easier.

In Argentina colours, though, it has been an entirely different matter.

Following the 2018 World Cup finals, Messi has now played in eight major international tournaments: World Cups in 2006, 2010, 2014 and 2018, and Copa Americas in 2007, 2011, 2015 and 2016. Those eight competitions saw seven different managers in charge, with none of Messi's Argentina coaches, other than Tata Martino, managing to stay in the post from one tournament to the next (and by the time this book is published, another new coach will have been appointed).

Those relentless coaching changes culminated in a merry-go-round of four managers in four years leading up to the most recent World Cup (Alejandro Sabella, Martino, Edgardo Bauza and Jorge Sampaoli), with the constant toing and froing also resulting in a staggering number of 44 different players being used during the 18 games of the 2018 World Cup qualifying campaign.

When Argentina finally arrived in Russia, rather than a dose of much-needed stability being applied, the changes continued at a rapid pace. Although Sampaoli had practised with a 4-2-3-1 formation for a full week before the tournament started and also employed that strategy in the opening game against Iceland, he then changed drastically to a three-man defensive line with a 3-4-3 formation in the disastrous loss to Croatia. In the last group game Sampaoli rolled his dice again, going with a 4-4-2 in the victory over Nigeria, before instigating yet another new formation – 4-3-3 with Messi playing as a false nine for the first time in more than three years – in the last-16 defeat against France.

Four managers in four years; 44 players in 18 qualifying games; four different formations and tactical systems in four World Cup games ... it's no surprise that Argentina lurched through their hapless campaign in Russia looking as though they'd never been properly introduced to each other. Developing a coherent team framework under such frenetic circumstances is close to impossible, with the number and scale of changes leaving no solid foundations upon which to construct a smoothly functioning team.

As we saw in Chapter Four, the chaos of Argentina's World Cup preparations in the summer of 2018 made it impossible for Messi to enjoy the same freedom of expression that he experiences with Barcelona, in turn preventing him from fulfilling the severe personal responsibilities with which he was saddled. At club level, he has a framework which gives him freedom; for much of his international career, he's had neither framework nor freedom.

Heading into the ill-fated World Cup in Russia, if Argentina had been collectively asked that vital question which confronted Adrian Moorhouse after he retired from swimming – who am I? – they would have had no answer to give. They just didn't know who or what they were. They had no identity.

No wonder they failed.

Messi's underlying stability

If Messi has benefitted from stability on a collective level during his career with Barcelona, he has also enjoyed personal stability – like Adrian Moorhouse during his swimming career – from the simple fact that he has always been a footballer.

His specific role in his teams has changed and changed again, and so too have the identity of his team-mates and coaches. Once, he idolised and emulated Ronaldinho; now, Ousmane Dembele idolises and emulates him.

Opponents have also come and gone: when his career started, AC Milan were the dominant force in European football, winning two Champions League titles in four years. Now he's being challenged by Manchester City and Paris St Germain, two teams who were non-entities when he started out, while Milan are struggling to even qualify for the Champions League. And although Real Madrid have always been his grand domestic rival, they look very different now than they did then – once, his nemesis was Pepe; now, it's Casemiro. Once, Jose Mourinho was his greatest antagonist on the sidelines; now, he's barely an afterthought. And now, for the first time in nearly a decade, he doesn't even have Cristiano Ronaldo to measure himself up against.

Messi is getting older, too. He can't do some of the things he used to do, like dribble past entire teams from the halfway line, but has instead found some new areas in which to excel instead. He's become a better passer, a better free-kick taker, and a more patient constructor of play from deep.

Amid all the changes, though, one thing has stayed the same: football.

Football has been with Messi throughout. Football has accompanied him through his greatest and bleakest moments. Football has been the reason for him to get up every morning, to continually strive to improve, to relentlessly hunt down new challenges and new ambitions.

Football, as we will now discover, has given him everything.

Chapter Seven
A Better Life

Barcelona 3-1 Manchester United
Champions League Final
Saturday 28 May 2011, Wembley Stadium, London

Twisting and turning; feinting and weaving; darting and dodging; prodding and probing. Changes of pace and bursts of acceleration, subtle touches and delicate flicks, a shimmy here and a shake there, occasionally standing physically still but always mentally alert and engaged.

Lionel Messi delivers one of his very finest masterpieces in the 2011 Champions League Final against Manchester United.

His first touch comes after just 20 seconds, a deft header to find Sergio Busquets in midfield.

Four minutes later he pops up on the right wing, exchanging a teasing quartet of first-touch short passes with Dani Alves. By the ten-minute mark he is really starting to enjoy himself, spinning into space on the edge of the box to create a chance for David Villa, whose shot is blocked.

Even at this early stage it is clear United are struggling to handle Messi, with the central midfield duo of Michael Carrick and Ryan Giggs unable to pick him up as he drifts between United's lines. Red Devils skipper Nemanja Vidic is looking distinctly uncomfortable as he is forced to break out of his central defensive position to close down Messi, who is also attracting the attention of Park Ji-sung, drifting inside from the left flank.

Midway through the first half the Argentine brilliantly evades three challenges on the edge of the box and nearly tees up Pedro. Then comes another run to force Vidic into an excellent last-ditch challenge, and a couple of minutes later Rio Ferdinand has to do the same.

Two quick goals soon follow. Firstly Pedro latches on to a pass from Xavi to convert a fine low finish, before United get back on level terms against the run of play with a confident sweeping strike from Wayne Rooney.

Messi is unperturbed, launching his team's next attack with a dribble from the halfway line and drawing a desperate foul from Antonio Valencia, before another burst results in a pass for Xavi, who fires over the top. Before the break he is again denied by a tackle on the perimeter of the area, this time by Rooney. Then he nutmegs Vidic, passes wide to Villa and is inches away from connecting with a low return pass across the face of goal.

The same pattern continues in the second half, which starts with Messi finding Gerard Pique in a rare advanced position, then a pass to Andres Iniesta whose shot is blocked, before Messi himself delivers a goalbound strike which the retreating Patrice Evra does well to head clear.

Eight minutes into the second period, Messi finally makes the breakthrough he has been threatening throughout. Receiving a short pass from Iniesta 30 yards out, he drives towards goal. With Vidic back-pedalling and Evra only making a tentative effort to close him down, Messi opens up some space on to his left foot and unleashes a fierce low strike, which fizzes with brutal speed past the left hand of diving goalkeeper Edwin van der Sar.

Messi has put Barça back in front, and this time they will not let United respond. The trophy is there for the taking.

Messi remains at the heart of everything. Another dangerous run, another foul from Valencia. Another dribble past Ferdinand, another save from van der Sar. A cross from Alves, a flicked back-heel blocked on its way to goal.

Barcelona are turning on the style, flowing forward with irresistible grace to launch wave after wave of purposeful, penetrative attacks. United are visibly wilting under the physical and mental assault of the dizzying passing carousel, mesmerised by their opponents' cool command of possession and territory.

The third goal is inevitable, and it comes when Messi tricks his way past Nani to break into the box. He is challenged but the loose ball falls to Busquets, whose pass to Villa is met with a glorious curling strike high into the top right corner for one of the iconic goals of Champions League history.

From that moment the outcome is never in doubt, but Barcelona retain firm control and even in the 93rd minute Messi continues to jink and jive, bursting forward from the halfway line to find substitute Ibrahim Afellay for the final shot of the game, saved by van der Sar.

A few seconds later the final whistle blows and Messi stands briefly with his arms aloft in triumph, a beaming and wide-eyed smile spreading across his face. He turns to hug Xavi, then Pedro, before the victorious team gather together on the halfway line, arms interlocked in a wide circle for a leaping and laughing group dance of celebration.

Messi spends the next few minutes, while the post-game ceremonial presentations are being prepared, working his way around all his team-mates and the club's coaching and support staff, enjoying a lingering embrace with each one in turn. Then it is time to head up the steps and collect the trophy, his third Champions League winners' medal and the inevitable man of the match award. All the time, an unrestrained grin of deep satisfaction remains fixed on his face, full of unselfconscious glee. He is 23 years old, but from his expression he could be back on his childhood playing fields of Rosario, joyful and innocent, transfixed by the beauty of football and immersed in his pure love of the game.

As he celebrates victory at Wembley Stadium, only one simple but endlessly powerful word is required to describe his state of mind: Lionel Messi is *happy*.

Flowing into the zone

What is it about a ball that makes us happy?

Wherever we are in the world, the ball is always present. It can be big or small, hard or soft, a perfect circle or a flattened oval. It doesn't really matter. Kicking it, catching it, throwing it, hitting it, running after it or simply holding on to it ... the ball is everywhere, and the ball is everything.

As any parent can attest, our apparently universal love of the ball emerges very soon after birth. Even the smallest of babies quickly become enraptured and enchanted by the ball: the sight of it; the touch of it; the potential for self-expression it provides. We don't have to learn how to enjoy interacting with a ball – it's somehow just within us from the very beginning.

Evidence suggests this has been the case throughout the history of humanity. Most modern sports have only been formalised into their current rules in the last century or so, but older versions of many have existed as far back as history can reach: the Mayans of Central America played a game called pok-a-tok, similar to basketball, around 4,000 years ago, while the ancient Chinese game cuju – practised as long as 5,000 years in the past – is regarded by FIFA as the earliest version of football.

Although the contemporary world is dominated by the outlandish popularity of football, the few corners of the globe not yet colonised by the beautiful game still boast their own ball sports – whether it's ga-ga ball in Israel, snow polo in Switzerland or pesapallo in Finland, our desire to play ball-based games knows no bounds. Interacting with balls clearly fulfils some of our deepest human needs.

In the context of this surprisingly profound attachment to small round objects, it's only logical that taking part in ball sports is regarded as one of the easiest and most common ways for human beings to experience the strong sense of inner contentment known to psychologists as the state of flow, more commonly referred to as 'being in the zone' (the phrases are synonymous – if you have found flow, it means you are in the zone and vice versa – so they will be used interchangeably from now on).

The concept of flow was first examined and explained in detail by the Hungarian psychologist Mihaly Csikszentmihalyi, whose 1990 book *Flow: The Psychology of Optimal Experience* has become an influential classic of modern popular science.

Csikszentmihalyi advocated that finding flow is the best way for people to maximise meaningful and sustainable personal happiness on a practical, everyday level. After asking 'What really makes people glad to be alive?' he identifies eight ingredients necessary to achieve that cherished mental state which enriches human experience with 'joy, creativity, the process of total involvement with life'.

His eight ingredients for happy living are:

1. Challenge: undertaking a task which is challenging but which you are equipped to have a realistic chance of completing. You might not get in the zone in your first attempt, but if you are prepared to tolerate the initial frustration of being not very good at doing something and gradually become skilled, you're on your way towards flow. And as your skills increase, so too should the difficulty of the challenge.

2. Concentration: being able to focus on whatever you are doing. Various neurological studies have suggested that multi-tasking is not really possible on a meaningful level – you can do two things at once, but not very well (recall the System 1 and System 2 theory of Daniel Kahneman from Chapter Three, and the impossibility of driving in difficult conditions whilst holding a detailed conversation). Finding deep enjoyment only comes if you can avoid distractions and concentrate on the here and now.

3. Goal-based: the activity should have a defined purpose and an obvious objective. Rather than doing something which doesn't have a clear climax, a more powerful level of enjoyment can be derived from an activity which is directed towards a specific endpoint.

4. Feedback: you should instantly know how well you are doing, how much progress you are making and where you need to improve. If the efficiency of your efforts is uncertain or unclear, pleasure is diminished.

5. Immersion: feeling a deep involvement and absorption with the task at hand, allowing you to temporarily forget any other concerns external to the demands of the moment.

6. Control: a feeling that you are in charge of your actions and can exert a strong influence over the outcome

of the activity. You are exercising your free will to determine the course of events and, due to the skills you have accrued, the activity should feel effortless even when it is difficult.

7. Selflessness: you can 'forget yourself' in what you are doing, finding yourself unquestioningly carrying out whatever needs to be done to complete the activity rather than selfish personal desires or ambitions.

8. Time-warping: in a flow experience, the normal passage of time becomes irrelevant. A few seconds can feel like several minutes, and hours can flash by in the blink of an eye. Time flies, as they say, when you're having fun.

When we engage with an activity which fulfils these criteria, Csikszentmihalyi argues, we can enjoy the 'best moments' in life: 'When a person's body or mind is stretched to its limits in a voluntary effort to accomplish something difficult and worthwhile.'

Finding flow allows us to take 'control over the contents of our consciousness', to become mentally more complex ('we learn to become more than what we were'), and consequently to lead a qualitatively better life. Put simply, being in the zone makes us happy, in the sense of lasting inner contentment rather than short-lived cheap thrills.

Csikszentmihalyi cites many activities which allow flow to flourish, including dancing, rock climbing, sailing, sex, reading and even carrying out seemingly mundane factory jobs – indeed, one of the principal aims of his work is to argue that flow can be experienced at any time, any place, anywhere, if our minds are correctly attuned and creating the right conditions for flow rather than waiting for it to magically appear by itself.

He also acknowledges that one of the easiest and most common ways to get in the zone is by playing sport. And it is not very difficult to see how a game of football – or many other team-based ball sports – fits his requirements perfectly.

Let's run through the eight steps to happiness again, this time in the specific context of football:

1. Challenge: ideally, the two teams in a game of football are relatively evenly matched, with every player competing at the appropriate level to make a personal contribution to the collective effort. It's not much fun if one or two players are much better or worse than anyone else, and the most exciting games for players and spectators alike are those where the result is in the balance until the end.

2. Concentration: it's impossible to play football well without concentrating. The higher the quality of play, the more concentration is required – not just on the ball but also on the movement of team-mates and opponents, and the overall pattern of the game. Concentration is encouraged by restricting the action to a specific area and prohibiting access for anyone other than players, who would get in the way and provide a distraction. The pitch is a sacred area because it is a zone reserved for deep concentration and focus.

3. Goal-based: this ranges from the obvious to the subtle. The overall goal of the game, clearly, is to win, but at a finer level every player has more specific roles to fill such as 'mark the opposition left-winger' or 'create chances', which will help achieve the wider goal of winning. A football match provides every player with both macro- and micro-goals.

4. Feedback: it's self-evident from the scoreline and the overall pattern of the game how well teams and individual players are doing. We always know who is winning, while the success of micro-goals is also generally very clear: the opposition winger I am marking is delivering too many crosses; I have already created six chances for my team-mates.

5. Immersion: you don't have the time or mental energy to worry about unpaid bills, relationship problems or irritating bosses in the middle of a football match. Sport is often referred to as an 'escape from the real world' for its ability to transport us into a new reality.

6. Control: 'playing well', on an analytical level, really means exerting a strong level of control over the outcome. Good players can control the ball, control the power of their passes, control the direction of shots, control the movement of team-mates and opponents. Football is essentially about attempting to impose order upon chaos; controlling an uncontrolled environment. This is why we find random factors such as bad refereeing decisions, lucky bounces and poor playing conditions so frustrating – they escape the control of the protagonists.

7. Selflessness: no matter how good you are, the team has to come first. Individual ambitions, even if you are Lionel Messi, can only be realised through the success of the team, and every player has to learn to 'take what the game gives you'.

8. Time-warping: a football match might last 90 minutes, but the way those 90 minutes are experienced varies dramatically – when the teams are separated by just one goal in an important game, the final five minutes feel like five hours to the winning team, desperate for the whistle, but they flash by in five seconds for the losing team, desperate for more time to equalise.

It's easy to see how football, by satisfying all the criteria laid down by Csikszentmihalyi, is a great way for us to get in the zone. Football is flow. Football is happiness.

It is for Lionel Messi, in any case. One of the great joys of watching Messi is being able to vicariously share the deep happiness he so clearly experiences when he is on the pitch with the ball at his feet.

When Messi is on the top of his game, as he was in the 2011 Champions League Final, it looks effortless. Give yourself a treat by watching that game on YouTube, and you will be struck by how – even though he is playing in the most high-profile, high-pressured and demanding fixture in club football against top-quality opposition – everything he does appears to be perfectly straightforward and entirely natural. He makes it look easy.

It is also obvious that for every second of that encounter at Wembley, he is deeply immersed in the game and only the game. Just playing, playing, playing. No distractions, no complaining, no play-acting. He's just there, deep down inside the moment, looking for the ball, getting the ball, playing the ball and never tiring of what he's doing. Passing, dribbling, shooting, drifting into space, assessing the movements of his team-mates and opponents. Always fully focussed, always totally absorbed in the game.

For neutral spectators, a central part of Messi's appeal is that he plays with a sense of childish exuberance, lacking in cynicism or egotism. He carries an air of innocent joy, completely focussed on the game. Just the ball, his team-mates, the opposition, and nothing else exists. He even appears to accept bad challenges from defenders as an inevitable part of the game – how else are they going to stop him, after all? He almost seems to respect being fouled as a natural outcome of his excellence.

When Messi is in that special place, in the zone, he really is just flowing. A constant and effortless flow of pure football, clean and unsullied. When he is in the moment, just playing, it doesn't matter that he's one of the most famous people in the world, earning countless millions, performing in an endlessly stressful environment. It doesn't matter to us, and it doesn't matter to him. He's just a kid with a ball, like the rest of us, finding a burst of happiness by playing football. A living demonstration of optimal experience.

An example for us all to aspire towards. A vivid illustration of how to live a better life.

Just imagine if we could love life as much as Lionel Messi loves football. Imagine if we could all find something to do which makes us as happy as Messi that night at Wembley Stadium in 2011. Imagine if we could all share that joy, that deep and undeniable sense of satisfaction, achievement and unbounded fulfilment.

According to Csikszentmihalyi, we can. We might not be able to achieve it through playing sublime football, but we can all, if we follow the eight steps to happiness, find flow.

Journeying through an elite sportsman's zone

Not every football match involves winning the Champions League Final, and by now we are more than aware that Lionel Messi does not always love playing as much as he did at Wembley in May 2011. So can Csikszentmihalyi's appealing theory work in real life, or is it just that ... a theory?

Can elite professional athletes really and truly, after a relentless, intense and seemingly endless cycle of practising, travelling, playing, shouldering constant pressure, facing unfair criticism, dealing with media intrusion, being ripped off by agents, haggling with ungrateful clubs over contracts, suffering injuries, arguing with referees over bad decisions, jostling for status within the team's hierarchy, moving families at the blink of an eye ... after being assailed by all that hassle, day after day, year after year, can they still love their sport? Can they still find flow? Or does it become, at the end of the day, just a job?

Nando De Colo is one of the best basketball players in Europe. His professional career started with Cholet in his native France before a move to Valencia in Spain. Then came 125 games in the NBA with San Antonio Spurs and Toronto Raptors, before returning to Europe to join CSKA Moscow in 2014. Two years later he was named the Most Valuable Player in EuroLeague, the continent's elite club competition (the equivalent of football's Champions League), after helping CSKA win the title, and he is responsible for three of the eight highest-scoring seasons in the tournament this century. He is, therefore, perfectly placed to tell us about the realities of life at the sharp end of the sporting world, because that has been his environment for as long as he can remember.

We are sitting in a quiet corner of the plush lounge bar at the five-star Hyatt Regency hotel in Belgrade, where De Colo and his CSKA team are competing at the end-of-season Final Four to determine the 2018 EuroLeague champions.

Tomorrow night, De Colo and his CSKA team-mates will face Real Madrid in the semi-finals, hoping to advance to the Championship Game two days later against the winners of the other last-four tie, to be played between Turkish team Fenerbahce and Zalgiris Kaunas from Lithuania.

But for now, De Colo is reflecting on his love of his sport. As he does so, he unknowingly recounts with uncanny precision the ingredients outlined by Csikszentmihalyi as being necessary for the creation of flow – he presents a living exposition of what it takes to get in the zone, and to stay there. As De Colo talks, keep in mind the eight steps towards happiness.

1. Challenge
2. Concentration
3. Goal-based
4. Feedback
5. Immersion
6. Control
7. Selflessness
8. Time-warping

It all starts with being competent enough to have a realistic chance of completing a challenge. It starts with being able to manipulate the ball.

'My parents both played and coached basketball, and my sister played, so even when I was very young I was in the basketball gym all the time,' De Colo begins with a smile.

'I spent more time with a ball than with a book! I was just happy to have a ball and play. People tell me they remember when I was with my parents in the gym, I was two or three years old and all I wanted to do was dribble the ball. The first reason you will love something is because you're good at it, because you can control it. And playing with my sister, my parents and later on with my friends was something I just really enjoyed.

'I still enjoy playing now. The day I think it's boring or I don't enjoy it, I will stop. I think this is the way you need to see sport. For sure, it's my job and the team pays me to be professional. But there is never a question of basketball being only a job and nothing more. I remember when I was young and it was just a game. And now, even if I don't win, it's still just a game.'

In the same way that Lionel Messi loves football, it's clear that Nando De Colo loves basketball. He enjoys playing the game purely for the sake of playing the game, irrespective of the rewards or frustrations it may bring.

But to reach his current elite level as a France international and a key player for one of the strongest teams in Europe, 'loving playing' is not enough. In order to continue to maintain his status within the continent's elite, De Colo has been forced to relentlessly challenge himself to get better, adding ever greater complexity to his experiences on the court by committing himself to deep levels of concentration on his craft.

'To play a professional game, you need to be ready,' he asserts. 'You can't just turn up to a game and think, "Well, maybe I'll make shots today, maybe not." No. You get ready. You practise and get your rhythm, and the more you practise hard the better you can see if you're ready or not. And when you know you are ready to play, focussed on what you have to do, nothing else matters. You just play your game.'

OK, but that's just the game. To be truly meaningful, the experience of flow should be repeatable and long-lasting. If it's merely a fleeting feeling which comes for a few minutes in the thick of the action but then disappears forever, it would be much less worthwhile.

And although individual games – the hour and a half spent striving once or twice a week in pursuit of victory – might not offer lasting long-term benefits, when viewed from a more distant perspective the wider experience of being a professional sportsperson does: one game is always followed by another, interspersed with opportunities to improve through practice and interaction with team-mates; one season is followed by another, always presenting new environments with either a new team to play for, or new team-mates, or new coaches, or new opposition. Always new challenges to overcome, to learn from and to improve.

Reflecting on the endless nature of the challenge presented by his profession, De Colo reflects: 'All year long you fight for the title, you fight to win games, and it's not easy every day. A competition doesn't begin with the final – it begins with the start of the season and you have to give everything to get that far.

'And it's the same with a career. A career is not just one or two seasons – you have to be the best player you can every day for a lot of years. You've got to make a lot of sacrifices.'

In the long and self-fulfilling cycle of a professional career, even that unwanted old foe, defeat, can be taken as a positive. De Colo observes: 'You can still enjoy playing a game if you're losing. Even if the game is difficult and it isn't going your way, that just means you need to find a solution to change it.

'And then if you lose, it means you have to get better. Nobody is perfect and you need to analyse it and know what you did wrong, so you can get better for the next one. They say "you lose or you learn", and for me it's better to learn. Sometimes it's even a good thing to lose, to remind yourself that you need to keep working.'

To basketball fans, De Colo is perhaps best known for his remarkable free throw record. By the end of the 2017/18 season he had made 561 of his 599 free throws in EuroLeague games, giving him the best conversion rate (93.66 per cent) in the competition's history since accurate records began. For context and comparison, the NBA's all-time leader in free throw percentage is Steve Nash with 90.43 per cent.

De Colo believes that he hardly ever misses free throws for a simple reason: he is convinced there is no reason to miss free throws. He has spent hours and hours perfecting his technique, and whenever he steps to the foul line he is able to truly live in the moment and block out any distractions.

'My mother always told me there is no excuse to miss a free throw,' he says. 'There's nothing to think about other than the ball and the basket. Nothing else.

'The opponents, the fans, the situation in the game ... they don't matter. It's the ball and the basket. You just have to forget everything else and focus.'

Everything De Colo says here is very much in keeping with Csikszentmihalyi's concept of flow: he is deeply focussed on a challenging but realistic task which has clear objectives and provides instant feedback; he believes that he can exercise control over his actions and the outcome of games, and he adds ever greater complexity to his experiences by continually striving to improve.

'You need to be ready ... you practise ... you make sacrifices ... you can control it ... you need to keep working ... you just play your game ... nothing else matters ... you learn ... you need to find a solution ... you just have to forget everything else and focus.'

This is flow. This is the zone. This – if your mind is attuned in the right way – is the challenging but rewarding cycle of life as an elite professional athlete. And we can, of course, easily relate De Colo's story to the day in, day out journey of ups, downs and everything in between we have seen travelled by Lionel Messi over the course of his career.

We have seen how Messi has never stopped trying to improve, adapted to new challenges and responded to setbacks as an opportunity to learn, relentlessly demanding the best out of himself and making painful sacrifices to reach and stay at the top. Like De Colo, he does this day after day, year after year, in a self-fulfilling cycle of personal growth which – when everything comes together perfectly – occasionally climaxes in ultimate 'flow' moments like the 2011 Champions League Final against Manchester United.

The euphoria and deep satisfaction experienced by Messi at Wembley that night – and experienced in a similar way by De Colo when he won the EuroLeague title with CSKA Moscow in 2016 – would not have been possible without all the work he had undertaken to get that far. It was only so satisfying and so meaningful because it hadn't been easy, and because it came as the result of a long, hard grind which had demanded constant commitment every step of the way.

As De Colo notes, the season doesn't start with the final. If you want to reach the destination, you have to embark upon the journey from the beginning, and embrace everything that comes along the way. The good and the bad, the difficult and the easy, the highs and the lows, the fun and the boring ... they are all part of one unified whole; they all add up to comprise the total experience. Only by fully engaging with each individual fragment is it possible to truly appreciate the whole.

And doesn't that, if you stop to think about it, also sound a lot like life?

Competition, process and outcome

One of the main reasons that sport gives us the opportunity to get in the zone, and one of the most valuable functions it fulfils in modern society, is that it allows us – all of us, from top-level internationals like Nando De Colo and Lionel Messi to casual armchair fans – to express in a safe and controlled environment one of our most basic instincts: competition.

Like all other living beings, we are an inherently competitive species. It could not be otherwise – without an innate thirst for competition, we would have died out long ago. Even on a microscopic level, our genes are constantly competing to survive and reproduce, as are the millions of microbes which live inside us. Deep, deep down, in ways of which we cannot possibly be consciously aware, our very bodies are an arena of endless competition.

Our earliest ancestors were forced to compete on a daily basis for food, shelter, clothing and mates, and although civilised society disguises the cut-throat nature of competition and converts it into more socially acceptable manifestations, the instinct remains. From the moment we are born until the moment we die, we are competing – for friends, for qualifications, for sexual partners, for money, for possessions, for status.

Part of growing up is learning the rules of how the universal competitive instinct can be expressed. Those cute babies we met a few pages ago, happily immersed in the innocent enjoyment of their interactions with the ball, have no hesitation in brutally shoving a fellow cute baby out of the way if it means they can regain control of the ball. One of the key roles of parents, carers and teachers is to prevent such antisocial behaviour by teaching fairness, respect for others and playing within the rules. Children have to learn how to express their competitive urges and enjoy their time with the ball in a socially acceptable manner.

When that doesn't happen, at its worst, our thirst for competition manifests itself in war and violence, rape and pillage. Conversely, one of the safest and most acceptable outlets for our inherent competitive spirit is sport: we play hard and we play to win, but nobody gets killed, the rules are applied equally and fairly, it's only a game, and everyone can shake hands and be friends when it's all over. And that is not only achieved through playing sport, but also through spectating, through the phenomenon of fandom – if we support a football team, we are competing vicariously, fulfilling one of our most basic instincts through the efforts of grown-ups attired in a strange coloured uniform, running around on a field, chasing a spheroid and competing on our behalf.

Seen in this way, it's no surprise to learn that the competitive instinct, according to Mihaly Csikszentmihalyi, is a shortcut to achieving the state of flow: 'Competing is a quick way of developing complexity,' he writes. 'The challenge of competition can be stimulating and enjoyable.'

Competing gets us in the zone because it encourages us to focus on a specific challenge and act with a clearly defined sense of purpose. Rather than just playing aimlessly with a ball, competition gives us a reason to exert our energies, an obvious goal to aim towards: beating the opponent.

Competing facilitates flow, and flow facilitates further competition. Both reward the other. We enjoy playing for the pure sake of playing, and we also enjoy expressing our competitive instincts through the act of playing. So we play more, and we compete more. It's a virtuous cycle. A win-win situation.

Until, of course, we lose. The danger with competitive situations like sport is that the focus of our attention can very easily turn from the actual activity itself and instead fall upon the desired result of that activity. That way lies madness, not happiness.

Csikszentmihalyi believes this state of affairs can be avoided with the recognition that the best way to win, perversely, is by not focussing on winning. Instead, we should focus on doing the right things. Striving to improve and playing in the right way, and understanding that winning comes as a result of playing well, rather than trying to win. If we focus our minds on the task at hand, giving every effort to drag the best out of ourselves, the winning part should take care of itself. We should focus on the process, rather than the outcome.

Even for the greatest of players, sometimes the pressures of winning can become so overwhelming they end up inhibiting an ability to actually perform well. 'Choking' or suffering the 'yips' are common problems for amateur and professional athletes alike, and they can be very difficult to overcome.

In the case of Lionel Messi, an excessive focus on winning perhaps helps to explain his struggles to replicate his club form when he plays for Argentina.

Messi's international career has certainly not been bad: he has scored more goals and registered more assists than any other player in Argentine history, and played the most important role in taking the team to four finals. But he has only rarely been the unstoppable force of nature for his country that we have seen on an almost weekly basis for his club, as demonstrated by his surprisingly contrasting goalscoring ratios in those different arenas: 552 goals in 637 games for Barcelona (0.87 goals per game), compared to 65 in 128 for Argentina (0.51 goals per game) by the end of the 2018 World Cup.

His goalscoring record for Argentina is good, but it is not even close to the other-worldly stats he has compiled for Barcelona, and that reflects an overall wider impression that he just does not play as well in Albiceleste as he does in Blaugrana. Judging by his international performances alone, you would probably conclude that Messi is a very good player; judging by his club performances alone, you would probably conclude that he's the greatest of all time.

As we have seen throughout this book, there are many reasons for this – starting with the fact that he has played in far worse overall teams for Argentina than he has for Barcelona. There have been no Xavi, Busquets and Iniesta midfield combinations or Neymar and Suarez strike partners to help him through his World Cup or Copa America campaigns, and no Pep Guardiola on the sidelines to instil the necessary team structure.

But it's more than that. Messi doesn't only look below his best when he plays for Argentina, he also looks less happy. The boyish enthusiasm and exuberance he displays for Barcelona are conspicuous by their absence, replaced by far more frowns, sighs, complaints and general disgruntlement. He simply doesn't seem to *enjoy* playing for Argentina as much as he does for Barcelona – never more evident than that disturbing moment before the 2018 World Cup meeting with Croatia, when he was seen furiously rubbing his forehead in a clear state of anguish during the national anthems.

Another example of Messi's different state of mind on the international stage came in March 2017, when he earned a four-game ban (later reduced to one) for swearing aggressively at the linesman during a nervy and narrow World Cup qualifying victory over Chile. He hardly ever does this kind of thing for Barcelona, instead staying focussed on the game and leaving the task of berating the officials to others.

Although we are only speculating here, this could well be the consequence of Messi getting his priorities wrong. Because he has never won anything for Argentina, because it means so much to him, and because he has more responsibility to carry the team and do everything by himself, he is burdened by a far greater weight of expectation when he represents his country. That is exacerbated by the fact that opportunities to win are far scarcer due to the irregularity of international competitions: he has only played in eight major tournaments for Argentina, whereas with Barcelona five or six trophies are available every year (and he has already won 32 of them, giving him even more reason to be relaxed).

These factors combine, we can easily imagine, to force Messi into adopting, against his will, a different mindset when he steps onto the international stage: for Barcelona, he is primarily concerned with playing well, which leads to winning; for Argentina, his only interest is winning. Excessive pressure compels him to forget the importance of playing well. And that attitude – focussing more on winning than on playing well – paradoxically makes it less likely that he will win, because it negatively impacts his ability to perform at his best. He is focussing on the wrong thing.

This hazard was articulated by Csikszentmihalyi, who noted: 'There is no inherent problem in our desire to escalate our goals, as long as we enjoy the struggle along the way. The problem arises when people are so fixated on what they want to achieve that they cease to derive pleasure from the present. When that happens, they forfeit their chance of contentment ...

'When beating the opponent takes precedence over performing as well as possible, enjoyment tends to disappear. Competition is enjoyable only when it is a means to perfect one's skills; when it becomes an end in itself, it ceases to be fun.'

Not only does an excessive focus on outcome (winning) rather than process (playing) cause an activity to cease to be fun, but it also impacts negatively upon levels of performance – it creates 'a condition of inner disorder ... a disorganisation of the self that impairs its effectiveness.' Focussing on what we want to achieve rather than what we are actually doing takes us out of the zone, and stops our flow.

Most of the time, this is not a problem for Messi and one visible example of his love for the game in itself – his focus on the process rather than results – is the fact that he is hardly ever substituted or rested (and when he is, he makes it plain that he is unhappy about it).

Logically, especially now in his thirties, whenever Barcelona are cruising to a comfortable victory, three or four goals up with half an hour remaining, Messi should be substituted. The game is won, the points are safe, and it would be eminently sensible to take him off, give him some rest and avoid the risk of injury. But that hardly ever happens, because Messi just wants to play. In the last five seasons, he has only been substituted on 11 occasions in 174 games in La Liga – and four of those were due to injury. By contrast, during the same time frame Luis Suarez has been replaced 26 times, and Neymar in 23 games.

Messi's dislike of being substituted has occasionally been a hotly debated topic, with fans and media alike struggling to understand why he continues to tire himself out when he could be sitting on the bench with his feet up, victory already assured. It's clearly a touchy subject – on one of the rare occasions that he dared to replace Messi, during a routine home win over Athletic Bilbao in February 2017, Barça manager Luis Enrique was so irritated by the questioning on the topic that he snapped: 'I will not comment. You always want the story but I don't want you to write this. I'm not going to give you this information.'

The reason that Messi is so rarely substituted, in the light of what we have learned in this chapter, could be very easy to understand: he just wants to play. He is focussing on the process rather than the outcome, he's in full flow, and he's enjoying himself too much to stop. If there are 90 minutes of football to be played, he wants to play 90 minutes – not 65. With

Messi, more than the result matters. He wants to play because he wants to play, purely for the love of the act of playing.

Maybe his disappointments with Argentina would have turned out differently if he was able to maintain the same focus on process, rather than outcome, when he wears international colours. And if these speculations are correct and we accept Csikszentmihalyi's theory, he would certainly have enjoyed his international career a lot more.

Friendship and camaraderie

Football is not a solo pursuit and, as examined in the chapter on teamwork, no matter how much he enjoys playing for the sake of playing, focussing his energies on the process of manipulating the ball and letting the outcome take care of itself, all of Messi's undoubted devotion to his craft wouldn't mean anything at all without the involvement of other people.

Over the course of his professional career, he has shared a dressing room with around 200 team-mates, some of whom would be instantly recognisable to even the most casual supporter but many more who would only be recalled by devoted fans and stats fiends.

We could all easily recognise the likes of Sergio Aguero and Neymar, but who could pick out Sergio Rodriguez Garcia, who was on the pitch with Messi for a grand total of three minutes in Barcelona's victory at Albacete in December 2004? Or Ariel Garce, who travelled to the 2010 World Cup finals in South Africa alongside Messi in the Argentina squad but didn't play a single minute and was never selected again?

All of these players and many, many more have featured somewhere along the way in Messi's journey, but there is only a small number with whom he has forged a special bond to last a lifetime.

Dani Alves, for example, established a richly productive partnership with Messi during their eight years together at Barcelona. Off the pitch they were chalk and cheese, as the brash and boisterous Brazilian with a taste for outrageously garish clothing contrasted in spectacular fashion with the meek and mild Argentine and his boy-next-door mannerisms. Despite the striking disparity in their personalities, though, together they just clicked as Alves succeeded in teasing out the fun side of Messi's nature and kept him constantly entertained.

On the pitch, the close connection between Messi and Alves could be seen on a weekly basis through their insistence upon warming up together before every game, with their party trick of standing 40 yards apart and pinging volleyed passes to each other – a kind of long-range version of keepy-uppy – worth the admission money alone.

When that fun stopped and the action got underway they were electric together, with Alves's non-stop, fearless running and dynamic ball skills down the right flank acting as the perfect foil for Messi, who could trust that his team-mate would always be in the right position to stretch the opposition defence, receive passes and then unselfishly give the ball back. By the end of their time together, Alves had provided Messi with more assists than any other player.

Alves's place, in many ways other than positionally, was taken by another South American: Luis Suarez, who became Messi's new pre-game warm-up partner and chief dressing room confidante – partly thanks to their shared love of maté, the traditional South American tea-like drink, and the fact that they are next-door neighbours whose sons are best friends and attend the same school in their home town of Castelldefels, a coastal resort a few kilometres outside Barcelona.

Messi has never lined up alongside a more grateful strike partner than Suarez, who has enjoyed the most prolific phase of his outstanding career during their time together by rattling home 152 goals in 198 games for Barcelona by the end of the 2017/18 season, also winning the Golden Shoe award in 2016 for European football's highest league goalscorer after netting a career-best 40, many of which derived from Messi's precise passes.

Even more than Alves and Suarez, though, the two players with whom Messi will always be most closely identified in football's history books are Xavi Hernandez and Andres Iniesta, the chief purveyors of the short passing game which beguiled the world during Pep Guardiola's trophy-laden managerial spell between 2008 and 2012.

As seen in the 2011 Champions League Final against Manchester United, Messi's false nine role as a deep-lying forward allowed him to regularly drop deep into midfield and play close to Xavi and Iniesta, allowing the trio to weave endless passing triangles around bewildered opponents who just couldn't keep up. They shared an identical footballing philosophy, full of prods and probes, twists and turns, quick darts into space and perceptively angled passes, manipulating both the ball and the space to constantly carve out openings for danger.

Their influence is plain by the fact that the three of them top Barcelona's all-time appearances chart, amassing a combined total of more than 2,000 outings with Xavi in first place (767 games), Iniesta currently second (674) and Messi hot on his heels after making 637 appearances in the Blaugrana shirt by the end of the 2017/18 season.

Fittingly in the ultra-competitive arena of elite sport, they triumphed together but they also suffered together. The departure of Guardiola and the inevitable effects of ageing led to a gradual decline in standards and, eventually, first Xavi and then Iniesta moving on to finish their careers in Asia.

One of the most memorable triumphs inspired by Messi, Xavi and Iniesta was also one of their last, as they joined forces to temporarily delay the inevitable parting of ways for a little longer in March 2013 with a remarkable 4-0 victory over AC Milan in the last 16 of the Champions League, overturning a 2-0 first leg deficit in irresistible fashion.

Messi took less than five minutes to open the scoring by sweeping home a precise curling shot after slick build-up play involving both Xavi and Iniesta, and it was 2-0 before half-time when Xavi's through ball was cleared, Iniesta gathered possession and found Messi, who drilled home a low strike from the edge of the box. The third goal came early in the second half when Iniesta and Xavi combined to find David Villa for a precise finish, and the comeback was completed in the dying stages when Messi sprang a counter-attack which allowed Jordi Alba to convert.

It was a sensational performance from Barça in general but from their three talismen in particular, with Messi,

Xavi and Iniesta summoning all their strength and skill to stubbornly hold back the passage of time and deliver a telepathic masterclass of precise passing, intelligent interplay and mesmerising movement. But it also proved to be a defiant last stand: a few weeks later, the iconic trio were powerless to stop their team from falling to a humiliating 7-0 aggregate loss to Bayern Munich in the semi-finals, and they were never the same combined force again with Xavi becoming a marginal figure by the time of the treble under Luis Enrique two years later.

In addition to an ever-changing roster of team-mates, since he turned professional Messi has also worked under 15 different managers, from Diego Maradona to Frank Rijkaard and Edgardo Bauza to Jordi Roura, all of whom have left their mark in different ways. Two are worthy of special mention.

Firstly, of course, Guardiola was the man who trusted Messi to become the centrepiece of his team of stars, granting him the freedom (and, as we have seen, the responsibility) of playing in the middle of the pitch as his false nine and trusting the young Argentine – who had only just turned 21 when Guardiola took over as manager – to lead the team in the right manner.

Messi responded better than anyone could have ever expected, scoring 211 goals during Guardiola's four seasons as coach – including no less than 73 during their last campaign together (yes, 73 goals in a season) – and winning four consecutive Ballon d'Or awards. The faith that Guardiola showed in Messi, and the tactical and technical sharing of minds which allowed them to execute a near-revolutionary style of play, will never be forgotten by either man or by anyone who witnessed the fruits of their partnership.

The other colossal coaching figure in Messi's career is also a tragic one: Tito Vilanova. They first crossed paths during the Argentine's time in the youth ranks, where Vilanova was the first coach in Barcelona to take Messi away from the right wing and place him in the centre of the field.

Vilanova subsequently became Guardiola's trusted assistant before succeeding him as manager in the summer of 2012, but the tale took a horrible turn when he lost a three-year battle with cancer and died, aged just 45, in April 2014. The fact that

Vilanova, a deeply intelligent man who understood Barcelona inside-out, was never given the chance to remould the team in the post-Guardiola era is one of the great 'what if?' scenarios of modern football, and his death profoundly affected Messi on both a professional and personal level.

All the players and coaches listed above had a major effect on Messi's life, not just his career, and some of the friendships he created through football will continue long into the future.

Many more should be mentioned, especially Ronaldinho, whose powerful influence on the teenage Messi was outlined in the first chapter; Gerard Pique and Cesc Fabregas were both in Messi's youth side when he first arrived in Spain and later starred alongside him in the first team; Sergio Aguero and Pablo Zabaleta have been close friends of Messi's since they all played together in the Argentina team which triumphed in the 2005 World Youth Championship; Carles Puyol was an inspirational captain; Eric Abidal was an incredible example of willpower during his successful battle with cancer; Neymar helped Messi deliver some of his most breathtaking attacking football; Sergio Busquets and Javier Mascherano have been indispensable companions for a decade and more.

This is not an exhaustive list, and nor is it meant to be (so no offence to anyone excluded). Rather, it is a demonstration that even one of the most individually gifted human beings on the planet needs other people, not only to become successful but also for the sake of his identity.

Look at Messi's reaction to winning the Champions League Final at Wembley in 2011: he turned straight to his team-mates, enjoying the moment of triumph with them. First Xavi, then Pedro, then everyone else: when Messi's greatest moment of glory in club football arrived, it only had meaning because it was shared with his colleagues.

Look at the way he played during that game, relentlessly associating with his team-mates all over the pitch, sharing the ball and keeping it moving in a hypnotic collective dance: from his first touch – a header to Sergio Busquets – to his last – a pass to Ibrahim Afellay – he was always applying his individual efforts for the good of the team, getting into the zone and finding flow with the help of others.

No man is an island, and Messi's reliance on other people to help him find fulfilment on that triumphant night at Wembley offers a succinct metaphor for life: without the friendships, relationships, alliances and connections we build with our fellow human beings as we go about our daily business, without other people to share our triumphs and tragedies, we would be unable to forge a sense of identity and our lives would ultimately be empty and meaningless.

Just like the rest of us, Lionel Messi defines himself by, and finds happiness through, his interactions with others.

Family, club, country

How, exactly, does Lionel Messi define himself? We can only guess, because he is a man of few words and, on the rare occasions he does speak, he is stubbornly determined to give away as little as possible, revealing next to nothing about his deep and innermost feelings.

We can, however, glimpse a revealing clue about how he perceives himself – about his own sense of identity – in the form of two images.

Firstly, there is a backpack he uses for away games, which has been embroidered with pictures of his first two sons, the word 'family' and the Argentine national flag. The second image is the trophy room in his house where he keeps all the medals, footballs and jerseys he has collected over the last 15 years.

The shirts are neatly hung up and, as you would expect, the names on the back read like a roll call of the greatest players in the world this century: the jerseys of fellow Barcelona stars like Gerard Pique, Luis Suarez, Andres Iniesta and Cesc Fabregas are all present. So too is his idol as a youngster, Pablo Aimar, and several great opponents he has faced including Iker Casillas, Raul, Francesco Totti and Philipp Lahm (although, interestingly, Cristiano Ronaldo does not seem to be represented, suggesting that Messi's claim not to regard CR7 as a personal rival may not be entirely accurate).

In this dazzling room of priceless collector's items, Messi has taken the additional step of framing only two of the jerseys separately: one of his own playing shirts from Barcelona, and another from Argentina.

Those images – Messi's personalised backpack and his two framed shirts – speak a thousand words, tempting us to conclude that Messi has three cornerstones to his self-identity: his family, his country, and FC Barcelona.

We all have these cornerstones: the foundations of how we perceive ourselves and our place in the world – the kind of information we will offer up to a new acquaintance at a party, for example, or perhaps place on our social media biographies: name, home town, profession, hobbies, family.

Judging by his travelling backpack and his home décor, Messi, if engaged in conversation at a wedding by a stranger who somehow didn't know who he was, would define himself with the following information: my name is Leo, I come from Rosario in Argentina, I'm married with three children and I play football for Barcelona, where I have lived for nearly 20 years.

These are, evidently, indisputable facts about Messi's life. But they weren't always facts about his life. When he was 13 and moved to Europe, all he had to rest upon was that his name was Leo and he came from Argentina. He would have added, no doubt, that he loved football, plus perhaps that he was very small, and maybe that he was very shy as a consequence of his lack of stature. But he did not, at that time, have a place in the world. He was still gingerly groping his way towards selfhood.

Now he has fully developed that sense of self, and it is a very contemporary and contradictory one.

Until relatively recently in human history, the vast majority of people were born in a small settlement, lived there until they died and rarely ventured much further than the nearest town. A sense of community, and with it a sense of identity, was automatically bestowed by accidents of geography and tradition, and outsiders were viewed with suspicion. The opportunity for self-invention was minimal.

In recent years, however, the advent of high-speed travel, increased social mobility, technological advances, the erosion of national boundaries and the widespread adoption of liberal, secular, capitalist values have combined to drastically change that picture. Now, rather than being born into a certain identity which is retained without question for life's duration, most of us have much more freedom to actively choose who and what we are – to define our own place in the world.

Messi, through football, has found a long-term home in Barcelona – the only place he has ever lived in his adult life. But he's not *from* Barcelona, nor has he adopted the local customs or really even fully integrated into local life: he is still very close to his family, he married a friend of his cousin's from Rosario, he has never learned Catalan (unless he hides it extremely well), he doesn't mingle in the local community, many of his best friends have been fellow South Americans (from Ronaldinho and Zabaleta to Neymar and Suarez) and his children attend an international school where they are educated – mainly in English – alongside other members of the region's sizeable and diverse expat community.

This is an unusual and transient world, but it is Messi's reality – and it is a reality that Messi, through the opportunities afforded by his profession and the onset of maturity, has created for himself.

It is also a reality he appears to be comfortable with. Everything we see about Messi now, from the way he holds himself in his rare media appearances to the way he has grown into his physical looks, developing the confidence to cover his body with tattoos and his face with a sculpted beard, suggests he is now very much at ease with himself – he appears to have found inner peace, a sense of happiness which is separate from but just as important as the 'flow' form of happiness we discussed earlier in the chapter. Messi finds happiness in *what he does*, but also in *who he is*.

The unique and somewhat contradictory reality of 'who Messi is' also reflects the identity of his lifelong employer, FC Barcelona. The club – 'More Than A Club', according to the famous motto – is a key cultural representative of its region, and has played an integral part in the campaign for Catalan independence from Spain in the last few years. But brand Barça also has a huge global presence and has attracted countless millions of fans from all over the world, many of whom have never been to the city, don't know anything about the region and have no interest in the club's grassroots activism as backers of Catalan independence.

In the modern world of social media, a multitude of marketing possibilities are wide open to any high-profile and internationally aware organisation, and Barça has embraced them wholeheartedly: at the time of writing, the club's English-language Twitter account has 28.8 million followers; its Spanish equivalent boasts 13.5 million and the Catalan version just 5.6 million. Does that mean the club's global, English-language fanbase is five times more important than its Catalan supporters, who are in turn less than half as significant as the Spanish-speaking fans? What is FC Barcelona's identity: local Catalan family club or global corporate giant?

Really, of course, it is both – those two strands of brand identity are not mutually exclusive and the club can operate on many different levels at the same time. And so can Messi himself: he is proudly Argentine despite not having lived in the country since he was 13; he is an iconic symbol of Catalonia's most revered institution despite barely speaking a word of Catalan; he is a husband and a father; a son, a brother and an uncle. And, of course, he is a footballer.

Through football, he is no longer the shy little kid who was laughed at for being so small; now, he is a global star, revered in every corner of the planet, with his deep and intense attachment to Barcelona best exemplified by the way he famously held up his shirt in celebration, cockily mocking Real Madrid fans, after netting a dramatic last-minute winner at the Bernabeu in 2017. But despite developing that strong sense of self which allows him to be at ease with his superstar status, he is also still just his mum's son, and his children's dad.

He is all those things and more and, in these often rootless times, the personal journey he has undertaken to establish his multifaceted identity can resonate with all of us. Across the world, traditional notions of community are breaking down: old barriers are being swept aside; countries are being colonised by capitalism; families and religion have lost much of their past power, and as a consequence of these rapid developments in the chaotic and fast-moving digital world it can sometimes be unclear who or what we are.

By examining Messi's personal story – and seeing how he has found his place in the world by sharing a stage with

Brazilians, Uruguayans, Spaniards, Frenchmen, fellow Argentines and many more besides, living in a foreign country yet still maintaining his emotional links with his homeland, forging a confident sense of self by existing in a bubble of his own making – we can all, if we wish, try to follow suit.

Old roots are being pulled up and swept away, but we can still find inner peace by laying down our own new roots, however we want and wherever we want. The world is out there waiting for us.

Epilogue

After everything we have considered in this book, perhaps the most profound and important life lesson we can glean from Lionel Messi's football career still lies in the future.

When it stops.

Despite occasional appearances to the contrary, Messi is only human (or, at least, his extra-terrestrial status has not yet been confirmed) and even he will not be able to permanently slow the hands of time and vanquish the inevitability of retirement.

Retirement can be an incredibly difficult adjustment for sportspeople who have dedicated their whole lives to endlessly setting new goals and pursuing new achievements. For years, their existence is shaped by a reliable rhythm: one season finishes, another one begins. There's no time to dwell on past disappointments or successes because fresh challenges always lie just around the corner.

A cyclical routine of striving and competing is created, always with new mountains to cross, always with improvements to make and always with adversaries to confront. Always with reasons to look forward with positive intent, providing a natural, strong and genuine meaning and purpose to life.

Always ... until the time comes – retirement – when no more challenges are possible. When the clock stops and the hands cannot be reversed.

That fate, in due course, will also befall Lionel Messi.

He can delay the end for as long as possible by eating well, looking after his body and avoiding unnecessary risks, but that will only provide a temporary respite: time will ultimately defeat him, as it defeats all of us. However much he might fight it, Messi's career is finite and one day it will end.

One day, he will lace up his boots for the last time, play his final game, and then it will all be over.

All he can do in the meantime, rather than worrying about the half-death of retirement that looms ahead, is continue to extract everything he can out of the remainder of his career. He can enjoy every game to the maximum. He can dedicate himself to ruthlessly hunting down more success. He can embrace new team-mates, new coaches, new opponents, new seasons and new demands on his body as he loses his pace and his physical capabilities change.

If he does the right things and is given the right help, it could lead to plenty more goals, more trophies and more accolades. Maybe a few more La Liga titles with Barcelona. Maybe a fifth and sixth Champions League crown. Maybe a sixth and seventh Ballon d'Or. Maybe even (but don't hold your breath) a senior trophy with Argentina.

But Messi has already learned that some of his most cherished ambitions, like winning the World Cup, will probably always elude him. Even the greatest can't win everything, and some of his biggest dreams will inevitably remain unfulfilled when his playing days come to an end.

Like Messi's career, our own lives will also one day come to an end. Like Messi, we can attempt to delay the inevitable for as long as possible – by eating well, looking after our bodies and avoiding unnecessary risks – but time will catch up with us as it will catch up with him. In the end, our clocks will also stop.

Like Messi's failure to win the World Cup, our own lives will probably come to a conclusion without every ambition having been fulfilled or every aspiration having been achieved. But if we can align our lives with the trajectory of Messi's career, we will conclude that's OK. In fact it's inevitable, because that's football, and that's life.

In any case, even if not every objective is met, perhaps the greatest success we can achieve is enjoying life for the sake of life itself, in the same way that Messi enjoys football for the sake of football itself – not only for the results or the rewards it will bring. We can enjoy the process, and let the outcome take care of itself.

We cannot defeat death, and Messi will not be able to escape retirement. But we can be inspired by his example and try to extract the maximum potential from our lives in the same way that he has made the very most of his career.

We can do our best to become successful, while accepting that defeat is sometimes unavoidable. We can learn to live in harmony with others, understanding and accepting our individual strengths and limitations, and embracing the role we play in collective endeavours.

We can deal with setbacks and accept criticism, however unfair. We can endure tough times by knowing that better days might be just around the corner, and that giving up is not an option.

We can accept and embrace our responsibilities to ourselves and to others. We can try to maintain the innocent spontaneity and playful joys of childhood. We can find meaningful fulfilment by immersing ourselves in our passions.

We can try to make good decisions and brave decisions, and look for solutions rather than excuses. We can allow ourselves to be judged by our actions rather than our words. We can commit ourselves to hard work, believing it will bring rewards in due course. We can adapt to change, knowing that nothing stays the same forever.

And if all else fails, we can look deep inside and ask ourselves a simple question: what would Messi do?

Bibliography

Aristotle, *Nicomachean Ethics* (Hackett)

Guillem Balague, *Messi: the biography* (Orion Publishing)

John Carlin, *Playing the Enemy: Nelson Mandela and the game that made a nation* (Atlantic Books)

John Carlin, *Knowing Mandela* (Atlantic Books)

Mihaly Csikszentmihalyi, *Flow: the Psychology of Happiness* (Random House)

Heraclitus, cited in Jules Evans, *Philosophy for Life and other dangerous situations* (Random House)

Michael Jordan, quoted in *Nike Culture: The Sign of the Swoosh* (1998), by Robert Goldman and Stephen Papson, p. 49

Geir Jordet, *When Superstars Flop: Public Status and Choking Under Pressure in International Soccer Penalty Shootouts* (Norwegian School of Sports Sciences)

Daniel Kahneman, *Thinking, Fast and Slow* (Farrar, Straus and Giroux)

Kenan Malik, *The Quest for a Moral Compass: A Global History of Ethics* (Atlantic Books)

Daniel Memmert, *Teaching Tactical Creativity in Sport: Research and Practice* (Routledge)

Daniel Memmert, (2017), Kaufman, Glaveanu, Baer, the Cambridge Handbook of Creativity Across Domains. (New York Cambridge University Press)

Daniel Memmert, Joseph Baker and Claudia Bertsch (2010), 'Play and practice in the development of sport-specific creativity in team ball sports' (*High Ability Studies* Vol. 21, No. 1)

Daniel Memmert & Matthias Kempe (2018), '"Good, better, creative": the influence of creativity on goal scoring in elite soccer' (Journal of Sports Sciences)

Rafa Nadal with John Carlin, *My Story* (Hachette UK)

Plato, *The Republic* (Cambridge University Press)

Theodore Roosevelt, *The Strenuous Life* (Digireads.com)

Robert Trivers, The Evolution of Reciprocal Altruism (*The Quarterly Review of Biology*)

Lama Yeshe Losal Rinpoche, *Living Dharma* (Dzalendara Publishing)

Website Articles

Angel Di Maria, https://www.theplayerstribune.com/es-es/articles/angel-di-maria-argentina-english

Carol Dweck [on growth and fixed mindsets], https://onedublin.org/2012/06/19/stanford-universitys-carol-dweck-on-the-growth-mindset-and-education/

Eddie Jones [on Danny Kerry], quoted in https://www.theguardian.com/sport/2016/sep/13/england-coach-eddie-jones-tap-into-team-gb-knowledge

ESPN interview with Messi, https://www.youtube.com/watch?v=uUwqnrhkDHI

Lionel Messi, quoted in http://www.goal.com/en-gb/news/3277/la-liga/2012/11/01/3494282/messi-my-team-mates-know-i-am-not-a-little-dictator

minutouno.com, https://www.minutouno.com/notas/118619-por-que-lio-messi-juega-tan-mal-la-seleccion-y-nunca-levanta

sportslens.com, http://sportslens.com/internazionale-beat-juventus-3-2-and-a-star-is-born-in-milan-mario-balotelli/5501/

tribalfootball.com, http://www.tribalfootball.com/articles/inter-milan-president-moratti-excited-balotelli-sensation-167656

Universal Declaration of Human Rights, http://www.un.org/en/universal-declaration-human-rights/